Rethinking the Mathematics Curriculum

Studies in Mathematics Education Series

Series Editor: Paul Ernest, University of Exeter, UK

The Philosophy of Mathematics Education
Paul Ernest

Understanding in Mathematics
Anna Sierpinska

Mathematics Education and Philosophy
Edited by Paul Ernest

Constructing Mathematical Knowledge
Edited by Paul Ernest

Investigating Mathematics Teaching
Barbara Jaworski

Radical Contructivism
Ernst von Glasersfeld

The Sociology of Mathematics Education
Paul Dowling

Counting Girls Out: Girls and Mathematics
Valerie Walkerdine

Writing Mathematically: The Discourse of Investigation
Candia Morgan

Rethinking the Mathematics Curriculum
Edited by Celia Hoyles, Candia Morgan and Geoffrey Woodhouse

Studies in Mathematics Education Series: 10

Rethinking the Mathematics Curriculum

edited by

Celia Hoyles, Candia Morgan, and
Geoffrey Woodhouse

FALMER PRESS
Taylor & Francis Group

UK   Falmer Press, 1 Gunpowder Square, London, EC4A 3DE
USA   Falmer Press, Taylor & Francis Inc., 325 Chestnut Street, 8th Floor,
         Philadelphia, PA 19106

First published in 1999

A catalogue record for this book is available from the British Library

ISBN 0 7507 0939 1 cased
ISBN 0 7507 0938 3 paper

**Library of Congress Cataloging-in-Publication Data are available on
request**

Jacket design by Caroline Archer

Typeset in 10/12 pt Times by
Graphicraft Limited, Hong Kong

*Printed in Great Britain by Biddles Ltd., Guildford and King's Lynn on
paper which has a specified pH value on final paper manufacture of not
less than 7.5 and is therefore 'acid free'.*

Contents

Contents

List of Figures and Tables

Acknowledgments

This book comprises an outcome of a conference held at the Institute of Education, University of London in October, 1996.

First we wish to thank the Nuffield Foundation for their generous sponsorship of this event.

Second, we express our appreciation to our colleagues in the Mathematical Sciences group at the Institute of Education, for the stimulating discussions both at the conference and since, which have helped to shape the book.

Our grateful thanks go to Sue Cranmer, Wendy Robins and Pippa Howell for their administrative support at the conference, and for their painstaking work in helping us to put the book together.

We thank all the participants at the conference whose contributions informed and enriched the chapters that now form the book.

Finally, to authors of chapters for their contributions and patience during the long editorial process, our sincerest thanks.

Series Editor's Preface

Mathematics education is established world-wide as a major area of study, with numerous dedicated journals and conferences serving ever-growing national and international communities of scholars. As it develops, research in mathematics education is becoming more theoretically orientated. Although originally rooted in mathematics and psychology, vigorous new perspectives are pervading it from disciplines and fields as diverse as philosophy, logic, sociology, anthropology, history, women's studies, cognitive science, semiotics, hermeneutics, post-structuralism and post-modernism. These new research perspectives are providing fresh lenses through which teachers and researchers can view the theory and practice of mathematics teaching and learning.

The series Studies in Mathematics Education aims to encourage the development and dissemination of theoretical perspectives in mathematics education as well as their critical scrutiny. It is a series of research contributions to the field based on disciplined perspectives that link theory with practice. The series is founded on the philosophy that theory is the practitioner's most powerful tool in understanding and changing practice. Whether the practice concerns the teaching and learning of mathematics, teacher education, or educational research, the series offers new perspectives to help clarify issues, pose and solve problems and stimulate debate. It aims to have a major impact on the development of mathematics education as a field of study in the third millennium.

A perennial question which faces the mathematics educator, and society in general, is what should be the shape and nature of the mathematics curriculum? What school mathematics content, teaching methodologies, resources including information and communication technologies, and assessments are appropriate for today and for the third millennium? Politicians are very ready to impose answers to these questions, all too often based on superficial analyses of utility and societal need. The present volume addresses these questions from a deeper set of perspectives. The role of mathematics in society has changed with the deepening impact of information technologies on commerce, industry, government and all aspects of cultural life. But the implications for mathematics education depend on the aims of the enterprise. Is it for preparing skilled workers, for fostering critical citizenship in democratic societies, or for other purposes? How should mathematics, mathematics teaching and mathematics teacher education respond to these changes? There are no simple answers to these questions, and this volume brings together a divergent set of expert perspectives which show the depth of the issues without reaching any simple consensus. There are views from several countries, including the Pacific Rim countries whose success in mathematics has been much trumpeted, as well as contributions from across the worlds of policy, administration, science, education and research. Any attempt to rethink the mathematics curriculum needs to address the questions and issues raised here. Politicians and policy-makers would do well to learn from this volume about the complexities involved, as well as considering the conclusions drawn by the panel of experts assembled here, before plunging into further reforms of the mathematics curriculum.

Paul Ernest
University of Exeter
1998

Introduction

At the turn of the millennium, it is appropriate to reflect on the mathematics education that will be needed for the future — by the 'educated person', by the employee in an environment of constantly developing technology, and by the scientist — and how this may be achieved.

A conference, 'Mathematics for the New Millennium', sponsored by the Nuffield Foundation, was held at the Institute of Education, University of London, in October 1996 to discuss these issues. This book is one outcome of the conference. Contributions were invited from 39 participants including mathematicians, scientists, technologists, policy-makers, and educators coming from research, teaching, administration, industry, and commerce. The meeting had an international flavour, with input from nine different countries and four continents. The contributors were asked to address the following themes, with freedom to identify their own priorities:

- What will it mean to be a mathematically educated person in the new millennium?
- What is the likely impact of technology on mathematics and mathematics education?
- What are the implications of changes in the labour market, for example, the decline in the need for unskilled labour?
- How will the increasing need for scientists and technologists be addressed in education?

The contributions to the conference ranged as widely as the backgrounds of the participants. The discussions were notable for their quality and candour, and moved the debate forward in a way that was refreshingly open and unprejudiced. The chapters in this book reflect those constructive debates. They follow from the authors' original contributions to the conference and include their revisions after the three days of discussion.

Any discussion of mathematics education must begin with a discussion of the nature of mathematics and the purposes of learning it. These are not simple questions. Every individual, and therefore every potential discussant, has a unique, personal knowledge of mathematics and mathematics education. Individual motivations for learning (and not learning) are diverse. Different cultures, societies, and economic systems have different perspectives on the nature of mathematics and the purpose of mathematics education. And all of these are changing over time. Recent advances in technology have added a new dimension to the debate. Some argue that, from the point of view of personal or national utility, most people will shortly need little more than basic arithmetical skills. Others argue to the contrary, that in order not to be disempowered either as citizens or as employees individuals will need more and better mathematics, and that if nations are to develop culturally and economically their populations will need to become more sophisticated mathematically. Most agree that, as we enter the 21st century, mathematics curricula in schools will have to be organized around 'something new'. We shall need clarity about what school mathematics is, could be, and is not, and about the legitimate — and helpful — demands that may be made of it.

This is not the first time that school mathematics has come under the spotlight. Chapters 1, 3 and 14 chart, in different ways, the history of mathematics education over the 20th century: how mathematics curricula have been adapted, sometimes quite suddenly, to meet changing perceptions of the needs of individuals and society; how politics, both within and outside education, have influenced developments, and how the personal sufferings of learners of all abilities have left a legacy of failure and resentment. Chapter 12, however, set in a longer time-frame, observes the continuing *democratization* of mathematics through periodic, empowering changes in technology and accompanying innovation elsewhere. Many of our contributors express hope in the possibilities that information technology offers for transforming students' experience of mathematics. But it will be essential to ensure that any proposals for change are subjected to criticism, and if accepted are put effectively into practice and monitored rigorously thereafter. History tells us that this process will not be straightforward: in particular, we can predict that a great deal of rotten information technology will be aggressively marketed.

Not for the first time, either, do we hear calls that publicly funded mathematics education should serve national economic needs. Yet the mathematics that is actually done in the workplace is often not easily recognized. Chapters 3 and 4 offer detailed exposés of this more hidden kind of mathematics, drawing lessons for classroom practice. Chapter 2 analyses the more obvious, but still imperfectly understood, role of IT in a scientific/technological environment and its implications for the school curriculum. Chapter 7 describes a practical attempt to provide, and assess, a mathematics curriculum in the context of a vocational qualification in science.

This theme of mathematics in context, or mathematics as servant, is taken up by a number of chapters concerned with a new pedagogy. What emerges is a relatively convergent vision of a mathematics curriculum built around the construction and interpretation of quantitative models. Authors show, from their different perspectives, how modelling is used in practice in the workplace, and how it motivates learning in schools. Modelling also provides a pivotal role for information technology, which in turn raises new questions: How does IT affect the nature of mathematics as it is used in the workplace? What is its potential for attracting students to engage in mathematics? What are the limits to the use of technology, and how far will it change what mathematics is and how it is done? We know that outside Europe, Australasia, and North America rather little use is made of technology in mathematics teaching. While acknowledging the potential for learning and teaching mathematics in new ways, some contributors from other countries expressed scepticism at the conference about current uses and suggested that their own countries might have different priorities in relation to the use of technology in schools. Their written contributions recognize that the influence of IT is likely to be critical, though they remain unsure of what that influence will be. What is the 'kernel' of knowledge, skills, and concepts that we should teach our students in order to exploit appropriately the new technology of the 21st century?

These and other fundamental questions — of values as well as means — are addressed in the final chapters of the book, by authors from three countries on the Pacific Rim. Despite their students' well documented prowess in certain manipulative skills, educators and policy-makers in those countries are looking for more creativity and problem solving in their mathematics curricula. Their contributions highlight the need for rational and collaborative methods to arrive at national solutions, which bring all agencies together without prejudice and draw on practices from other countries to challenge fashionable trends in any one area. Teacher education, for example, will be crucial in preparing an education system for the new millennium, and Chapters 15 and 16 are devoted to it. Its problems are similar in different countries — how to build strong connections between theory and practice — but the solutions put forward are very different. In the UK, practical classroom experience is being increased at the expense of theoretical grounding, while the French have radically increased both academic and professional training in two-year postgraduate courses. Refreshingly also for the UK reader, the French acknowledge the need to utilize collective competence, and take advantage of research.

The need to strengthen a relationship between educational research and professional practice is a theme visited by several of our contributors. Mathematics education is about issues central to *all* of education and can potentially offer ways to address them. For example, it is important for learning in general that students should be able to move from one representation to a more general one, and play with different representations. Thus the book lends support to the conjecture that mathematics education in the third millennium will be not just about teaching and learning mathematics, but about the nature of knowledge and the place of mathematics in society.

These issues are elaborated in the following pages. We trust that the book will confirm the view expressed by one of our conference participants, that there is still energy and hope in mathematics education — even in British classrooms.

Celia Hoyles, Candia Morgan, Geoffrey Woodhouse, 1998

What Is Mathematics and What Is It For?

When you bring together people with disparate experiences and interests in relation to mathematics, as we did for this conference, you discover very quickly that 'mathematics' means different things to different people. Perhaps one thing on which all the contributors could agree was that mathematics needs to be viewed as much more than the 'traditional mathematics' of the school curriculum — as a living, changing discipline. Mathematics has roles beyond the basic functionality associated with numeracy and simple algebra: as a powerful language for sharing and systematizing knowledge, and as a part of human culture. The chapters in this section each start from a very different position, yet taken together they provide strong support for the ubiquity of mathematics. In some guise it appears in all areas of life and education; *we* can see this, but at a time when the privileged place of mathematics in the curriculum may be in question we need to think carefully about how to communicate it to others in a way that makes its importance clear.

While part of the importance of mathematics is its utility, Johnston Anderson reminds us that mathematics is also a discipline in its own right and a part of our cultural heritage. He argues that appreciation of this should not be reserved for the tiny minority who are destined to become professional mathematicians, but should be part of the education of all 'generally educated citizens'. Anderson's review of the course of school mathematics in England and Wales in the 20th century raises important issues about the choices that will need to be made as we move into the 21st. Society is changing, the technological tools available to us are changing, and mathematics itself is changing. Increasingly, the question 'Why should we study mathematics?' is asked as students become more sophisticated and want to see a direct pay-off for their efforts. The reward for studying mathematics is the power that it provides for understanding — beyond mathematics itself. Willibald Dörfler's chapter argues that the utility of mathematics lies not just in its 'application' but in the 'thinking tools' it provides. His examples suggest how mathematical notions such as relation, function, and set, by becoming part of our 'everyday' language, can provide us with ways of thinking about the world and of considering alternatives.

When thinking about the future of mathematics and mathematics education, we cannot afford to be inward-looking, concerned only with the views of the mathematical and educational communities. As Rogers Hall argues in his chapter, if we think that mathematics is important for everyone, 'we need to know more about the "everywheres" these people are likely to inhabit'. Several chapters in this section deal with concrete questions about what mathematical tools are actually used and needed in the 'real world'. Michael Clayton draws on his experience of working in the telecommunications industry to address the issues raised for mathematics education by the increasingly widespread use of information technology. While this has brought benefits for quality and productivity, it has also brought 'traps for the unwary'. Clayton identifies the importance of teaching the principles and techniques of mathematical modelling, including the appropriate, critical use of IT tools and an appreciation of the importance of validation and verification.

After Clayton's look at the use of mathematics in industry from the inside, the chapters by Rogers Hall and by Celia Hoyles, Richard Noss and Stefano Pozzi look at mathematical thinking in work practices that the participants themselves might not label as mathematical. Both these chapters describe innovative methodologies for studying mathematical practices — and both raise issues for the future of mathematics education. Hall's case study examines how quantitative reasoning and modelling are used within the interactive process of architectural design. He explores the ways in which this knowledge, and knowledge of how participants with different expertise communicate with each other and make sense of each other's contributions, may inform classroom-based activity. As well as identifying 'mathematizable situations' in the practices of nurses and bank workers, Hoyles et al. discuss how making the mathematics of the situation more explicitly visible to the practitioners might bring benefits to them. They describe how computer-based modelling can allow practitioners to make connections between mathematics and their practice. Here we see how new developments in technology not only change mathematical activity in the workplace but also have a role in changing mathematical education. Contributions in later sections develop this theme.

Chapter 1

Being Mathematically Educated in the 21st Century: What Should It Mean?

Johnston Anderson

Introduction

The history of the development of mathematics indicates that, until recently, mathematics was a subject studied and practised by an élite few. In 19th-century Britain, 'grammar' and 'public' (which, in the quaint English cultural tradition, actually means *private*) schools catered for only a small minority of children; the mathematics that was taught in their classes was either of a pure type, such as the study of geometry, or topics which 'would be useful to a nation of inventors and engineers'. For the majority of young people, anything other than the most basic education was regarded as a waste of resources. Battles were fought in Parliament against compulsory schooling, on both political and financial grounds. Eventually, the Education Act of 1870 introduced compulsory education for the first time, although, as we shall see, the standards to be achieved in mathematics were limited. Over the next 100 years, other Education Acts have followed, culminating in 1988 with the introduction, for the first time, of a National Curriculum in England and Wales (though other countries had long gone down this road).

Part of the rationale behind the National Curriculum was a realization, first articulated in the 1960s and 1970s, that it was in the UK's economic interests to have an educated, skilled workforce and that too many school pupils were leaving school both earlier and less well qualified than their continental counterparts. Soon came the further realization of a similar threat posed by the emerging economies of the Far East. In this chapter, we review some aspects of mathematics and mathematics teaching, as they have developed in the 20th century. With this perspective, we may then speculate as to what might constitute the answer to the question posed in the title.

Mathematics in the 20th Century

In 1900 David Hilbert gave a seminal address to the International Congress of Mathematicians in Paris. In it he discussed 23 unsolved problems which he forecast would occupy the attention of mathematicians in the 20th century. Mathematics, both pure and applied, had accomplished much by 1900; however, the formalization of analysis under the influence of Weierstrass and abstract algebra in the shape of group theory and determinants were less than 50 years old, the works of Cantor and Dedekind, and Felix Klein's Erlanger Program, even more recent.

Whole new areas of mathematics have sprung up in this last century: mathematical statistics, discrete mathematics and its applications, graph theory (even though its roots may have been in the 19th century), quantum mechanics, chaos, and game theory represent just some of the more novel ones; but geometry and analysis have advanced, almost out of all recognition, in the last 100 years, fusing and separating, enriching and being enriched by their applications to disciplines such as mathematical physics. The foundations of mathematics have been shaken, by Gödel and others; we now know that there are propositions which are undecidable and that there are problems whose solutions are, from a practical point of view, unreachable. It is claimed that there are more mathematicians actively working today than the sum total of all mathematicians throughout recorded history (though how one validates that claim might be an interesting exercise!). To Hilbert's agenda has been added a vast compendium of new challenges. The frontiers of mathematical research are today more remote from the average educated person than they have ever been. For one person to make major contributions to half a dozen different areas of mathematics, as some (Euler, Gauss, Cauchy, Poincaré) have done in the past, looks increasingly unlikely. It was Hilbert himself, quoted by Weyl (1944), who said

> The question is forced upon us whether mathematics is to face what other sciences have long ago experienced, namely to fall apart into subdivisions whose representatives are hardly able to understand each other and whose connections, for this reason, will become ever looser. I neither believe nor wish this to happen; the science of mathematics as I see it is an indivisible whole, an organism whose ability to survive rests on the connections between the parts.

The story of professional mathematics in the 20th century has confounded this hope; what then are the implications for those teaching and learning the subject? In order to try to answer this, we look at how the content and style of what has been included in school mathematics has changed.

Some Aspects of Mathematics in Schools

Following the introduction of compulsory schooling, 'standards of instruction to allow a school to be certified as efficient' were published in 1876:

- 50 per cent of those above 7 years will be individually examined (in reading, writing and arithmetic). One half of the children examined ought to pass in two subjects. One half of the children so passing ought to pass in arithmetic.

- 7–8 years: Form (from dictation) figures up to 20. Name at sight figures up to 20. Add and subtract figures up to 10, orally and from examples on the blackboard.
- 8–10 years: Simple addition and subtraction of numbers of not more than four figures. Multiplication tables to 6×12.
- 10+ years: The four simple rules to short division (inclusive).

In view of current concerns and pronouncements on standards in schools, it is perhaps salutary to note the following comments from HMI and others over the last century or so (McIntosh, 1977):

> In arithmetic . . . worse results than ever before have been attained — partly attributable, no doubt, to my having framed my sums so as to require rather more intelligence . . . but the failures are almost invariably traceable to radically imperfect teaching. (Farm, Stafford and Derby, 1876)

> The accuracy of the work in Standards I and II are all that can be desired, and in many cases marvellous; at the same time, the oral test shows that the children are working in the dark. In these standards, at least, far too much time is given to the mechanical part of the subject. The result of this unintelligent teaching shows itself in the inability of the upper standards to solve very simple problems. (1895)

> 62% of Standard V [typically 12 years old or over] could take 1 from 10 000 correctly. (1910)

> There is a prevailing opinion that London children are slower and less accurate in computation than they were ten years ago. I have searched for evidence in support, but failed to find it. But even if there has been a loss in accuracy, there has been a great gain in intelligence and intelligence is an equipment incomparably more valuable than facility in calculation. (Board of Education, 1912)

> Instruction in many primary schools continues to bewilder children because it outruns their experience. (Plowden, 1966)

> In general, the results show that teachers of first-year secondary children should not, except in the case of very bright children, take their understanding of multiplication and division for granted. (Brown, 1977)

There was much confusion in other reports (for example, Hadow, 1931) about the relative merits of learning principles and being actively involved as opposed to acquiring 'facts' and memorizing rules. So the current debate on the claimed shortcomings of alternative approaches to learning mathematics is nothing new. It is also of interest to compare the content of mathematics examinations taken by pupils around the age of 16, who attended 'grammar' schools.

Elementary Mathematics II, from the year 1933, contained 10 questions. The rubric stated 'Logarithms, Slide-Rule, or Algebra, may be used in any question'. The composition of the paper can be roughly broken down as follows:

- 3 questions on 'pure' geometry
- 2 questions on practical arithmetic (conversion of units, ratio)
- 1 question each on scale drawing, (piecewise-linear) graphs, trigonometry, algebraic manipulation, and number and proof

Typical of the geometry questions is:

> Give a construction for drawing two tangents to a circle from an external point, and prove that the tangents so obtained are equal in length.

> Prove that if the sides of a parallelogram touch a circle, then the four sides of the parallelogram are equal.

Sixty years later, the effects of the virtual disappearance of Euclidean geometry from the curriculum of many British schools can be seen from the evidence that, of a class of 50 third-year mathematics undergraduates in 1995, less than a quarter could complete the first part and the majority made little progress with the latter part, introducing all sorts of extraneous, unnecessary, and often unhelpful, construction lines into their diagrams.

While the word 'prove' is consistently used in the geometry questions, 'show' occurs in another question:

> Show that the sum of a number of four digits and the number formed by reversing the digits is always divisible by 11.

Clearly, the ability to translate the information given into an appropriate general algebraic form, i.e. getting to the expression $1001(a+d)+110(b+c)$, is a key process being tested. One suspects that verifying the result in a small number of cases would not have gained many marks.

In 1949, 16 years later, *Elementary Mathematics II* had 12 questions, of which four were compulsory and at most five others were to be attempted (in two hours). There were

- 3 questions on 'pure' geometry (one compulsory)
- 2 questions on practical arithmetic (one compulsory)
- 3 questions involving accurate drawing and measurement (one compulsory)
- 3 questions on algebra (one compulsory, on the factor theorem)
- 1 question on graph-drawing ($y = x^2$ and $2y = x + 4$)

As in 1933, apart from the geometry, there is little in the paper that involves *proof*. The word occurs in question 8:

> It is given that
>
> $$x = 1 + \frac{p}{p - q} \text{ and } y = 2 - \frac{3q}{p + q}$$

Prove that

(i) $\dfrac{x}{y} = \dfrac{p+q}{p-q}$; (ii) $\dfrac{3}{x} + \dfrac{1}{y} = 2$

But the question is simply one of algebraic manipulation (and of a fairly trivial kind).

The mathematics being taught to these pupils could be regarded as the comfortable outcome of an unwritten conspiracy between the grammar schools and the universities, to preserve the supply of professional mathematicians and not to worry too much about any other national needs.

The 1960s saw the beginnings of a new wave of mathematical change in schools (see also Griffiths, Chapter 13, below). The Schools Mathematics Project (*SMP*) was just under way. The main thrust in the construction of the syllabus was that it was primarily for those *who would do no mathematics beyond O-level*, while at the same time being also suitable for those who would wish to take it further. The 1964 rationale for the proposed syllabus (Schools Mathematics Project , 1971) stated:

> for this reason, any reform of GCE syllabuses, in our opinion, must begin in the lower school and it would not be sound policy to attempt to initiate the first changes at A-level.

Thirty years on, we have seen a whole raft of reports and initiatives, some implemented, some rejected: N and F levels (Institute of Mathematics and Its Applications, 1978; Schools Council, 1980), Cockcroft (1982), Department of Education and Science (1988) and the National Curriculum (1988), revised several times since and to be yet again revised. However, there are other stated aims in the *SMP* report about which one feels there would be a considerable consensus:

- to make school mathematics more exciting and enjoyable
- to impart a knowledge of the nature of mathematics and its uses in the modern world
- to encourage more pupils to pursue further the study of mathematics
- to bridge the gulf between university and school mathematics (in both content and outlook)
- to reflect the changes brought about by increased automation and the introduction of computers.

In the light of some of the strictures made in the recent report of the London Mathematical Society (1995), on the lack of algebraic and manipulative facility among contemporary incoming undergraduates, it is interesting to read that in the *SMP* syllabus

> we have constantly tried to shift the emphasis towards mathematical ideas and away from manipulative techniques.

While it is conceded that facility in manipulation is indeed required by those who would aspire to be mathematicians (and physicists, and engineers) more controversial is their view that

> it is [our] opinion that the acquisition of techniques is best left until the post-O-level stage; then, technique will come more rapidly, because the need for it will be more apparent. It will also free the pupil who stops at O-level from much *unnecessary* learning.

The new *SMP* O-level, and similar initiatives in Scotland with the almost simultaneous introduction of the Scottish Mathematics Group's Modern Mathematics for Schools (MMS) brought a change in focus, not only in the way mathematics should be taught, but also in the content. The widening of access to more and more pupils, coupled with successive raising of the school leaving age (the age at which pupils were no longer required to attend compulsorily) meant that curricula had to cater for a far wider range of abilities. Although there was to be an increased emphasis on algebraic structure ('conveying the nature of algebraic concepts rather than [merely] imparting a body of knowledge'), definitions and axioms would 'grow out of concrete illustrations' (a theme later taken up by Skemp, 1986) while *proof* was to be accorded a significant role. The nature of geometry would change: though the merits of formal deductive geometry for a minority were conceded, for the majority of pupils it 'offers little training in logical reasoning' and simply forced them into 'memorising theorems and proofs of no particular worth'. Instead, transformation geometry, with its links to matrices, was introduced, and more attention was devoted to three-dimensional geometry and the construction of polyhedra. Also making an appearance were topics such as inequalities, treated both graphically and algebraically, elementary statistics and probability, estimation, and degrees of accuracy. A typical *SMP* paper of the time (Paper II, 1971) comprised

- 4 questions on geometry
- 2 questions on graphs
- 1 question each on inequalities, probability, composition of functions, and number.

The change in style can be seen in the following geometry question. The question is not only contextualized but also concerned with measure and calculation rather than with proof.

> An isolated hill standing on a plain has the shape of a perfect circular cone. *A* and *B* are points at the foot of the cone, *A* being due North and *B* due South of the summit. The distance from *A* to *B* over the summit is 600m while the direct distance through the hill is 540m. Sketch the shape you would cut out to make a cardboard model of the hill (showing all necessary measurements).
>
> There is a path over the slope of the hill, following the shortest route from *A* to *B*. Show this path in your sketch and find its length. Find also the shortest distance from the summit of the hill to the highest point on the path.

Table 1.1 Numbers of entries at GCE Advanced level (A-level) in England and Wales in four options of mathematics, by year and sex

		Maths	Further Maths	Pure Maths	Applied Maths
1984		42854	6286	8744	6948
	M	34699	4729	5787	5090
	F	13555	1557	2957	1858
1987		43746	5567	6180	7669
	M	30829	4171	3911	5431
	F	12917	1396	2269	2238
1992		54889	4180	3176*	1271*
	M	35249	3096	2021	982
	F	19640	1084	1155	289

*Note: *partly attributable to a change in definition*

Table 1.2 Numbers of entries at GCE Advanced level (A-level) in the four principal named options of mathematics (single-subject), 1992, by sex

Maths	M	14669	(66.5%)
	F	7378	(33.5%)
Pure and Applied	M	9606	(71.0%)
	F	3938	(29.0%)
Pure-with-Mechanics	M	3859	(76.3%)
	F	1198	(23.7%)
Pure-with-Statistics	M	7115	(50.0%)
	F	7126	(50.0%)

Such changes in emphasis were not universally acclaimed at the time, as the polemic by J.M. Hammersley (1968) showed.

The 1980s and 1990s have been characterized by a number of significant changes (some already alluded to), in the style and the content of school mathematics, at both GCSE (the integrated successor to the distinct qualifications of O-level and CSE) and A-level. There has been a marked shift away from 'Double Maths' at A-level, as shown in Table 1.1.

By 1992, there was apparent an equally significant shift towards syllabuses such as *Pure-Mathematics-with-Statistics* and away from *Pure-Mathematics-with-Mechanics*, notably among female candidates.

The proportion of female candidates taking mathematics at A-level, over all combinations, had risen steadily from 28.4 per cent in 1984 to 33.6 per cent in 1992, but the composition of different single-subject entries showed considerable variation. For example, the figures for 1992 for the four principal named qualifications were as in Table 1.2.

In addition, in the A-level examinations of 1992, there were 73 different examinations (as distinct from papers) available leading to a qualification with the word 'mathematics' in the title; there were also two separate statistics examinations as well as numerous ones in computing. Since then, the introduction of 'modular'

A-levels has further dented, for sixth-form students, Hilbert's hope of an indivisible discipline. The new agreed common core represents about half the material in any syllabus for single-subject 'mathematics'. The inference seems to be that, in the 21st century in the UK, one mathematically educated person is likely to know something quite different from another mathematically educated person.

The restructuring of school mathematics in England may have contributed to other side-effects. In international comparisons, England (and Scotland) appear to fare badly, but such comparisons frequently exclude topics such as statistics, and credit for good performance (for example in problem-solving, in which England recently came second, behind the Republic of Korea) is often grudging. Personal experience of teaching undergraduates from the Far East shows them to have good technical competence, high motivation to absorb (and regurgitate) new knowledge, but relatively poor ability to adapt this knowledge to novel situations and to tackle non-standard or open-ended problems. It should be noted, however, that other countries also suffer anxiety about the state of their mathematical education. The Japanese see a crisis in mathematics, and the natural sciences, in their schools (Fujita et. al., 1996). They too call for an increase in the time-allocation given to mathematics at high school (particularly the formative junior high school level) and for a widespread 'mathematical literacy' for all pupils, because of the increasing impact of mathematics in the social sciences and humanities, implemented through a 'flexible and enjoyable' curriculum, which progresses systematically from elementary school through to college level, and which develops the cognitive processes central to the study of mathematics. They also note that the lowering of entrance qualifications (in mathematics) for colleges and universities has created a vicious circle in which, because less of a premium is placed on mathematics, less time gets spent on the subject at high school, resulting in a further erosion of mathematical skills.

Technology

One of the most significant developments in the last 20 years has been the widespread availability of cheap but powerful calculators and computers. The UK has perhaps, in its schools, embraced the calculator culture more enthusiastically than many countries. Most A-level examining boards in mathematics now recommend that the student has access to a 'scientific' or 'graphical' calculator both during the course and in the examination. Calculators are now available which are capable of handling complex numbers, inverting matrices, and finding eigenvalues and eigenvectors, as well as many advanced statistical functions. Algebra packages such as *Maple*, *Mathematica*, and *Derive* are commonplace in personal computers in university departments; the last is now incorporated in the recently released *Texas TI-92* calculator also. The Open University makes extensive use of information technology (IT) in its forthcoming entry courses *Using Mathematics* and *Exploring Mathematics*. It is therefore disappointing that the use of IT in mathematics teaching in school is claimed to be as little as once per term on average (Taverner, 1996). However, more significant than the use of computers as a tool to overcome drudgery is the opportunity they offer to develop mathematics as an *experimental* subject, though the point is well made (Tepper Haino, 1995) that while there is a place for experimentation and conjecture, and while these may take place with or without the assistance of a computer, part of the essence of mathematics is the central role of rigorous proof. Technology-based developments in teaching, which include both computer-aided-learning packages as well as interactive and dynamic teaching materials (such as dynamic geometry software, and the software discussed by Kaput and Roschelle in Chapter 12 of this book) have the capability to transform the way pupils understand and learn mathematics. The richness and variety of the visual presentation of mathematical knowledge through these media, in contrast to the some-what one-dimensional world of the textbook, will open new horizons for pupils of all abilities, but particularly for those who find verbally presented data more diffi-cult to comprehend. The increasing availability of CD-ROM materials will make access to all sorts of information potentially universal. How, therefore, can we best equip the average school-leaver of the future, in order that they can make use of this mathematical information, participate in a process of lifelong learning, and adapt to ever-changing demands for new skills? In the final section, I look at some implications for mathematics within the political and social structure of the UK and try to offer some tentative suggestions.

Mathematical Education in the 21st Century

As we have seen, the growth of mathematics, both as a subject in its own right and in its fields of application, has been accelerating throughout the 20th century. Most of this has been undertaken, and is understood, by only a tiny minority. The majority of the population is unaware of the impact of mathematics, through its interaction with developing technology, on people's everyday lives. Unfortunately, in the popular conception, 'mathematics' is synonymous with 'number' and various forms of computation. Freudenthal, as usual, has something germane to say (1973). Commenting that 'mathematics' is now often used to describe what is really *arithmetic*, he adds:

> Soon 'mathematics' will be taught in the lower grades of the schools of quite a few countries by people who do not even know what mathematics is.

The lack of a sense of what mathematics can and cannot achieve means that political policy-makers, who may take advice on all manner of issues from civil servants using mathematical models, often lack any means of judging whether those models are appropriate, or indeed what questions they should be asking. This situation arises in part because mathematics is perceived, not just as difficult, but as remote, opaque in its language and symbolism, and 'lacking a human face'. It is no accident that, among a range of books purporting to explain the new subject of chaos, one of the most popular was that by James Gleick (1988) — not because he explained the mathematics of chaos particularly well (there are many books that do this better) but because he turned it into a story of human endeavour, in which the reader could relate to real people. The history of mathematics and its symbiosis with the development of advanced societies is a missing dimension in its teaching, at all levels.

What, then, should be taught, and to whom? A major problem is to cater for the needs of the minority who will eventually become professional mathematicians (or who will, at least, practise mathematics in some form) and at the same time equip the generally educated citizen and tax-payer with both the mathematical skills they will need and an appreciation of the role, place, and power of mathematics as a discipline in its own right. Freudenthal (1973) reminds us that:

> A mathematician should never forget that mathematics is too important to frame its instruction to suit more or less the needs of future mathematicians.

There are many laudable sets of principles upon which an instructional programme might be constructed. For example, the Mathematical Association Teaching Committee suggested (Mathematical Association, 1976):

- the acquisition of basic skills and knowledge necessary for everyday life
- the acquisition of further skills pertinent to particular careers
- the development of the ability to think and reason logically . . . including spatial thinking
- an appreciation of the idea of a mathematical model (and therefore of the role mathematics can play in a wide variety of situations)
- mathematics as queen and servant — as a tool in mankind's control of its environment and as an intellectual activity . . .
- mathematics as a social activity, in its conduct, its existence, and its applications, with concurrent emphasis on communication skills — verbal, graphical, and written
- mathematics as a language
- an appreciation of the problem-solving powers of mathematics through personal experience of investigation and open-ended problems.

If such a set of aims as these is to be implemented, then there are some tricky political problems that need to be addressed, before one can get down to such relative trivialities as deciding what the content of appropriate mathematical syllabuses should consist of. Two such problems are: the supply of *teachers* capable of delivering this mathematics, and the amount of *time* that should be devoted to mathematics (in the widest sense) within the curriculum at different stages.

Geoffrey Howson (1996), in a recent article, surveys the educational scene in mathematics over the last century and concludes that the most important and crucial lesson to be learned from history is the central position of the teacher. He points out that 75 per cent of all mathematics graduates in 1938 entered the school-teaching profession, compared with less than 10 per cent 50 years later, and makes the assertion that 'the probability of a bright 11–16 year-old having a (mathematics) teacher who can comprehend and meet his or her needs would seem markedly less today than 30 years ago'. The mathematically educated person of the next century will require the instruction and intellectual leadership of good teachers of mathematics.

In England and Wales, mathematics is now compulsory for all pupils up to the age of 16. If we are serious about providing basic skills (with sufficient practice for fluency) as well as building the platform that will encourage the further study of the subject (to whatever level), then mathematics will need to be assigned more time within the school curriculum. It is perhaps worthy of note that in the Pacific Rim economies of Japan, Korea, Taiwan, and Hong Kong, the time devoted to mathematics in the school curriculum is considerably more than in the UK and probably many other western countries. Not only, for example, do Taiwan schools teach for 222 days a year, compared with 190 in England but, more strikingly, the typical pupil will spend around 15 hours a week on mathematics (including classes, homework and extra 'cramming'), which is probably three times as much as a typical pupil in Britain. That there may be a downside to this, in terms of a wider cultural education, is discussed by Lin and Tsao (Chapter 19). But an increase in the time allocated to mathematics, either within the standard school day or as part of a general expectation of pupils, will not happen unless the mathematical community can make out a case for the unique importance of learning and appreciating mathematics that will either (a) persuade other subject areas to concede some of their time allocation (not very likely) or (b) convince political agencies that the school day or year needs to be extended to cope with these demands (perhaps marginally more plausible, since other subject areas might see some self-interest in supporting such a move).

Post 16, the situation is more complex. There is, I believe, a rational argument to be made that some mathematics ought to be a compulsory part of a Baccalaureate-style education (while those intending to become mathematics specialists at universities might follow a 'Mathematics Baccalaureate', which could be different in depth and quantity). The hard part, again, is deciding the content of this compulsory 'Mathematics for the majority'. What follows is inevitably a personal view, for which I do not claim any special position of authoritativeness.

In trying to define what being mathematically educated might mean, perhaps one should distinguish between mathematics as a discipline in its own right and part of our cultural tradition (akin to music, literature, and the arts), and mathematics as a necessary tool for coping with and understanding the complex world in which we live. The mathematically educated person should certainly have encountered both facets.

Under the first heading, I would hope that the mathematically educated person would have an appreciation of principles in mathematics (such as the purpose of abstraction and of generalization, and the role of proof), an understanding of why the tools work and which tools are appropriate in given circumstances, and especially an awareness of interconnections within mathematics. One would like to see the mathematically educated person being exposed to an account of the major concerns of contemporary mathematics (a current example would be some of the things in Ian Stewart's book *From Here to Infinity*, 1996), as well as learning about the historical impact of the subject in the development of the modern world, its symbiotic relationship with the growth of science and technology, and the industrial consequences of these two.

Under the second heading, it would be nice to aspire to a state where the mathematically educated person would have an appreciation of such things (beyond standard numeracy and geometry) as probability and risk, and what statistical analysis can tell one. Is it unreasonable to hope that this person could work out for themselves why the odds against winning £10 in the UK National Lottery are about 57 to 1, and could interpret the parameters μ and σ in the normal distribution and so realize that μ specifies the centre of the curve, while σ determines whether the bell is tall and narrow or short and wide, and interpret this in context?

There are questions about computability and its limitations (what can and can't be solved by computers); chaotic and deterministic behaviour; the idea and some of the methods of mathematical proof as opposed to empirical theory (see Anderson, 1996a, 1996b); generality (including infinite processes); isomorphism (recognizing the same structure in superficially different situations); and invariance (the preservation of some aspect, notwithstanding other changes).

Conclusion

It has been my aim to draw attention to the fact that there are many constituencies to be addressed when debating mathematics for the new millennium: pupils who will need some basic mathematics as part of their 'life skills', employers who may require not only mathematical techniques and knowledge but also transferable skills such as the ability to reason logically and to be organized and systematic, policy-makers and decision-makers (for example, in Government) who need to be able to weigh up both qualitative and quantitative evidence, not to mention parents, teachers, and mathematics professionals.

The accelerating pace of change that has been apparent throughout the 20th century shows no sign of slowing. This applies not only to the technological changes which have transformed life in the 'First World', with rapid travel and communications making technology much more widely and quickly accessible, but also to the development of subjects such as mathematics. Driven by all kinds of demands, from innovative industries to arms developments and hi-tech projects such as the space race, mathematicians are pushing forward the boundaries of their subject to the extent that no individual can be knowledgeable about more than a part. A striking feature of this is the mathematization of subjects which, 20 or so years ago, would have been generally thought of as having little scope for such treatment: biology, medicine, and the life sciences are examples. This creates its own dilemma for professional practitioners of mathematics: on the one hand, the subject is expanding beyond the capability of the ordinary person to understand and appreciate — on the other, this remoteness is an obstacle to persuading the ordinary person that mathematics at a more elementary level is a worthwhile activity for them to become engaged in. But, as the world in which we live becomes even more complex and its problems more difficult and challenging to solve, it becomes even more important to strive for the means of comprehending those problems.

The continuing health of mathematics as a subject depends not only on recruiting students for advanced study, but also on creating a wider understanding of why mathematics should be financially supported. This in turn requires changing the perception of mathematics as a difficult, arcane, and minority pursuit to one in which the acquisition of mathematical skills, understanding, and knowledge is valued, and its exactness and rationality provide a counter against numerology and spurious beliefs. In promoting the view that no-one in the 21st century can claim to be educated unless they are, *inter alia*, mathematically educated perhaps the last word should be left to Brown and Porter (1995):

> There is a general lack of appreciation of what mathematicians have accomplished, and the importance of mathematics. Some of this has come about through mathematicians themselves failing to defend and explain their subject in a global sense to their students, to the public and to government and industry. It is possible for a student to get a good degree in mathematics without any awareness that research is going on in the subject.
>
> Another danger is the growing reliance on computers as a black box to give the answer, without understanding the processes involved, or the concepts which are intended to be manipulated. . . .
>
> We need in society a real understanding of the work of mathematicians, and of the way mathematics has played a role in the society in which we live. It is our responsibility to the subject we love to find ways of developing this understanding.

The goal is to achieve as wide a mathematically educated populace as is possible. If the mathematical community can't or won't do it, then no-one else will: it is in our own hands.

References

ANDERSON, J.A. (1996a) 'The legacy of school: Attempts at justifying and proving among new undergraduates', *Journal of Teaching Mathematics and Its Applications*, **15**, 3, pp. 129–34.

ANDERSON, J.A. (1996b) 'The place of proof in school mathematics', *Mathematics Teaching*, **155**, pp. 33–9.

BROWN, R. and PORTER, T. (1995) 'The methodology of mathematics', *Mathematical Gazette*, **485**, pp. 321–34.

COCKCROFT, W.H. (1982) *Mathematics Counts*, London: HMSO.

DEPARTMENT OF EDUCATION AND SCIENCE (1988) *Advancing A levels* (The Higginson Report), HMSO.

FREUDENTHAL, H. (1973) *Mathematics As an Educational Task*, Dordrecht: Reidel.

FUJITA, H. et al. (1996) 'Mathematics education at risk', *Mathematical Gazette*, **488**, pp. 352–5.

GLEICK, J. (1988) *Chaos*, London: Heinemann.

HADOW REPORT (1931) *The Primary School*, London: HMSO.

HAMMERSLEY, J.M. (1968) 'On the enfeeblement of traditional mathematical skills by "modern mathematics" and similar soft intellectual trash', *Bulletin of the Institute of Mathematics and its Applications*, **4**, pp. 66–85.

HOWSON, A.G. (1996) 'Looking back — and looking forward', *Mathematical Gazette*, **487**, pp. 129–36.

INSTITUTE OF MATHEMATICS AND ITS APPLICATIONS (1978) *The N and F Proposals in Relation to Mathematics: Proceedings of Symposium*, Institute of Mathematics and its Applications, London.

LMS/IMA/RSS (1995) *Tackling the Mathematics Problem*, London: London Mathematical Society/Institute for Mathematics and its Applications/Royal Statistical Society.

MATHEMATICAL ASSOCIATION (1976) *Why, What and How?*, Mathematical Association, Leicester.

McINTOSH, A. (1977) 'When will they ever learn?', *Forum*, **19**, 3 (also reprinted in *Mathematics Teaching*, Primary Supplement 86, 1979, pp. i–iv).

NATIONAL CURRICULUM (1988) *Mathematics for Ages 5 to 16*, National Curriculum Council, Mathematics Working Group, Dep of Education and Science.

SCHOOLS COUNCIL (1980) *Examinations at 18+: Report on the N and F Debate*, London: Methuen Educational, Schools Council Working Paper, 66.

SCHOOLS MATHEMATICS PROJECT (1971) *The First Ten Years*, The Schools Mathematics Project, Southampton.

SKEMP, R.R. (1986) *The Psychology of Learning Mathematics*, London: Penguin.

STEWART, I. (1987) *The Problems of Mathematics*, Oxford paperbacks: Oxford University Press.

STEWART, I. (1996) *From Here to Infinity*, Oxford: Oxford University Press.

TAVERNER, S. (1996) 'Comparing boards in A-level mathematics', *Mathematical Gazette*, **488**, pp. 362–6.

TEPPER HAINO, D. (1995) 'Experiment and conjecture are not enough', *American Mathematical Monthly*, **102**, 2, pp. 102–12.

WEYL, H. (1944) *Obituary Notices of Fellows*, Royal Society, London, **4**, 13.

Chapter 2

Industrial Applied Mathematics Is Changing As Technology Advances: What Skills Does Mathematics Education Need to Provide?

Michael Clayton

One of the most remarkable features of our present-day society is the ubiquity of information technology (IT). In any industrial or commercial workplace, the chances are that most employees will have a computer on their desk, and will spend a significant proportion of their day working with the information that it presents to them. This widespread use of IT has had a tremendous impact on working practices everywhere, with consequent changes both in the number of people employed and in the skills that they now require.

In the electronics industry where I work, many of the software tools which support our businesses are based on mathematical principles and techniques, and require a variety of mathematical skills in their application. Users can be design engineers working on new components or systems, planners specifying, scheduling, and controlling projects, or managers largely concerned with financial matters. I meet a fair cross-section of all these types of people in the course of my work, and consequently have a good view of how the advance of technology is changing the ways in which organizations operate, and in particular the use they make of mathematics. In this chapter, I shall try to describe both positive and negative aspects of these changes, and hence identify the attitudes and skills that businesses will be likely to need from their future employees as IT assumes an increasingly important role in the workplace. I shall also suggest how education can help to make students aware of the power and relevance of mathematics for modelling real-world situations, and encourage them to make appropriate use of IT during their time at school.

The opinions that I shall present are, of course, purely my own, and should not be interpreted in any way as representing a corporate view from my employers.

How Applied Mathematics in Industry and Commerce Is Changing

My experience of applying mathematics relates mainly to the telecommunications industry, where, for the past 30 years, I have been involved in the design and development of new systems. Most of my immediate colleagues have been mathematics graduates, and our work has involved modelling, theoretical investigations, mathematical analysis, and computer simulation. We liaise closely with other design and development staff, as well as the production engineers responsible for manufacturing the systems which we have helped to specify.

From the early days when telephone exchanges were first invented, mathematics has been applied to analysing the performance of telecommunications systems, and in the past 70 years it has played a vital role in providing the foundation for technical design. This extends to all aspects of telecommunications: information transducers that turn speech, images, and other data into an electronic form suitable for communication; transmission systems that use wire, cable, radio, or optical fibre to send information from place to place; switches and networks that provide the facilities for interconnecting communicators. As in other branches of applied mathematics, the analysis generally has three main phases:

- create a symbolic description of the physical situation being modelled
- manipulate the mathematics to provide understanding and the basis for numerical calculation
- carry out detailed numerical calculation on cases of interest

with iteration at any stage as dictated by the results produced. Initially, when calculations had to be carried out by hand, the balance was quite strongly towards parsimonious modelling, with considerable emphasis on symbolic analysis for understanding, and to produce expressions that would allow quantitative performance predictions. Some direct simulation was carried out, but usually only in situations involving genuine randomness, such as modelling the flow of telephone calls through exchanges.

In recent years, the availability of powerful computer systems and modern software has made quite a difference to the way in which my colleagues and I work. It is still important for us to formulate our problems using mathematical symbolism, but, in many instances, solutions are achieved through direct numerical modelling and optimization rather than specialized mathematical manipulation. For example, to design selective filters that separate radio waves of different frequencies — such as those used in mobile telephone base-stations — engineers now have computer-based tools which accept performance requirements directly, maybe via a graphical interface, and generate numerical values for the circuit components. This contrasts with the original design methods which were based on manipulations of rational functions of a complex variable: locating poles and zeros to achieve the desired performance, and then decomposing the associated rational functions in particular esoteric ways to determine component values.

Beneficial Results of New Technology

Similar changes have taken place in all areas of science, industry, and commerce, generally with very positive effects on quality and productivity. The benefits can be grouped under four broad headings.

Michael Clayton

Synergy of Human–Machine Interaction

In many situations, it is now possible to carry out initial design evaluations by means of 'computer experiments' rather than having to resort to the traditional expensive alternative of constructing hardware 'breadboard' prototypes on which to make measurements. IT tools provide a rapid response for quantitative performance assessment which gives designers, planners, and controllers the ability to perform a number of alternative prospective ('what-if') investigations before making decisions. This 'human in the loop' approach to optimization can be very productive, not least because it provides information directly to the person making decisions. Much of the synergy derives from linking human intelligence with the data manipulation and visual presentation options available from modern software, thereby facilitating insight, understanding, generalization, and hypothesis building. A typical interaction takes the form: 'I wonder what happens when . . .? Ah, now I think I see what's going on . . . so what I need to do is . . .' As the range of IT tools grows, different, complementary modules can usefully be integrated into 'environments' or 'workbenches' from which the user can select whichever is most appropriate. This flexible accessibility encourages alternative problem formulations and improves the chance of obtaining successful solutions.

Extended Range of Soluble Problems

As computer processing has grown faster and more powerful, solution methods requiring large amounts of calculation have become feasible. At the same time, increased memory capacity and rapid data transfer to and from disc storage mean that computers can easily handle problems that involve large datasets. Software integration is important here too, offering easier links between different aspects of the modelling process, so that in the course of a single investigation one might use tools to carry out symbolic algebra, numerical solution of differential equations, and multi-dimensional data display and exploration, all accessible from within a coherent environment.

Quantifiable Effects of Uncertainty

The use of computers to perform Monte Carlo trials based on pseudo-random number generators makes it possible to carry out investigations by direct simulation of situations that are inherently stochastic in nature such as congestion in road traffic or telecommunications networks. Similar techniques can also be used to establish the sensitivity of a mathematical model to changes in one or more of its parameters whose values are uncertain.

*Better Communication and Broader Applicability of
Mathematical Modelling*

General-purpose IT tools such as spreadsheets, and mathematically based environments and workbenches such as *MathCAD* and *Matlab* have made it easier for engineers, dealers, salesmen, managers, and others to construct their own models and refine them for specific applications. When time is of the essence, the value of these tools lies in the rapid prototyping that they allow: initial modelling ideas can be investigated by potential users, and the resulting interaction often leads to an improved match between the model and the users' requirements.

Modern graphical user interfaces (including virtual reality where appropriate) can be designed to make even the most sophisticated special-purpose models accessible to the people who need to use them, helping to remove the 'ivory-tower' and 'back-room' images that have sometimes been attached to mathematicians in the past. Communication is further improved once report generation is integrated with the modelling and problem-solving process.

IT Can Be Counter-productive — Traps for the Unwary

In some situations, particularly if they are used by unskilled or inadequately trained people, the introduction of IT modelling tools can lead to problems and difficulties that might not have arisen previously. It is important that educators and trainers should recognize the dangers, and ensure that students are brought up to follow working practices which avoid them. Otherwise we shall frequently have cause to regret the truism: 'A fool with a tool is still a fool!'.

Inappropriate or Uncritical use of Modelling

There is a growing tendency for modellers to provide a fully detailed characterization for every component or sub-system in their overall model, since the power of IT tools to handle complex objects significantly reduces the incentive to create simple, understandable representations to think about. Although the fidelity of the model is likely to benefit, the resultant demands on analysis resources can be severe. With such a complex model, it is often much harder to gain any creative insight about the situation or problem being investigated, and difficult to determine the limitations of the model itself.

A second concern is that, too often, users incline to the view that 'the computer is always correct'. Not enough attention is currently directed to establishing what accuracy should be attached to quantitative estimates derived from IT tools. It is particularly noticeable that, when a result is presented to (say) four significant figures, graduates who should know better tend to quote them all, without attempting a proper uncertainty analysis. This type of checking is also one way of preventing the use of incorrect or unreliable data — an ever-present danger in any modelling exercise ('Garbage in; garbage out!'). It is particularly easy for this to happen with unthinking application of IT tools: users need to be constantly aware of the possibility.

Verification and Validation Difficulties

The widespread use of IT tools creates important problems associated with verification and validation — how does one know whether or not to trust results, models, or analysis tools provided by other people? In particular, what is the structure of the models incorporated in a particular tool? What hidden assumptions might be built into it? What is the range of applicability over which its predictions will be valid? For example, some methods for predicting signal degradation in radio communications implicitly assume that the transmission channel is only slightly perturbed from its ideal distortion-free state. In certain circumstances, using values of the model parameters that violate this assumption produces nonsensical predictions; in other cases, the results can be plausible, but wrong!

Wasteful Use of Resources

Not enough attention is paid to the design of computer experiments. Thus we quite often hear remarks which could be paraphrased as: 'Let's set up a detailed system simulation, vary all the parameters that might conceivably be important, and see what happens'. One thing that almost certainly happens in this type of simulation is that data are produced in such profusion that they conceal the essential behaviour of the system being investigated. Unfortunately, it is all too easy to generate large, obscure datasets by asking IT tools unfocused questions. The volume of data is likely to cause processing problems at later stages of the investigations, and will often hide important facts under an excess of irrelevant information.

Future Demands for Mathematical Skills and Attitudes

There is every reason to suppose that in the future the power of IT tools will continue to increase as the performance of both hardware and software improves. Further advances in visualization methods will improve the way that information is presented, and hence make communication easier — both person-to-person and at the human-to-computer interface. I believe that this continuing development will confirm that the main value of IT tools to industry, commerce and science lies in the synergy that derives from properly organized partnerships between people and computers, working with carefully developed models of real-world situations. Most people working with computers and mathematics will be *using* tools, rather than developing them, and any problems are likely to be associated with misuse arising from the illusion of machine infallibility. Consequently, I think that employers will be seeking people who have the ability to think about real-world problems analytically and formulate symbolic relationships between observable entities in ways that will make them amenable to further investigations using mathematics and computer-based tools. In short, employees will need:

- symbol sense (Arcavi, 1994) for constructing mathematical models and manipulating them in order to acquire understanding
- an awareness of how mathematics and IT can be applied synergistically
- experience in solving problems, making use of IT where appropriate
- an appreciation of the importance of verification and validation in any modelling application, but particularly when IT is involved.

I think that there will also be an increasing demand for staff who are capable of handling uncertainty — both in data and behaviour — as sophisticated tools make this aspect of modelling more widespread.

The Role of Mathematics Education

My conclusions lead me to suggest that an important aim of mathematics education should be to make students properly aware of the value of mathematical modelling in a wide range of situations, and to train them how to apply IT tools most effectively. The benefits that will accrue are essential for the survival and future growth of commerce, industry, and science, and there are opportunities for them to be realized at every level of employment.

To help our young people acquire the necessary skills and use them profitably in their later employment, I hope that schools and colleges will be enabled and encouraged to maintain a balanced mathematics syllabus that includes:

- mathematical techniques and analysis methods taught in contexts that show how they can be used
- the principles and application of mathematical modelling
- numerical methods including direct simulation, and the use of appropriate technology
- the effects of uncertainty — how they can be measured and analysed.

In this type of learning, IT, with its power to produce graphical images and manipulate symbols, objects, or numbers, has an important role as a tutorial assistant: illustrating mathematical concepts, encouraging directed investigations, and aiding visualization in the exploration and transformation of data.

The scope of mathematics can usefully be broadened to provide the basis for a disciplined approach to problem solving across the whole curriculum, in which mathematical modelling and IT tools are used to enhance understanding and derive quantitative results in a wide variety of subject areas. If such activities are carefully planned they can be used to ensure that the principles of verification, validation, and accuracy estimation are understood and properly applied in the construction and application of mathematical models.

Implications for 16–19 Courses and Examinations in the Future

In the UK, all of the points raised in the previous section are already included in the requirements for the current core for mathematics at A and AS level, as it was defined in 1993. Therefore I had hoped that there was a willingness to begin an evolution of school mathematics to meet future needs — a process that will require a significant change of emphasis. Students must be convinced that mathematics in general and, more importantly, the mathematics they are asked to learn have a real relevance to a wide range of post-19 opportunities and careers. In my opinion, cross-curricular links should be encouraged — to subjects such as geography, economics, business studies, and biology as well as the physical sciences. This is likely to require syllabus modifications in order to encompass opportunities for more investigative modelling activities, while ensuring that these are based on solid mathematical foundations. I also hope that mathematical comprehension becomes something that every A and AS student is required to demonstrate, with particular emphasis on an ability to understand what conclusions may or may not justifiably be drawn from the results of modelling investigations or data analysis. Such changes will necessarily require careful planning, together with full support for teachers as they too adapt to the new and different mathematical requirements.

However, despite all the evidence which is accumulating to support the need for evolution, as shown for example in Chapters 9, 15, and 17 of this book, the recent (1996) revision of the UK subject core for mathematics at A and AS level has removed all reference to mathematical modelling and the mathematics of uncertainty, retreating to a position which could leave students dangerously ill equipped for the future. As Bernard Cornu said at our conference: 'One does not learn teamwork other than by being part of a team; one does not learn how to use technology other than by using technology'. I would add: 'One cannot learn mathematical modelling other than by building and investigating mathematical models in realistic contexts'.

Reference

ARCAVI, A. (1994) 'Symbol sense: Informal sense making in formal mathematics,' *For the Learning of Mathematics*, **14**, 3, pp. 24–35.

Chapter 3

Following Mathematical Practices in Design-oriented Work

Rogers Hall

Introduction

While educational reform and policy documents regularly refer to the workplace in calls for 'realistic' or 'authentic' mathematics in school classrooms, we still know relatively little about the organization or development of mathematical practices in the workplace. This is relevant to research on mathematics education for several reasons:

- our basic assumptions about cognition, teaching, learning, and assessment may change as a result of research into mathematical settings in the workplace
- workplaces are changing rapidly, so detailed, extra-curricular images of mathematics in use may help the educational community to think about the content and organization of reform-driven mathematics pedagogy
- it may be useful to carry these images into classrooms, so that the recurrent problem of 'motivating' mathematics for students can be approached with something other than curricular fictions about other places called 'every-day' or 'work.'

The Math@Work Project

The Math@Work Project is a three-year study to compare the organization and development of mathematical practices in school and work settings where design is a leading activity. Project researchers and teachers work together to conduct detailed cognitive and ethnographic studies of mathematical activity in classrooms that are reorganizing as part of educational reform movements, and in workplaces that may provide career targets for school students. Studies in the workplace over-lap with a summer 'workshop' for participating teachers; school studies are then conducted in the classrooms of these teachers, who use project-based curriculum units (for example, the Middle School Mathematics through Applications Project 'Antarctica' unit, 1996) developed around similar types of work. We use these studies of work and school in a comparative fashion, asking how the teaching and learning of mathematics might be reorganized to take advantage of activity that we find in the workplace.

The project focuses on *quantitative reasoning* and its role in the modelling of complex systems. By quantitative reasoning we mean the processes of selecting attributes of a situation that can be measured, identifying units and schemes of numeration appropriate as measures, and inscribing these in one or more systems of representation. This approach treats quantity as something that people construct in specific domains (diSessa et al., 1991; Greeno, 1983; Hall, 1996; Kaput, 1991; Schoenfeld et al., 1993; Thompson, 1992). Attending closely to the practical contexts in which quantitative reasoning occurs reflects the challenge of studying mathematical activity outside laboratory or school settings that can be manipulated to emphasize generality, and a theoretical approach in which learning and doing mathematics depends on specific resources available in particular settings.

By modelling we mean a process of assembling and coordinating related quantities that are taken to be a representation of some situation, usually under a negotiated set of social agreements (Nunes et al., 1993, pp. 128–31). Subject to these agreements, a model can be used to explore the behaviour of a complex system as it is projected into different scenarios during the process of design (Carrol, 1994). It is the dual nature of modelling — agreeing on what quantities and relations are reasonable and then exploring their implications — that we are following. Quantitative reasoning and modelling provide a general framework for studying how mathematics is used when people explore trade-offs in the design of complex systems.

Our research has included three adult workplaces: a large civil engineering firm (OutBack), a medium-sized architectural design firm (JC Architects), and an interdisciplinary research group studying the chemical taxonomy and community ecology of forest insects (BugHouse). Having analysed the field materials, we are taking cases of interesting mathematical activity into two middle-school mathematics classrooms. This chapter reports on our findings with material collected in the architectural design firm. Other papers from this project follow comparisons across workplaces (Hall and Stevens, 1996a) and between workplaces and middle-school mathematics classrooms (Hall and Stevens, 1995, 1996b; Hall and Torralba, 1997). All these studies share a common concern with how mathematics is used in places where people work together to design things.

Imaging Mathematics for the New Millennium

The research reported here contributes to a much-needed expansion of what we think mathematics is and how we should communicate this understanding to people who are learning and teaching mathematics. The mathematics we find in design-oriented work is only part of a much larger and extremely diverse body of lived mathematical practices. A growing body of research on these diverse practices includes studies of:

- urban candy sellers in the streets of Brazil (Nunes et al., 1993; Saxe, 1991)
- professional mathematicians at work in university and industrial settings (Clayton, Chapter 2 of this book; Livingston, 1986; Restivo, 1992; Rotman, 1993)
- insurance agents in California's rapidly changing economy (Darrouzet et al., 1996)
- carpenters and their apprentices in Africa (Milroy, 1992)
- women studying to become carpenters, pipe-fitters, or electricians in a community college 'Skilled Trades for Women' programme (Castellano, 1996)
- navigators aboard military transport ships and Polynesian canoes (Hutchins, 1995)
- dieters preparing meals under strict measurement guidelines in their kitchens (de la Rocha, 1986)
- nurses administering drugs in the oncology ward of a paediatric hospital in London (Hoyles, Noss, and Pozzi, Chapter 4 of this book)
- assembly-line workers and machine-tool engineers working in the automotive manufacturing industry in Detroit, Michigan (Smith and Douglas, 1997)
- store owners and their customers as new users of currency in places like Tibet and New Guinea (Beach, 1992; Saxe, 1991)
- warehouse loaders and delivery truck drivers working in a dairy plant (Scribner, 1986)
- school children and teachers participating in a variety of new (or at least vigorously recycled) approaches to curriculum development (for example, Goldman and Moschkovich, 1995; Kaput and Rochelle, Chapter 12 of this book; Lehrer et al., 1997; Saxe, 1991; Saxe and Guberman in press).

I have listed these studies of practice in haphazard order to call into question what we think mathematics is as a cultural activity. Is there a single account of mathematics that can help us to understand all these diverse, site-specific practices? Mathematics instruction, at least as it has developed in the United States since the turn of this century (Cohen, 1982; Resnick, 1987), has largely assumed that the answer to this question is yes and that we can find out what counts as mathematics either by asking professional mathematicians or by studying people in laboratory settings. We can find out a great deal in this way, but I argue that this strategy will never allow us to map out this larger corpus of heterogeneous mathematical practices. If mathematics is to be 'for everyone' (National Research Council, 1989; Lacampagne et al., 1995), then we need to know more about the 'everywheres' these people are likely to inhabit.

How to Follow Mathematics at Work

Our field studies attempt to link together three levels of analysis:

- the interactional structure of local work with different representational forms — for example, how do architects and structural engineers coordinate plan views of a building with formulae and thresholds that appear in state or municipal 'code' books?

- the manner in which this local work shapes and is shaped by recurrent activities in the organization — for example, how are design alternatives, proposed by an architect, held accountable to the analysis of structural engineers and the code requirements of government agencies?
- the ways in which people take up discipline-specific forms of identity in this kind of work — for example, how does participation in these activities lead an architect to describe their work as being 'beautiful' or a civil engineer to describe the work of a 'good engineer' as being 'creative' and 'very cool'.

The types of data we collect include: *field notes*, written in the course of ethnographic observation and indexed to provide contextual information for analysis of other forms of data; *video records* of recurrent activities in field settings, usually filmed either to follow the activities of a particular person or to capture activities that pass through a specific site (for example, a shared table surface during a design meeting); *conversational interviews*, either when study participants talk with us during breaks in their work or when we schedule taped conversations about specific topics, and *working design documents* that are used during the sessions we film or as these documents circulate through phases of a design project. No particular data source is privileged over others in our analysis. For example, to understand the significance of a design alternative, drawn over a plan view (i.e. a moment of interaction, captured in a video record, indexed on to a design document), we need to know how this alternative relates to the broader history of the design project (i.e. observations made in field notes and statements from participants during interviews).

Analysis of these data follows interpretative techniques used in the development of grounded theory (Glaser and Strauss, 1967; Strauss, 1987; Strauss and Corbin, 1990). Field notes and interviews help to identify records of project work that are good candidates for a close analysis of interaction (Goodwin and Heritage, 1990; Jordan and Henderson, 1995). Detailed analyses are then used to develop categories of learning and doing mathematics that can be checked against participants' own accounts of their work, and these categories are systematically extended across a broader sample of field data. The cycle of generating empirically grounded theoretical categories continues until we can demonstrate adequate coverage of the three issues, listed above, that lead the research. The purpose of developing this kind of grounded theory is to respecify mathematical problem solving, teaching, and learning in terms that do justice to the distributed, context-specific character of actual work practices (Suchman, 1995).

A Case Study: Making a Building Stronger

This case study is an analysis-in-progress, taken from ongoing research in an architectural firm we call JC Architects (JCA). The name of the firm is a pseudonym, as

Figure 3.1 The social and physical setting for a preliminary design meeting to retrofit two public libraries

a The JCA design team in action

are the names of study participants. JCA is a medium-sized firm (two principal architects and four juniors) located in a light-industrial neighbourhood of Berkeley, California.

Background to the Case

A neighbouring city has commissioned a feasibility study for seismic retrofitting of two public libraries (Taraval and Portal), and they have now asked JCA to present a preliminary design proposal on how to strengthen each library. These libraries are located close to an active fault line, and their exterior walls are made of unreinforced masonry and could either collapse or produce lethal debris during a major earthquake. Since such an earthquake is expected within the next 20 years, most communities in Northern California are raising public moneys for seismic retrofitting projects. Counterbalancing the need to retrofit these structures, both libraries are Carnegie-era buildings and so have great historical value. Furthermore, their 'program' (i.e., intended use) is a matter of fierce and conflicting community interest.

The excerpt chosen for analysis here comes from an early design development meeting. Figure 3.1(a) shows the design team seated around a large table covered with design drawings and various code documents. The disciplinary specialties of

Figure 3.1 (cont'd)

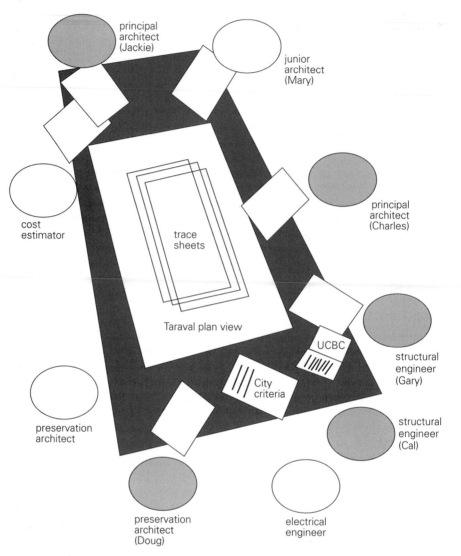

b Their various specialties and the distribution of design documents over the table surface

team members are shown in Figure 3.1(b), along with the location of different design documents. The meeting was led by the principal architects (Charles and Jackie), and they, along with an historical preservation architect (Doug) and two structural engineers (Gary and Cal), contributed most of the conversation to be examined.

This excerpt was selected for several reasons: it contains a sustained discussion about how to satisfy city and state codes governing the strength of public buildings in California; this discussion makes explicit use of several important quantities; much of the conversation balances the different but complementary contribution of architects and structural engineers; and there is serious discussion of whether or not the assumptions underlying the codes are accurate or even adequate for judging the strength or safety of a building. As a result, this excerpt contains extended stretches of activity in which people actually do the things that the Math@Work Project is attempting to follow. That is, they engage in *quantitative reasoning* in the service of *modelling*, and both are densely negotiated processes that need to be held accountable to surrounding activity structures. While we have not fully analysed all field materials from JCA, this meeting does not appear to be atypical.

Two quantities were at the centre of the design conversation. The first is called 'h over t', which for a local component of the building's structure, like an external wall, is the ratio of the height of the component to its cross-sectional area. In an earthquake the ground accelerates rapidly, so limits are placed on allowable h over t ratios for buildings made out of unreinforced masonry. These limits vary according to different 'procedures' for retrofitting (what Gary calls 'general' and 'special' procedures). The second quantity is 'demand/capacity ratio', which is an overall measure of the building's resistance to shaking and is calculated by accumulating h over t ratios. For example, a demand/capacity ratio of 1.0 indicates that the resistive capacity of the building would meet expected forces in a seismic event of some given size.

A quick overview of the case will be helpful, before showing a sequence of detailed exchanges and considering the nature of mathematical activity we can find. In this meeting, team members are hoping to find one or two design alternatives that can be presented to the city architect's office and, later, at a public review meeting that will include the library governing board. One of the historical architects makes an important proposal: the bottom floor of the library is partly below ground, so they can strengthen it and call it the foundation. By redefining the bottom floor, they can change their analysis of the strength of the entire structure, and their proposal might meet city and state codes. This leads to an extended discussion of two things: (a) whether the structural engineers, who are 'on the line' concerning the integrity of the design proposal, can 'live with' excess stresses that exceed code limits and (b) whether the design team should challenge the studies that were used to set these code limits in the first place. After carefully framing their leading proposal in a way that makes structural elements 'stronger', one of the structural engineers sketches an engineering approach that 'just might work'. This final contribution completes the request for a design 'concept' made by the project leader at the beginning of the case.

In the sequence of episodes that follow, my analysis will be concerned with the following questions:

- How do quantitative reasoning and modelling emerge in design activity, given that these are not the organizing purpose of the activity?
- How do designers manage tensions between the specific, local conditions of a design project and more general constraints that govern their work?

- How are different interests and forms of accountability aligned or articulated together when moving a design forward?
- Can we find teaching/learning events in this work and, if so, how are they organized?

Episode 1: Charles Frames Today's Task As Finding a Design Concept

In this first episode Charles, the principal architect on the project, lays out the purpose of the meeting: they need to 'walk through the applicable standards' to find a 'concept of what it is we want to do'. This concept will be presented both to the city and to the public. As this is a case study of the negotiated character of mathematical practice, two things are particularly important to notice.

First, the term consists of a number of different specialists. For example, Doug represents the discipline of preservation architecture and Gary represents structural engineering. While these two have overlapping understandings that allow them to work together, they have been brought together precisely because their specific understandings do not completely overlap. Instead, what they are expected to know and do are complementary: they are part of a multi-disciplinary team. Within the work of the team, individuals are asked to speak from discipline-specific perspectives on a common design problem, for example the principal architect asks the structural engineers if they are 'comfortable' with a proposed challenge to code. We should expect team members to have different views of 'standards' or what makes for a reasonable design 'concept'. This is a good start for an analysis of how assumptions are negotiated when describing a complex system in mathematical terms.

Second, there are many interests to satisfy in this design project, and there are conflicts among them. While Charles does not list them all in this episode, our ethnographic work at JCA can be used to highlight the most important of them. The *public* wants to be sure these library buildings are safe, but also to preserve their historical character, to award construction contracts to local builders in a way that mirrors the ethnic diversity of the community, and to minimize disruptions in service while the work is in progress. The *library staff*, on the other hand, has concerns about losing private workspace to accommodate the retrofit and would like to include building improvements wherever possible. The *city*, operating with a restricted budget and a variety of state and federal design guidelines, needs to ensure safety and access within this budget. In terms of our analysis, then, we should expect that negotiations about assumptions will be contentious and extend well beyond the disciplines represented by members of the design team.

Managing potentially incommensurable interests and the constraints they imply is what makes design problems difficult. Consider how Charles opens the work of the team meeting. As he sets it out, their work is to find a 'concept' for strengthening the libraries. Even in the structure of Charles's opening utterance, we find there are multiple interests in this design problem, and the team needs to find some way of articulating[1] these together if they expect to make a successful proposal. But how are interests not present in the room brought into this working conversation?

In the first major segment of his opening utterance, Charles proposes that the design team 'walk through the applicable standards here' to arrive at a 'concept of what it is we want to do.' In this, he describes the collective, present-time work of the design team, as it relates to a variety of municipal and state regulations. The second major segment, in contrast, shifts into future-time and brings in the perspectives of two groups who are not present in this meeting. First, he describes talking to 'the city, we're gonna have to go through this exercise of explaining to them very clearly what their choices are'. Second, he describes going before 'the public' and, within this description, he produces a sequential narrative that includes challenges from the public (for example, 'are the lives of our children not of value to you'), responses from the design team (for example, 'tell them, you know, why we've arrived at, you know, the choices we have'), and attempts to articulate public and city interests (for example, 'whether those are feasible or not feasible based on the budget'). It is this second major segment that starts the process of bringing other interests into the local, here-and-now work of the design team.

Episode 2: Gary Wonders If 'We Can Live with a Bit of Excess h over t'

In this second episode, Gary speaks about the libraries from the perspective of structural engineering, having partially analysed their stability in terms of the two conventional quantities (h over t and demand/capacity ratio). The Taraval library is not structurally sound (the demand/capacity ratio exceeds 1.0), yet he proposes that the team might be able to 'live with' this situation. Although this is a multi-disciplinary team, JCA is the firm legally responsible for the quality of its design proposals. Charles, a principal architect in this firm, understandably questions how they could 'live with' this excess. Gary works for a separate structural-engineering firm engaged as one of JCA's consultants. Cal, the more senior structural engineer in Gary's firm, acknowledges that the city might not agree to the excess in such a 'high-profile job'.

This is an interesting set of developments: the team is considering a design proposal that violates pre-established mathematical results; multiple interests and accountabilities are in play; and the outcome will apparently hinge on assumptions used to interpret two related quantities. From a mathematical perspective, we might think that structural features of the Taraval library can be unambiguously determined and then compared with code criteria that also are determinate. This second episode starts to unravel the unambiguous correspondence between mathematical description and the world, at least that part of the world that is made out of unreinforced masonry.

Consider first the different interests and accountabilities. By accountability I mean formal responsibility for the conduct of activity in which many different stakeholders may have an interest. Although interests, pursued over time, may lead to formal accountabilities — this, presumably, is how 'code' develops — the two concepts are not identical. If they were, designers would face problems that have either determinate solutions or no solutions at all. Instead, designers more often face dilemmas in which solutions will involve trade-offs. In this kind of setting, mathematical description and analysis are resources for lining up interests and accountabilities, but they do not single-handedly determine stable outcomes and can sometimes be judged irrelevant (Hall and Stevens, 1995; Kraemer et al., 1987; Latour, 1996).

Within the team, the structural engineers are the experts in negotiation, but the principals at JCA are legally accountable for the quality of the team's design proposal. This tension appears in Cal's initial response to Charles, where he shuffles the cast of characters who will talk to the city ('I think, I guess (that we, the) architect, is that what you're saying, we have to talk with the city'). Outside the team, the city architect's office is both legally and politically accountable to the public. As in Charles's previous narrative about public interests, Cal's final turn within this second episode animates the perspective of the city. He refers to the library retrofit as a 'high-profile job' and suggests that 'they' will want to 'go by the book'. In whatever way the design team proposes to alter the world to meet the code, each of these accountabilities needs to be met.

Second, the mathematical structure of code criteria becomes relevant when design activity breaks down, in this case when h over t and demand/capacity ratios are exceeded. Gary announces the breakdown qualitatively, saying these ratios are not 'OK' on Taraval, then gives his current, quantitative estimate of a demand/capacity ratio ('one point one'). He also describes an error interval around his calculations ('plus or minus 10 per cent'), raising the possibility that final calculations could be slightly lower or higher.

Even in the way that gestures are coordinated with talk (Gary's hands trace out symbolic derivations for h over t, while Charles's hands sweep out a vertical interval to show a 'range' and excess), we find evidence that people with different responsibilities understand and use quantities in different ways. Gary's perspective is that of someone deriving the quantities under discussion, while Charles's perspective is that of someone using these quantities in a context of justification. If their design is to move forward these different perspectives will need to be brought into alignment.

Episode 3: Doug Disagrees with Accepting the Code Limit

Immediately following the discussion of 'excess', Doug (historical architect) explores the possibility of breaking open the code. He steps in on the issue of code limits, talking over Cal to announce a bald disagreement ('No'). He argues that the original test data for setting code limits were analysed using 'arbitrary margins of safety' and, as a result, the team is 'close' enough to convince the community to 'accept it'.

As in Episode 2, we find evidence that talk and action together animate quantitative reasoning. In this case, Doug's challenge to code starts as a narrative about the process of creating code limits for h over t, something that other firms did in the past and in another setting. So, just as Charles brings interests from the public and the city into the conversation in Episode 1, Doug brings in a version of the actual process of developing code. As Doug speaks, his hands sweep up and down to show how averages were constructed in these earlier tests, then he shows how limits were set well below these values and argues that the size of these 'margins of safety' was arbitrary. Having animated the process of setting arbitrary limits, he then shows that the team is 'this close', using his thumb and index finger to juxtapose the excess in relation to the much larger 'margins.'

My analysis of Doug's challenge is based on what he says, on what is visible in the video record, and on a broader ethnographic understanding of how this design project proceeds. I argue that two things are important in this exchange. First, a mathematical result is challenged by opening up its history of development. In Doug's narrative we and the other members of the JCA team are given a tour through a process in which Doug claims 'arbitrary' assumptions were made about safety. Second, using this historical animation as a comparative backdrop, he manually assembles a spatial display in which 'margins of safety' are arbitrarily large, yet the excess is comparatively small or 'this close'. The quantitative comparison appears both in talk and in enacted spatial displacements. He then adapts this comparison, produced for the team, to the city ('in many communities they will accept it') and to the public ('in terms of public opinion').

We already see ample evidence for the negotiated character of modelling or mathematical description. The next question for the JCA team is what to do about the Taraval library in the light of Gary's and Doug's proposals for challenging code.

Episode 4: Jackie Asks If the Engineers Are 'Comfortable' Arguing against the Code

Episode 4 opens as Jackie, the second principal architect, explicitly asks the structural engineers, Cal and Gary, whether they are 'comfortable' with the idea of challenging code on the Taraval library design. They agree they can 'talk with the city' about this and when Jackie pushes for their justification, Cal refocuses the conversation on the demand/capacity radio, a quantity that combines multiple h over t ratios.

This episode provides an example of how the complementarity of the disciplines within the team is used by participants to assess a design proposal. Here, a principal architect emphatically asks the structural engineers for their perspective on a possible code challenge (Jackie says, '*You're* the structural engineers'), and the more senior engineer acknowledges 'our thing's on the line now.' While Cal and Gary think it will be possible to 'push a little bit', they do not yet explain how they would 'justify' or 'prove' to the city that exceeding the demand/capacity ratio would be acceptable.

When Jackie asks explicitly if they would 'recalc it', Cal notes that the calculations leading to code limits are already 'in the book' and repeats that they will need to justify the excess to 'them' (i.e., the city). Within 10 minutes of Charles's opening proposal that they walk through standards to find a design concept, the team is in the middle of a design dilemma:

- Gary, only part of the way through his structural calculations, has yet to explain how he thinks 'we can live with a little excess h over t'.
- Cal, who is co-owner of the firm that employs Gary, thinks the city will resist code exceptions on this high-profile job.
- Doug, an architect specializing in historical preservation, disagrees sharply with Cal. He claims that safety assumptions backing the code limits were arbitrary, that the library is sufficiently close to the code limit, and that he can produce the original test data if necessary.
- The principal architects, who are legally responsible for the design, turn repeatedly to the structural engineers, asking if they are 'comfortable' and how they would 'justify' a design proposal that exceeds code limits.

While different perspectives on the design are becoming clear, the relation between *h* over *t* and demand/capacity ratios is not. As Gary starts the next episode, we find that there is work yet to do in mapping the Taraval Library on to design guidelines.

Episode 5: Gary Frames 'Stronger' within Different Procedures

In Episode 5, Gary returns to his calculations-in-progress and begins to describe how they might 'live with' results that exceed code restrictions. Within the code, there are different 'procedures' for retrofitting unreinforced masonry buildings, and these procedures make different assumptions about structural components, for example 'crosswalls', and their behaviour during an earthquake. Gary explains the context for evaluating *h* over *t* within different procedures, suggesting that they work within a 'general' procedure. The general procedure will allow him to interpret components of the Taraval library as being 'stronger' in his calculations.

As Gary describes this strategy, Charles asks whether the general procedure considers 'cross walls' as strengthening elements. Gary repeats these terms, pauses, then carefully instructs Charles on proper terminology, saying 'this word is one word, crosswalls, OK?' Using the technical term 'crosswalls' would classify their design within the less stringent 'special' procedure. Gary instead proposes that they call these walls 'seismic resisting elements' and place them within the library at locations where they will collect lateral forces. If they do this, their design proposal will conform with retrofitting procedures in a way that the state interprets as making the building stronger. Rather than directly challenging assumptions made when the code was developed, as Doug suggested in Episode 3, Gary opens up alternative retrofitting procedures within the code. As he qualifies the language they will use in relation to state code guidelines, first Charles and then other members of the design team begin to laugh.

Two aspects of this episode are important for an analysis of mathematical practices. First, the exchange between Charles and Gary is an example of how discipline-specific understanding and design accountability come together. When Charles uses the term 'cross walls' Gary is careful to distinguish this from 'crosswalls', noting that these are different structural entities within the special procedure. He then shifts his talk to a context of justification — an event that occurs 'when we talk about it later' — and says they will call these entities 'seismic resisting elements'. As Charles laughs, Gary points out that this classification of walls will give them an advantage within the general procedure.

I interpret this as a teaching/learning event emerging out of Charles's imprecise use of technical terms for structural components. While Gary is the specialist in this technical register, Charles, as principal architect, may well be the person making the argument 'when we talk about it later.' Therefore, Gary carefully distinguishes between the meanings of three terms — 'cross walls', 'crosswalls', and 'seismic resisting elements' — and their interpretation under different procedures. Charles has asked for a justification, and Gary is hard at work describing what words to use, what they mean, and how they will figure in the justification. In our studies across different settings for design-oriented work, we find that teaching and learning often occur during breakdowns in discipline-specific understandings or when these understandings cross lines of accountability (Hall and Stevens, 1996a, 1996b). Stevens (1997) describes this kind of interaction as a matter of 'disciplined perception', in the dual sense that specialists see objects in discipline-specific ways and interact with non-specialists so as to discipline their perception in similar ways (see also Stevens and Hall, in press).

Second, this episode is a compelling example of the distributed character of mathematical description in design-oriented work. The team is attempting to alter an existing structure, which they have visited, carefully measured, and documented. Their work must meet complex analytical criteria — the code documents on the table. At the same time, they need to keep track of varied and potentially conflicting interests. What is striking is how many things and people are physically absent and so need to be represented: the libraries as physical entities, code developers and their testing regimes, librarians, volunteers from the Friends of the Library, and a host of city officials. Depending on how the JCA team maps the part of the Taraval library on to these guidelines and interests, they get very different results.

In this view, the laughter that builds across Episode 5 — starting with Charles's amusement at being instructed about the highly specific meaning of structural terms and ending with the entire team laughing about the same physical element being 'stronger' under the general procedure — can be interpreted as a collective response to the vigorously negotiated character of mathematical description in this meeting. These people are looking for a good design solution and to do this they must negotiate with each other, with an existing analysis of seismic stability for this type of building, and with a host of other people. Mathematical assumptions matter and are hotly contested, both in face-to-face interaction and in narrative projections of future events. As this episode ends, the feasibility of the entire project apparently hangs on whether a stretch of wall is called a 'crosswall' or a 'seismic resisting element'.

As the meeting continues, there are other requests for justification, and Gary carefully explains that h over t calculations are local, specific contributions to aggregate demand/capacity ratios. Many of these aggregate ratios will be calculated for the building. This means the team can distribute stress across the building in a way that makes the overall analysis of stability acceptable.

We turn now to the final episode, in which Gary reviews his alternative to a direct code challenge.

> *Episode 6: Gary Closes by Referring Back to Charles's Call*
> *for a Concept*

If the JCA team can stay within the general procedure, they can locate a 'seismic resisting element' along an existing wall in a manner that takes forces off the wall they have been discussing, parts of which exceed the h over t limit. The resisting elements will probably redistribute forces so that the demand/capacity ratios that Gary calculates drop below 1.0. Again, it is clear that the principal architects are learning from and appropriating parts of the structural engineer's proposal. In fact, Jackie and Charles collaboratively complete an interpretation of the desired value for demand capacity ratio ('So the demand is not greater than the capacity'). The episode ends as Gary refers back to Charles's original framing for their work today: this proposal, which 'just might work out', is Gary's conceptual scheme for the building.

Conclusions

Earlier in this chapter, I argued for studies that expand our view of what counts as mathematics, since these may help us in thinking about how to approach teaching and learning mathematics as we move into the next millennium. In conclusion, I turn to three features of design-oriented work, each grounded in this case study, and consider how they might also expand our view of mathematics as a cultural practice.

1 Complementary perspectives on design lead to different views and uses of quantity

Different disciplines are represented in the JCA team because they are complementary, so participants in this meeting are expected to have different perspectives on the same thing. An excess that Gary thinks 'we can live with' draws an immediate question from a principal architect, who wonders how an engineer could 'justify' this for other audiences. When the structural engineers equivocate, an historical architect begins to pick apart the studies used to develop code limits. We find evidence for different conceptions in the way that specialists coordinate talk and gesture when addressing what seems to be the same quantity. What an engineer constructs as a specific, symbolic derivation, a principal architect turns into a spatial display of excess, which a historical architect then deconstructs (spatially and comparatively) as an arbitrary assumption. There is no single view of the 'quantity' used to communicate between these specialists; instead, their different perspectives and uses become topics of conversation within the meeting. Differences in disciplinary perspective are a good place to look if we want to understand how mathematics is organized within specific cultural practices.

2   Multiple interests and different accountabilities drive the negotiated character of mathematical description

As we saw across this case study, narrative and gestural animation bring interests into design conversation, even though the people or institutions said to hold these interests (the stakeholders) may not physically participate in the interaction. These animated design conversations are one site for 'articulation work', a place where designers anticipate future events in which their proposals will be evaluated. People are also accountable to different things in a design project. For example, the principal architects repeatedly turn to the structural engineers, searching for some way to justify what appears to be a code violation. Getting to the point of being 'comfortable' with a design, in relation to future justification, can require extended negotiation.

3   Mathematics comes to the fore during breakdowns in design-oriented work

When a design proposal starts to break down (in this case by failing to meet 'code'), mathematical descriptions become both more detailed and hotly contested. Something has to give way if the design is to progress. We have followed two responses to such a breakdown: (a) directly challenging the history of development of an established result and (b) mapping the existing design proposal on to 'code' in a way that produces a more favourable analysis. Gary's proposal to map parts of the Taraval library on to code in a different way avoids a direct challenge on this 'high-profile' job.

4   Towards a grounded theory of mathematical practices in design-oriented work

The features of mathematical practice at JC Architects that we have described are consistent with a more general set of findings and conjectures that we have derived from studies in other workplaces. These include:

- Quantitative reasoning is commonplace in these kinds of work.

We do, in fact, find mathematical practices and can study them as we would any other form of naturally occurring human activity. The naturalistic research programme outlined in this paper is practically feasible and (we think) productive.

- This reasoning usually involves simple arithmetic combinations of routine quantities.

Although our studies in the workplace are still under way, we have yet to find people involved in extended episodes of doing abstract mathematics, for example, the kinds of activities we might expect to find among students working through homework sets in an advanced course in calculus. Quite the contrary, people in our work settings comment on the fact that they do relatively little of this, and they also regularly express a preference for making mathematical arguments as simple as possible. For example, a senior entomologist at our BugHouse site (population biology) tells a consulting statistician that he wants their analysis to use 'eighth grade math' so he can communicate effectively with his colleagues. When mathematical analysis is used to convince people that decisions or claims are 'reasonable', the reasoning of recipients is carefully anticipated. On the one hand, these findings tell us something about what kinds of mathematics are actually useful for people outside academic settings. On the other hand, this situation may be very productive for thinking about how to reorganize the teaching and learning of mathematics as a form of communication (National Council of Teachers of Mathematics, 1989).

- Routine quantities are complex historical artifacts, involving negotiated agreements about how to model processes and structures.

That quantities have histories would be surprising only if we took seriously the foreshortened character of 'problems' and 'solutions' in traditional school mathematics. A more expansive view of mathematical problem solving — particularly the nature of representation in mathematical sense-making — is already under way in research on mathematics education (for example, diSessa et al., 1991; Hall, 1996; Nemirovsky, 1996; Schoenfeld et al., 1993). It is my hope that studies conducted within the Math@Work Project can add weight to this movement in ways that will actually reach the classroom. Getting students to understand that challenging mathematical assumptions is even possible is one of our educational goals, and we think this is particularly important for students to see early in their mathematical careers.

- Agreements about how to model things break down under a variety of organizational conditions.

From a theoretical perspective, this tells us about the nature of mathematical activity as a demand-driven, social practice. This is not a description of how mathematics happens everywhere, but it does tell us a great deal about the nature of mathematics as it emerges in the context of other activities. To the extent that these kinds of breakdowns are prevalent in design-oriented work (and we think they are), our naturalistic methods for following mathematical practices can be powerful.

- It appears useful to approach breakdowns and renegotiated agreements as teaching/learning events.

This final point is important because it helps us to understand that school and work are not in a polar opposition that separates learning from doing. People do and learn in both settings, and we need to continue to develop theories of learning that look outside the institution of schooling, as it is traditionally conceived, for productive ways to organize both teaching and learning. We have the good fortune of being able to draw from a number of strong theoretical and empirical precedents (for example, Engestrom, 1990; Hutchins, 1995; Lave and Wenger, 1991; Nunes et al., 1993; Rogoff, 1993), and we hope that our studies help to move this growing tradition into the next millennium.

Note

1   Sociologists of science and technology describe the problem of making connections between potentially incommensurable interests as 'articulation work' (Clarke and Fujimura, 1992; Fujimura, 1987).

References

BEACH, K. (1992) 'The role of leading and non-leading activities in transforming arithmetic between school and work', Presented at Annual meetings of the American Educational Research Association, San Francisco, CA.

CARROLL, J.M. (1994) 'Making use of a design representation', *Communications of the ACM* **37**, **12**, pp. 29–35.

CASTELLANO, M.E. (1996) 'The tools of the trade: Women acquiring the discourse of the skilled trades', Doctoral Dissertation, Graduate School of Education, University of California, Berkeley.

CLARKE, A.E. and FUJIMURA, J.H. (1992) *The Right Tools for the Job: At Work in Twentieth-century Life Sciences*, Princeton, NJ: Princeton University Press.

COHEN, P.C. (1982) *A Calculating People: The Spread of Numeracy in Early America*, Chicago, IL: University of Chicago Press.

DARROUZET, C., GALLAGHER, L., HARDING, J., LINDE, C., LAWRENCE, N., MOSCHKOVICH, J., OLSON, L., POIRIER, C. and PRESTON, C. (1996) 'Enhancing life insurance sales through motivation and learning', Project Report. Palo Alto, CA: The Institute for Research on Learning.

DE LA ROCHA, O.L. (1986) 'Problems of sense and problems of scale: An ethnographic study of arithmetic in everyday life', Doctoral Dissertation, University of California, Irvine.

DISESSA, A.A., HAMMER, D., SHERIN, B. and KOLPAKOWSKI, T. (1991) 'Inventing graphing: Meta-representational expertise in children', *Journal of Mathematical Behavior*, **10**, pp. 117–60.

ENGESTROM, Y. (1990) *Learning, Working, and Imagining*, Helsinki: Orienta-Konsultit Oy.

FUJIMURA, J. (1987) 'Constructing "do-able" problems in cancer research: Articulating alignment', *Social Studies of Science*, **17**, pp. 257–93.

GLASER, B.G. and STRAUSS, A. (1967) *The Discovery of Grounded Theory: Strategies for Qualitative Research*, Chicago, IL: Aldine Pub. Co.

GOLDMAN, S. and MOSCHKOVICH, J. (1995) 'Environments for collaborating mathematically: The Middle School Mathematics through applications project', in, SCHNASE, J.L. and CUNNIUS, E.L. (eds) *Proceedings of The First International Conference on Computer Support for Collaborative Learning*, Hillsdale, NJ: Lawrence Erlbaum and Associates, pp. 143–6.

GOODWIN, C. and HERITAGE, J. (1990) 'Conversation analysis', *Annual Review of Anthropology*, **19**, pp. 283–307.

GREENO, J.G. (1983) 'Conceptual entities', in GENTNER, D. and STEVENS, A.L. (eds) *Mental Models*, Hillsdale, NJ: Lawrence Erlbaum Associates, pp. 227–52.

HALL, R. (1996) 'Representation as shared activity: Situated cognition and Dewey's cartography of experience', *The Journal of the Learning Science*, **5**, 3, pp. 209–38.

HALL, R. and STEVENS, R. (1995) 'Making space: A comparison of mathematical work in school and professional design practices', in STAR, S.L. (ed.) *The cultures of computing*, London: Basil Blackwell, pp. 118–45.

HALL, R. and STEVENS, R. (1996a) 'Teaching/learning events in the workplace: A comparative analysis of their organizational and interactional structure', in *Proceedings of the Eighteenth Annual Conference of the Cognitive Science Society*, Hillsdale, NJ: Lawrence Erlbaum Associates, pp. 160–5.

HALL, R. and STEVENS, R. (1996b) 'Assembling mathematical competence in school and work settings', Talk in a symposium on *Development through Work: Activity, Artifacts, and Persons*, Annual meetings of the American Educational Research Association, New York City.

HALL, R. and TORRALBA, A. (1997) 'Bringing images of design-oriented work into middle school mathematics classrooms', Talk in a symposium on *What Can Studies of Mathematics in the Workplace Tell Us about Teaching and Learning Mathematics in School?*, Annual meetings of the American Educational Research Association, Chicago, IL.

HUTCHINS, E. (1995) *Cognition in the Wild*, Cambridge, MA: MIT Press.

JORDAN, B. and HENDERSON, A. (1995) 'Interaction analysis: Foundations and practice', *Journal of the Learning Sciences*, **4**, 1, pp. 39–103.

KAPUT, J.J. (1991) 'Notations and representations as mediators of constructive processes', in VON GLASERSFELD, E. (ed.) *Radical Constructivism in Mathematics Education*, The Netherlands: Kluwer Academic Publishers, pp. 53–74.

KRAEMER, K., DICKHOVEN, S., TIERNEY, and KING, J. (1987) *Datawars: The Politics of Modeling in Federal Policymaking*, New York: Columbia University Press.

LACAMPAGNE, C.B., BLAIR, W. and KAPUT, J.J. (1995) *The Algebra Initiative Colloquium, Volumes I and II*, US Department of Education, Office of Educational Research and Improvement. Washington, DC: US Government Printing Office.

LATOUR, B. (1996) *Aramis, or the Love of Technology*, Cambridge, MA: Harvard University Press.

LAVE, J. and WENGER, E. (1991) *Situated Learning: Legitimate Peripheral Participation*, Cambridge: Cambridge University Press.

LEHRER, R., SCHAUBLE, L., CARPENTER, S. and PENNER, D. (1997) 'The Inter-related Development of inscriptions and conceptual understanding', Working paper, University of Wisconsin, Madison.

LIVINGSTON, E. (1986) *The Ethnomethodological Foundations of Mathematics*, London: Routledge and Kegan Paul.

MIDDLE SCHOOL MATHEMATICS THROUGH APPLICATIONS PROJECT (1996) *The Antarctica Project*, Palo Alto, CA: The Institute for Research on Learning.

MILROY, W.L. (1992) 'An ethnographic study of the mathematical ideas of a group of carpenters', *Journal for Research in Mathematics Education, Monograph Number 5*, Reston, VA: National Council of Teachers of Mathematics.

NATIONAL COUNCIL OF TEACHERS OF MATHEMATICS (1989) *Curriculum and Evaluation Standards for School Mathematics*, Reson, VA: National Council of Teachers of Mathematics.

NATIONAL RESEARCH COUNCIL (1989) *Everybody Counts: A Report to the Nation on the Future of Mathematics Education*, Washington, DC: National Academy Press.

NEMIROVSKY, R. (1996) 'Mathematical narratives', in BERNARDZ, N. and LEE, L. (eds) *Approaches to Algebra*, Netherlands: Kluwer, Kieran, C., pp. 197–220.

NUNES, T., SCHLIEMANN, A.D. and CARRAHER, D.W. (1993) *Street Mathematics and School Mathematics*, New York: Cambridge University Press.

RESNICK, L.B. (1987) 'Learning in school and out', *Educational Researcher*, **16**, pp. 13–20.

RESTIVO, S. (1992) *Mathematics in Society and History*, Dordrecht: Kluwer Academic Publishers.

ROGOFF, B. (1993) 'Observing sociocultural activity on three planes: Participatory appropriation, guided participation, apprenticeship', in WERTSCH, J.W., DEL RIO, P. and ALVAREZ, A. (eds) *Sociocultural Studies of Mind*, Cambridge: Cambridge University Press, pp. 139–64.

ROTMAN, B. (1993) *The Ghost in Turing's Machine*, Stanford, CA: Standford University Press.

SAXE, G.B. (1991) *Culture and Cognitive Development: Studies in Mathematical Understanding*, Hillsdale, NJ: Lawrence Erlbaum and Associates.

SAXE, G.B. and GUBERMAN, S. (in press) 'Emergent arithmetical environments in the context of distributed problem solving: Analyses of children playing an educational game', in GREENO, J. and GOLDMAN, S.G. (eds) *Thinking Practices*, Hillsdale, NJ: Lawrence Erlbaum and Associates.

SCHOENFELD, A., SMITH, J. and ARCAVI, A. (1993) 'Learning,' *Advances in Instructional Psychology, Volume IV*, Hillsdale, NJ: Lawrence Erlbaum and Associates, pp. 55–175.

SCRIBNER, S. (1986) 'Thinking in action: Some characteristics of practical thought', in STERNBERG, R.J. and WAGNER, R.K. (eds) *Practical Intelligence: Nature and Origins of Competence in the Everyday World*, Cambridge, England: Cambridge University Press, pp. 13–30.

SMITH, J. and DOUGLAS, L. (1997) 'Surveying the mathematical demands of manufacturing work: Lessons for educators from the automotive industry', Talk in a symposium on *What Can Studies of Mathematics in the Workplace Tell Us about Teaching and Learning Mathematics in School?*, Annual meetings of the American Educational Research Association, Chicago, IL.

STEVENS, R. (1997) 'Disciplined perception: Learning to see at work and at school', Talk in a symposium on *What Can Studies of Mathematics in the Workplace Tell Us about Teaching and Learning Mathematics in School?*, Annual meetings of the American Educational Research Association, Chicago, IL.

STEVENS, R. and HALL, R. (in press) 'Disciplined perception: Learning to see in technoscience', in LAMPERT, M. and BLUNK, M. (eds) *Mathematical Talk and School Learning: What, When, Why*, Cambridge: Cambridge University Press.

STRAUSS, A. (1987) *Qualitative Analysis for Social Scientists*, Cambridge: Cambridge University Press.

STRAUSS, A. and CORBIN, J. (1990) *Basics of Qualitative Research: Grounded Theory Procedures and Techniques*, Newbury Park, CA: SAGE Publications, Inc.

SUCHMAN, L. (1995) 'Representations of work', Special issue of *Communications of the ACM 38*, **9**.

THOMPSON, P.W. (1992) 'The development of the concept speed and its relationship to concepts of rate', in HAREL, G. and CONFREY, J. (eds) *The Development of Multiplicative Reasoning in the Learning of Mathematics*, New York: SUNY Press, pp. 181–234.

Chapter 4

Mathematizing in Practice

Celia Hoyles, Richard Noss and Stefano Pozzi

The mathematization of intellectual and social life is gaining pace (Weizenbaum, 1984). In order for citizens to cope fully with this process, it seems that people at every level need to come to some functional appreciation of mathematical structures and relationships. We know that most adults are unaware that they are engaging in mathematical or quasi-mathematical activity even when they are involved in quite complex numerical or geometrical activities (Wolf, 1984), and that for many (at least in the UK), the suggestion that they do so engenders hostility, fear, and even guilt (Buxton, 1981). We also know that people usually make sense of everyday situations in ways that do not involve explicit mathematical descriptions: they are geared towards solving particular problems framed by personal or professional practice and not towards seeking out structures or general solution strategies. More generally, as the mathematical structures which underpin many professional practices become less visible within various technologies, it becomes more necessary (and more difficult) to study the complex ways in which mathematics enters into the picture. An important agenda is therefore to study the links between implicit mathematics used in practice, and more explicit and formal mathematical activity.

We hypothesize that there is a range of settings, which we will call 'mathematizable situations', where there is a 'pay-off' for making the mathematics visible in terms of personal or professional empowerment, and there are settings where there is little or no pay-off. The task is first to distinguish between these two classes of situations and then, for the former class, to identify possible mathematical approaches, to study how individuals can come to appreciate them, and to tease out any benefits that might accrue.

The research that we describe in this chapter is in the context of two practices: personnel working in a large investment bank and paediatric nurses working in specialist wards.[1] We will describe our methodology, outline some of the mathematizable situations we have identified in the two practices, and show how the process of computational modelling can serve as a window on how connections might be forged between implicit and explicit mathematical thinking.

Each study is divided into two phases with distinct questions and methods. In Phase 1 a mixture of interview and ethnographic observation is employed, with data collection taking place over several months *in situ*. This observation phase is guided by four questions:

- What kinds of activities which we judge to be mathematizable do people undertake in their workplace?
- How are these activities integrated into professional knowledge and goals?
- How do different technologies shape the relationship between these activities and professional knowledge and goals?
- Which of the identified mathematizable situations are amenable to mathematical modelling?

In Phase 2 we seek to study the ways in which a more explicit mathematical approach may broaden the ways professional situations might be conceived. In this phase interviews are conducted and experimental work undertaken away from the workplace. Explicit questions include:

- What are the participants' responses to questions about the underlying structure of the mathematizable situation?
- What kinds of computer-based mathematical models might prove useful to practitioners?
- Can practitioners make sense of such models in terms of their own practice and are they able to construct models for themselves?
- How does the process of model building illuminate the role of mathematics in practice and its connections with other areas of expertise?

In what follows we illustrate Phase 1 by reference to our study of nurses[2] and Phase 2 by reference to our work with bankers[3].

The Nursing Study: Phase 1

After obtaining access to a paediatric hospital we conducted exploratory interviews with senior nursing staff and undertook a comprehensive review of the literature on nursing mathematics. Most of the work reported starts with professional considerations, such as the need for new nurses to carry out a range of numerical calculations competently and accurately. Thus, the majority of studies focus on the mathematical preparation of nursing students, especially in arithmetic, where competence is assessed by means of paper-and-pencil tests (see, for example, Gillies, 1994; Pirie, 1987). Although we do not doubt the importance of this kind of training, the starting point of our research is that nurses' performance in paper-and-pencil tests bears rather little relationship to their competence *in practice*. Indeed, one longitudinal study by Hutton (1998) suggests that most learning goes on in the first two years after qualifying and that mathematical proficiency at the beginning of or during a training course is not a good predictor of how nurses use mathematics once they have gained experience after qualifying. Therefore, in order to study nurses' actual competence, we needed to investigate any mathematical activity carried out by experienced nurses as it arose on the ward.

After consultation we identified 12 volunteers from three specialist wards, to whom we gave a short questionnaire to find out their personal details, such as educational background and employment history. We then audiotaped interviews with each subject, to illuminate their work routines, their attitudes to work, the extent to which they felt they used mathematics at work, their descriptions of this mathematical use, and what they had felt about mathematics in school.

After the interview we observed each subject on the ward for a total of 10 to 12 hours over a number of visits, taking notes, audiotaping their interactions with doctors and other nurses, noting the resources used, and copying nurses' records and charts where appropriate. Our aim was to find out as much as possible about how nurses carried out the parts of their practice which were — in any way we could see — concerned with mathematical thinking. At this stage we took a broad and unrefined view of what 'concerned with mathematical thinking' might mean. Our observations changed their emphases as we proceeded, being rather open for the first one or two visits and becoming more focused as we learned to 'look for' rather than merely 'look at' the professional expertise we were observing (see Walker, 1981). At the end of an observation period we interviewed the nurse to probe her perception of some of the situations we had found interesting and to follow up outstanding issues which had emerged from our preliminary data analysis.[4]

Data Analysis

As usual in ethnographic studies, we were continually revising our view of the wealth of data we were collecting and attempting to structure more clearly our understandings of what we were seeing. We attempted to clarify a number of questions which kept reappearing as critical: did it make sense to re-articulate nursing practice mathematically? Were we simply imposing our view of what mathematics was on to the practice? What, indeed, did we mean by mathematics-in-practice? This process was useful as a way of beginning to classify some of the data we had collected, and helped us to make a first cut through the data based on *arenas of nursing activity* in which both we and the nurses agreed mathematics clearly played some role. These were: drug dosages; infusion preparation and monitoring; monitoring of drug level; interpreting laboratory reports; dialysis management; monitoring fluid balance; reading and constructing charts; and reading measurements from instruments.

This was the first step. We were interested not only in documenting how nurses used professional routines (for example, when calculating drug doses), but also in how they conceptualized their practices where there was no routine or formulaic response, and how mathematics did or did not feature in this conceptualization. These conceptualizations were most visible in 'conflict' situations, when routines had come to a halt either because of a divergence of opinion between nurses or because a nurse judged some information or prescribed procedure to be 'not right'. We therefore made special efforts to document all the details of any conflicts we happened to observe. An example of such a situation is given in the vignette below.

Changing the Frequency of Drug Doses

Many drugs are given at regular intervals, but occasionally a drug is given first at one frequency and then at another, the 24-hourly dose remaining constant. In the following scenario a patient was prescribed an antibiotic — vancomycin — at 600 mg every 6 hours for 24 hours, then at 1200 mg every 12 hours thereafter. As with many drugs, the dosage level in the blood needs to be kept high enough to be effective but if the level is too high the drug becomes toxic. Our observation starts at midday when two nurses, Wanda and Betty, check when to give the first 12-hourly dose, the last 6-hourly dose having been given at 6 o'clock that morning. Wanda thinks they can give this 12-hourly dose now, but Betty points out that the prescription chart states that it should be given at 6 pm:

W   Because if anybody's going 12 hours after low dose, your blood level is going to go right back down again isn't it?
B   So why are they giving them 12 hours later then, if that's what's happening?
W   Well, I don't know. . . .
B   No, nor me. I'll just go and ask [She leaves to ask doctor.]

Before Betty returns from seeing the doctor, Wendy tells the researcher what she sees is the main issue and explains that there is a difference of opinion among staff:

W   When you give vancomycin, you give 4 times the dose over 24 hours, then it goes BD [twice a day], but does it go twice a day after 6 hours or after 12 hours?
I   What do people generally do?
W   Well, it depends who you ask [Betty returns.]
B   Ella [the doctor] says she doesn't mind, so give it now.

Betty later explained that it is quite common to change the drug times to allow more effective use of nurses' time, although such changes need to be cleared with the doctor and recorded. That said, Wanda and Betty's initial concern was not time management but drug level: they thought the drug in the body would fall below the therapeutic level if they waited a full 12 hours after the last 6-hourly dose.

The hidden complexities of this particular issue became more apparent when we decided to describe this scenario to other nurses during our post-observation interviews. Like Wanda and Betty, Cathy would also give the first high dose 6 hours after the last low dose, although her reasoning was slightly different. Her explanation is based on preserving the 24-hour cycle of dosages. The scenario was put to her and she immediately responded:

C   There is a lot of debate on that one. I would have said working it out in my head, that the 24-hour dose doesn't change — the 24 hours have ended at 6 am, if we started previously, 6 o'clock before, so therefore you go midday

Figure 4.1   Cathy's drug level graph

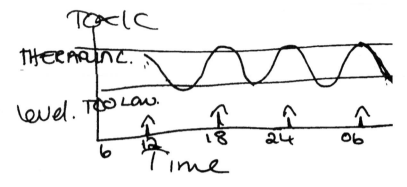

midnight because that is the next 24 hour clock because otherwise you are losing the 6 hours. If I waited until 6 pm, I would be gone into the next 24 hours.

Cathy has a clear view of how the level of drug in the blood changes and advocates administering the double dose 6 hours after the last 6-hourly dose. She could even visualize a graph of this model which she sketched on paper (see Figure 4.1).

She described her representation as follows:

C   I think that the reason why you do four lots first of vancomycin then 12 hourly, is that you want to get the blood level up. It's an incline up to your peak to the amount that should be in the body, then it is a gradient away and then it peaks again when you do the next one. What you are going to do is not let the gradient go too low — that there is a low peak. What you want to do is keep it and then let it drop slightly, so it goes up again, so you get like a 'U' horseshoe shape. Quite a broad shape . . . therefore to get to the level you want you do the four times to keep it up, to push up.
I   Without getting it too low?
C   Yes, you get the gradient up first.
I   Does it go up and go up further like that, do you think?
C   No, I think it always hits the same peak, because it is a certain amount of blood level. You only want a certain amount in the blood, you don't want to overdose the child, and then you mustn't go too far down, because then it wouldn't be therapeutic at all.

In contrast, another nurse — Amy — said she would give the first high dose 12 hours after the last low dose. Her main concern was the total amount of drug given in the first 24 hours which led her to the idea of a *maximum daily dose*:

A   They have a total of 2400 mg in that 24 hours [. . .] my motto is, if you have given them 600 mg here at 6 am, you will leave it go for 12 hours so their next BD dose is going to be at 6 pm, rather than [midday], because if you give them

Figure 4.2   Two different plans of action for changing the frequency of dose

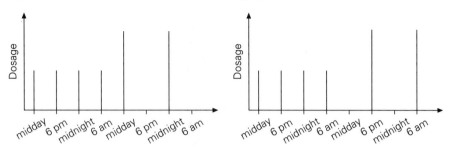

that 600 mg at 6 am, you are giving 1200 mg at midday and you are giving
1200 mg at midnight, you have actually given them a 3000 mg in 24 hours.
That is toxic so you can't do that [. . .] it's worked out that they can only
have 2400 mg.

I   So that 2400 mg is the maximum . . .

A   Maximum daily dose.

So, for Amy, the main issue is a notional 24-hour dose, and whether the timing of
the drug over the midnight-to-midnight 24-hour period exceeds this. Yet a third
view is offered by Frances, a nurse on a renal ward, who first said she would wait
the full 12 hours after the 6-hourly dose, but then revised this to 10 hours. Her
explanation is based on clinical issues arising from her own experience of kidney-
failure patients, and she contrasts this with the possible normal renal clearance of
the patient described to her:

F   I wouldn't give it straight after [. . .] because Vanc' can cause deafness. They
gave it at 6 am so it would have [. . .] I probably would have given it at 6 pm
[. . .] Or you could wait . . . at 4 [pm]. It's a very potent drug. It depends on
your renal clearance as well. He probably has normal renal function. We give
out Vancomycin every 48 hours, because the levels of it stay high. Because
obviously if your kidneys aren't working, the levels stay high, so we only give
small doses. We only give 10 mg per kilo [. . .] But even 10 mg per kilo — if
you looked at their blood and our children's blood, they're the same peak
height levels.

What can we learn from this incident, and the interviews subsequent to it?
Firstly, the fact that there is disagreement means that the issue is unresolved within
the questioning culture of the staff. Secondly, the nurses' justifications seem to be
based on alternative models of the drug in the blood. All the nurses mentioned that
the problem could be solved empirically, by checking the drug level with a blood
test. But given such tests are usually only taken on the third day, sometimes the
only course of action left open is to try to justify a particular decision from the basis
of a conceptual model of drug level over time. The two main plans for action are
illustrated in Figure 4.2.

In our preliminary analysis, we identified four basic models:

1   Wanda and Betty's model involving the assumption that a drug only lasts for the period between doses, so a 6-hourly dose will be eliminated in around 6 hours.
2   Cathy's model, though involving a choice of time identical to Wanda and Betty's, has a different base; that is preserving a 24-hour cycle regardless of the frequency of dosage. So, for her, if the four 6-hourly doses started at midday, the subsequent 12-hourly doses should start at midday the next day.
3   Amy's explanation is based on finding a maximum daily dose by aggregating drug doses over the first 24 hour period, then checking whether any change in prescription involves exceeding this daily limit.
4   Frances's model incorporates a clinical explanation based on her knowledge of patients with renal-clearance problems. Notice that it was Frances who was the most flexible in her response and the least certain of the 'right' answer.

All the models seemed to evoke a conceptual framework of drug levels rising then falling with each drug administration. This was evidenced mainly by the language used (for example 'go right back down', 'peak height' and 'gradient away') but also by gesture and, in the case of Cathy, by her use of a graphical representation. What is intriguing is that the nurses came to different conclusions, depending on the weights they attached to the variables in their models. We would argue that mathematizing this situation would illuminate more clearly how nurses come to decisions about these weights and about the nature of the relationships between the variables. For example, Wanda and Betty felt the need to question the doctor's prescription as they made the reasonable assumption that a 6-hourly dose lasts for around 6 hours, but also because they could manage their time better if they could give the drug at midday. Models of drug levels are only one of the tools nurses use in making decisions — there are other issues such as efficient time management, the specifics of drugs, illnesses, and treatments, the authority of doctors, and prior experience of similar situations. It is also becoming increasingly apparent in our structured interviews prior to Phase 2 that nurses' practices are shaped by the resources used to record the time of dosages. Whether mathematizing this scenario would support the nurses' models and plans for action or lead them to question them is a question we hope to answer in Phase 2 of the project.

We now go on to describe a study in which we *did* offer mathematized views of banking concepts to banking staff.

The Banking Study: Phase 2

A major multinational investment bank came to us in May 1994 with a problem. Apparently many of its employees had insufficient mathematical appreciation of the models underpinning the financial instruments they were working with — not surprisingly given their complexity. They found difficulty in spotting mistakes and recognizing the limitations of the models: the bank was losing out. Mathematics, which provided the infrastructure of the operation, was largely taken for granted or ignored in pursuit of banking objectives. However, when errors arose (for example, when there was a mismatch of capital at the time of exchange) the tools became noticed and the implicit shifted to the explicit. The situation described by the bank highlighted the problematic relationship between using and understanding mathematical tools, a relationship which has previously been studied mainly in the context of elementary mathematics.

As in Phase 1 of the nursing project, we set out initially to immerse ourselves as far as possible in the practice of banking, to seek to understand the essence of financial mathematics by talking to a wide range of employees, watching them at work, interviewing them, and reading the literature on the mathematics of finance trying to make sense of the new language we found there. Every field has its own language and banking is certainly no exception. We used questionnaires and interviews to probe the ideas held by the bank employees, particularly concerning the relationships of time and quantity and their interpretation of graphs.

What became clear was the dominance of a data-driven rather than relationship-driven approach: the shape of any graph was predicted and read by reference to pointwise calculations as opposed to any appreciation of the trends in any underlying model. This is not surprising given the practice of the bank — computer screens surround the traders (it is not unusual for one individual to have four or five) and these are routinely full of numbers in tables. Where there are graphs, they are mainly graphical representations of these numbers, or predicted values of them — pictures of pieces of data. Yet in order to make predictive calculations, the bank employs theoretical models based on mathematical relationships, typically functions from $\mathbb{R}^n$ to $\mathbb{R}$ (where n is suitably large!).

As we stated at the outset, this example will focus on Phase 2. Pedagogically, our approach was broadly constructionist (Harel and Papert, 1991). We structured our activities around starting points meaningful to the participants, which could be seen as jumping-off points for broader investigation and exploration of banking. We tried to incorporate a range of striking examples and intriguing questions. Why should we not expect interest rates to move by full percentage points in 1995 while this was the norm at the turn of the century? What happens to an investment as the frequency of compound interest payments is increased, and why?

Our struggle was to keep the connection of mathematics with banking, so that meanings from one domain could feed into the other and *vice versa*. This approach was completely novel to our bank employees. On the one hand, as far as we could tell, financial mathematics courses simply taught the relevant mathematical tools as a system separated from banking practice, leaving frustration and anxiety in their wake. On the other hand, the books we read left most of the mathematical work invisible: it was bypassed with deliberately opaque phrases such as 'it can be shown' or 'this can be proved mathematically'. Such devices inevitably leave the reader in a powerless state, unless they have the resources (intellectual and computational) and the confidence to fill in the gaps in the text which, as we can now testify, was by no means a trivial task.

We had to find ways in which our students could abstract relationships *within* (rather than away from) their working practices — or at least situations which mirrored these practices. We wanted to find ways to respect the classification of financial instruments and other objects used by our students, while bringing to their attention the relationships between them and their underlying structures. In short, we wanted to encourage our students to think about their familiar practices in ways which *included the mathematical*, rather than by replacing them by 'mathematics'.

The challenge was to design an environment which afforded rigour with meaning, ways of expressing relationships mathematically without the presupposition that students already knew what we were trying to teach. We decided to adopt the same approach as that which we had tried and tested with children, to open a window for the bank employees on to mathematical ideas through programming, using a dialect of the programming language Logo. First, we constructed in Logo our own computer models of a range of simplified financial situations. Building models helped *us* to connect our mathematics to banking, and to sort out what might be the big issues from a mathematical point of view. We trusted that the same process of model building would work in the other direction for our banker students, connecting their knowledge of banking to mathematics.

Our approach was to view all financial instruments in terms of their common mathematical structure, using the concept of function/program to provide the glue with which different financial instruments could be compared, contrasted, and modelled. We planned to immerse students in a programming environment, not as a quick way to represent and manipulate data, but as a means for building representations of relationships symbolically and graphically.[5] By building simple models themselves, we wanted our students to learn to look at a graph as driven by an underlying model rather than as a collection of data points, like share prices. Alongside our intention to make mathematics more visible, we wanted our students to make the practice of banking more visible for us. Thus, our students were co-designers; we wanted to learn (and incorporate into subsequent versions of our materials) how a more systematic, mathematical, view of the banking world could assist in understanding banking practice. We wanted examples from our students which they could work on and explore in the context of their professional practice, and from which we could then learn.

Our first task was to distinguish and name a small number of functions as fundamental building blocks for modelling financial instruments. One such building block which epitomizes the function/program idea is `fvs` ('future-value-simple'), which calculates the future value of an amount invested in a simple-interest account. We note that since `fvs` is a function, it can be combined with other functions, and in particular has an inverse function, `pvs` ('present-value-simple'), the essential building block in pricing instruments (see Figure 4.3).

The simplicity of these programs masks a number of interesting programming mathematical issues. We comment on one. Some variables can be considered as *parameters* in the expression of the function in which case they are stored in *text*

Figure 4.3   The building blocks fvs *and* pvs

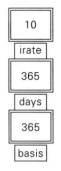

```
to fvs :amount
output :amount * (1 + irate / 100 * days / basis)
end


to pvs :amount
output :amount /(1 + irate / 100 * days / basis)
end
```

Figure 4.4   The pvs-days *function*

```
to pvs-days :days
output amount / (1 + irate / 100 * :days / basis)
end
```

boxes: so, for example, *irate* is the name of a text box whose value is the interest rate[6]; days holds the number of days for the investment; *basis* specifies the number of days taken to be in a year — which varies across countries between 360 and 365. Since we were using functions and graphs as a way of representing a relationship between two quantities (the functions were from $\mathbb{R}$ to $\mathbb{R}$), we put considerable stress on the idea that a function has a single input and a single output. But we often came upon situations which could be considered as functions of more than one variable. In such cases we asked students to choose one variable as the input or independent variable and insert the others into text boxes as parameters. In this way, *all* functions could be displayed graphically, and families of graphs could be produced for different values of the parameters. This approach, which clearly distinguished two mathematical objects — variables as inputs to procedures and parameters held in text boxes — proved important for understanding both mathematics and banking.

After the students had constructed and played with fvs and pvs together with their graphs, they were able to construct further programs by simple interchange of variable and parameter. For example, to examine how the present value of some future capital changes over time to maturity, students were able to rewrite pvs by interchanging a variable (:*amount*) with a parameter (*days*) (see Figure 4.4).

Students could use the new function pvs-days graphically, exploring the present-valuing relationship between time and money, and go further by plotting a family of graphs of this function for different interest rates. We were interested to see if the students could predict the shape of the curves and wondered if modelling the curves would provide a step to thinking about the relationship between time and money: specifically, maturity and price. The family of graphs produced is illustrated in Figure 4.5, where the horizontal axis is time (0 to 36 000 days)[7] and the vertical axis is price.

Figure 4.5   *A family of price risk graphs*

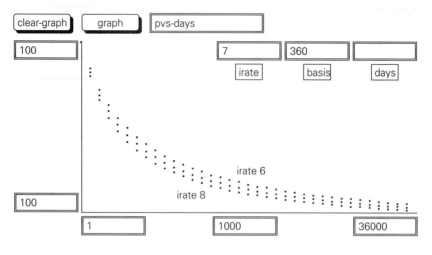

Each curve shows how price drops with time to maturity. But the *family* of graphs illuminates more — most notably that there is a *price risk*: that is, if interest rates increase, there will be a drop in the price of the financial instrument, since, for example, the curve for 7 per cent interest is always below that for 6 per cent. One student, Simon, wanted to go further. He noticed that the vertical distance between the curves was not constant. In other words, Simon made an important discovery: that *price risk varied with time to maturity.* Moreover, he noticed that the size of the gap between the 6 per cent and 7 per cent curves was different from that between the 7 per cent and 8 per cent curves — so price risk varied with prevailing interest rate. We had not noticed this, or if we had, we had not thought it interesting. But Simon had a sense from his practice of these influences on price which tuned his sensitivity in this direction. For example, he was very clear that a fall of one percentage point had a greater impact on securities trading at a lower yield (rate) than on those trading at a higher rate; and that a 100-point fall in rates in a country with a very high interest rate had a less dramatic effect than the same fall in the UK. Here was the opportunity to look at this phenomenon explicitly rather than tacitly.

Simon wanted to see what happened to price for different times to maturity, when interest rates changed. He wanted to investigate *functions of his functions* by taking a 'cross-section' through his first family of graphs (this description is ours not Simon's) and plotting a new family of differences in price over time for different prevailing interest rates. For him, the curves of price risk had become familiar objects and he had formulated an implicit and powerful meta-theorem: functions reveal structure. This activity spread through the class with some students becoming convinced that there should be a consistent pattern in the price-difference curves, leading them to investigate proportional changes in interest rate (instead of a fixed amount) while others (who knew a little calculus) plotted differentials.[8]

In the real banking world price risk is considerably more complex than in our model, as interest payments are compounded and the prevailing interest rate is in constant change. None the less, this activity brought price into focus and made it susceptible to mathematical analysis rather than treating it as a banking entity only. What was so exciting about this work was that it provided confirmation from a dramatically different context of how to teach and to learn mathematics: how mathematical and banking ideas and their respective motivations can be woven together to produce a powerful and motivating synergy (for us and our students) — a *Banking Mathematics*. The power of the computational modelling approach was that it facilitated this interconnectivity, as students could to some extent take control of the investigations and shape them according to their banking experiences.

Discussion and Conclusion

In an influential classification of individuals' progress from novice to expert knowledge, Dreyfus (1972) suggests a five-fold model which reflects changes in skills performance. Benner (1982) uses this model to classify nurses' behaviours, and states two general aspects of the Dreyfus model:

> One is a movement from reliance on abstract principles to the use of past, concrete experience as paradigms. The other is a change in the perception and understanding of a demand situation so that the situation is seen less as a compilation of equally relevant bits, and more as a complete whole in which only certain parts are relevant. (Benner, 1982, p. 402)

Each of these aspects deserves attention: we will begin with the first. The suggestion is that, in the beginning, novices rely on 'abstract' rules, algorithms, and principles, and that, with developing familiarity and knowledge, they begin to draw on their concrete experiences. Our first observation is that this characterization of expertise, one which certainly fits with our findings, is in direct contradiction to the assumptions which underlie school-based learning. In the latter, it is usually assumed that the trajectory of learning moves *from* concrete *to* abstract, and that the litmus test of expertise is the stripping away of contextual, concrete and experiential knowledge in favour of abstract, decontextualized knowledge.

However, our findings suggest a way of extending Benner and Dreyfus's framework. Although the movement from general principles to concrete experiences provides a useful axis along which to classify emerging expertise, we can also see an opposing trajectory. Specifically, while the bankers' expertise in their professional practice was based on the concrete and the specific, we saw how an appreciation of generality could add to their knowledge base, by helping to connect disparate pieces of their practice. Our nurses too, when pressed, were able to reflect on models of drug concentration in ways which were unnecessary (and inefficient) in normal practice, but which were useful in discussing the rather special situations we offered them. Thus Benner's second observation, that expertise involves selection and prioritization of knowledge is only partial. It ignores the expertise which can derive from general or unifying principles, a viewpoint which — as our data illustrates — adds a dimension to expertise in situations where routines break down.

In seeking to redefine abstraction in this way, we are in fact suggesting that abstract and concrete are, in practice, two sides of the same coin, rather than disparate kinds of activities, a point we have argued elsewhere (see Noss and Hoyles, 1996; and, for a seminal paper on this point, see Wilensky, 1991). Benner is right to point out that 'concept' or 'theorem' are insufficient in themselves to diagnose illness or specify treatment:

> Experience, in addition to formal education preparation, is required to develop this competency since it is impossible to learn ways of being and coping with an illness solely by concept or theorem. (Benner, 1982, p. 406)

What then is the relation between abstract and concrete? We would suggest an alternative formulation: namely, that expertise grows as a web of interconnected knowledge (for more on the notion of webbing, see Noss and Hoyles, 1996). The nurses' models of drug levels and the bankers' ideas of price risk, acquire meanings through use. Once such meanings are acquired, they become part of the conceptual framework of the practitioner and remain available as a flexible resource for the expert. Thus general rules and concepts are shaped by practice but, we argue, if mathematized, they can gain further meaning from connections to mathematics (for example, by being able to mobilize alternative formulations of proportionality or different types of graphs).

If 'abstract' means 'decontextualized', then Benner's observation amounts to noticing that contextualized meanings derive only from 'real' activity. We believe this reflects a one-sided notion of mathematics as essentially meaningless and that, on the contrary, it is possible for mathematics when used as a tool to generate meaning in its own right by its intra-mathematical connections. Benner and Dreyfus pointed to experts' holistic ways of knowing. We are convinced they are right here: that the move from an undifferentiated network of knowledge fragments to a connected and structured one is a significant distinction between novice and expert. But what our data are beginning to show is that 'abstract' knowledge (we are using the term strictly in the Benner/Dreyfus sense) can serve as one set of connections or as a resource for webbing connections.

The bankers and the nurses were, of course, in somewhat different situations, and it would be wrong to rely too much on the similarities between them. One way to make sense of these similarities is to notice that both scenarios involved implicit models of practice — of the concentration of vascomycin in the blood in the case of the nurses, and of price risk in the case of the bankers. Through conflict on the ward in the first case, and a planned process of modelling in the second, these models became more *visible* as circumstances forced reflection upon them.

The notion of visibility is meant to evoke the way in which, by some rupture or other in the practice, the workings of that practice became evident, and our professionals came to look *at* their practices rather than *through* them. Consider the notions of time that were held by our bankers and nurses. In their working situations these notions were not the isolated constructs that mathematicians sometimes take them to be, stripped of their connections with people and places. On the contrary, the ontology of time is quite implicit and situation-specific. For the bankers even the number of days in a year is not fixed and they measure time backwards — as days to the maturity of an investment. The nurses' idea of time is intimately harnessed to the notion of what constitutes a day, the management of time within it, and the asymmetry (for practical purposes) between day and night.

This is hardly a surprising conclusion: when we say that Paris is three hours away, we are implicitly acknowledging the details of current practice and techno-logy which completely specify the meaning in ways that are quite apparent to the 'expert'. The knowledge depends on the situation, and abstractions (Brussels is 15 minutes further than Paris) are immersed within it. Provided the situation is well defined and familiar (for example, we are talking about trains, not cars) it can remain implicit. If not, understanding will necessitate making visible the mathematical (and other) assumptions which underpin it.

At a time when the aims of mathematics teaching, its role in social and eco-nomic life, and the influences of new technologies remain unclear, further clarifica-tion of how mathematics is used is urgently needed to plan curricula for the new millennium. The dialectic we are beginning to describe between mathematics and practice illustrates how much more complex is the situation than mere 'application' of mathematical skills or knowledge. Recognizing that complexity is a first step in redefining mathematical education in the new millennium.

Notes

1 Paediatric clinical nursing is generally regarded as more mathematically intensive than other areas of nursing, partly because of the greater variety of drug dosage levels required for babies and children. Our choice of occupational groups is to some extent arbitrary, although both have clearly identifiable mathematical practices and involve the the use of mathematics as a tool. However, these considerations are balanced by our ability to gain access to the workplaces and collect data in a relatively straightforward way. We also intend to study the work of airline pilots using a similar methodology.

2 We acknowledge the support of the ESRC-funded project 'Towards a Mathematical Orientation through Computational Modelling", Grant No. RO22250004. Phase 2 of the nursing project has not yet started.

3 The example we give is largely based on that in Noss and Hoyles, 1996, 245–50.

4 We also posed each subject a small set of problem situations, as close to 'real situations' as we could, in order to study more closely the range of responses which were deemed professionally appropriate to issues which had emerged as interesting and important during our observations. These are currently being analysed and we do not discuss them here.

5 We used *Microworlds Project Builder* (MPB) again because it provides a suitable set of primitives so that models could be relatively easily built. Unfortunately it must be admitted that it also (at least on the PC machines we were using) has one almost fatal flaw: its numerical accuracy is severely limited. We survived this difficulty by a number

of 'fixes', none of which was completely satisfactory. We wish to express our appreciation to Uri Wilensky for his assistance in writing our graphing utility.

6   In *MPB*, a text box is like a visible function which simply gives up its value when called. Readers unfamiliar with the idea will not suffer by thinking of `irate` as the value of a global variable — although this is not actually the case.

7   Time is exaggerated to discern trends more clearly in the graphs.

8   The project briefly outlined above led to the discovery of an apparent maximum price risk (something which nobody in the bank, as far as we can find out, knew before) and its later debugging in terms of banking practice.

References

BENNER, P. (1982) 'From novice to expert', *American Journal of Nursing*, March, pp. 402–7.

BUXTON, L. (1981) *Do You Panic about Maths?*, London: Heinemann.

DREYFUS, S. (1972) *What Computers Can't Do: A Critique of Artificial Reason*, New York: Harper and Row.

GILLIES, R. (1994) 'Drug calculations for nurses: More than a formula and a calculator?', Proceedings of the Australian Bridging Mathematics Network Conference, Sancta Sophia College, pp. 56–66.

HAREL, I. and PAPERT, S. (eds) (1991) *Constructionism*, Norwood, NJ: Ablex Publishing Corporation.

HUTTON, M. (1998) 'Do school qualifications predict competence in nursing calculations?', *Nurse Education Today*, **18**, pp. 25–31.

NOSS, R. and HOYLES, C. (1966) *Windows on Mathematical Meanings: Learning Cultures and Computers*, Dordrecht: Kluwer Academic Press.

PIRIE, S. (1987) *Nurses and Mathematics: Deficiencies in Basic Mathematical Skills among Nurses*, London: Royal College of Nursing.

WALKER, R. (1981) 'On fiction in educational research: And I don't mean Cyril Burt', in SMETHERHAM, D. (ed.) *Practising Evaluation*, North Humberside: Nafferton Books, pp. 147–65.

WEIZENBAUM, J. (1984) *Computer Power and Human Reason: From Judgement to Calculation*, Harmondsworth: Penguin Books.

WILENSKY, U. (1991) 'Abstract mediations on the concrete and concrete implications for mathematics education', in HAREL, I. and PAPERT, S. (eds) *Constructionism*, Norwood, NJ: Ablex Publishing Corporation, pp. 193–204.

WOLF, A. (1984) *Practical Mathematics at Work: Learning Through YTS*, Research and Development Report No. 21, Sheffield, U.K.: Manpower Services Commission.

Chapter 5

Mathematics Provides Tools for Thinking and Communicating

Willibald Dörfler

The turn of a millennium is very appropriate for pondering on the past and the future of all aspects of life — though this point of time is only an artefact of our decimal counting system. To recognize this some simple mathematics is needed — there are different counting systems — and mathematics helps to demystify what would otherwise be a highly peculiar event. This example points the direction in which I believe mathematics education could and should develop: mathematics as a means for making sense of one's experiential world, for organizing and structuring it, and for realizing that all this is accomplished by people through their thinking and communicating. Perhaps such a goal sounds very demanding, but I believe that much can be achieved within quite elementary mathematics, as I hope to show by a number of examples.

I start by discussing some specific features of mathematics as a human activity which appear to me to contribute to this goal. Then I give my view on how to conceive of thinking and communicating: these human activities depend on, and are determined by, socially available means and tools. The rest of the chapter discusses examples of mathematical notions from the point of view of their being tools for thinking and communicating.

For whom would such a mathematics education be suitable? I think that a focus on mathematics as a cognitive tool is well suited to mathematics for all — though it would be of a different kind from the usual. This aspect can be treated in all topics of school mathematics, but of course it needs a very different kind of teaching and learning. The more technical and procedural parts of school mathematics, which dominate at present, should be reduced and transferred to the computer. The emphasis should shift from mathematics as a calculating tool to mathematics as a conceptual means for cognitive activities.

Remarks on Mathematics

Any kind of school mathematics is explicitly or implicitly, consciously or unconsciously, based on a particular view of what mathematics is. I want to expose here those features which guided my thoughts for this chapter. Mathematics is indeed a multi-faceted human endeavour and what follows is only one dimension of it, but I believe that these features demonstrate a special power of mathematics which hitherto has not been exploited adequately in school.

Many mathematical concepts have the potential to present *relations*. By their nature relations are not perceivable in the same way as the objects which they relate. They have to be inferred by an observer and are always of an abstract quality. To be able to talk about relations, to think about them, scrutinize them, change them and so on, we generally need a presentation which makes them 'visible' in some way. And this is just what mathematical notions can do for us: mathematics turns abstract relations into material objects — mostly symbols and diagrams. Detailed examples will follow but, for now, just consider the Cartesian graph of a function, or the arrow diagram of a relation such as partial order, or an algebraic formula, or a combinatorial graph such as a sociogram.

Mathematics education is already much concerned with visualizations as pedagogical devices. The focus I propose is to use these mathematical notions and their visualizations as 'thinking tools'. By materializing abstract relations we are enabled to manipulate them, to interpret them, to communicate them, and also to apply them to hitherto unstructured situations. We can use them as lenses to scan our experiences, or as templates to organize and structure them. For example, the notion of exponential function is a means for thinking about growth or decay processes, and its usual graph supports this very efficiently. In a very general and pretentious way I could say that, via the materialization of abstract relations, mathematics contributes to the human ability to organize and order one's experience.

Another feature of many mathematical notions is that they present formal schemas by using *variables* to denote structures and processes. These variables remain uninterpreted as long as there is no need for a concrete assignment of values to them. For example, think of the nodes of a network graph, or the reals as arguments for the exponential function (not yet interpreted as the values of some quantity). Through this use of variables the general becomes concrete and specific, and accessible to thought.

What is even more powerful is that mathematics encompasses the study of every conceivable schema: all kinds of relations, all kinds of operations, functions and so on. Thus in mathematics we have a department store for formal structures and schemas waiting to be used by everybody interested in them.

This supply of formal schemas and their various materializations empowers human thinking in several ways. First, it gives us the opportunity to *consider alternatives*. To make sense of a situation we can try to apply variations of a single schema, or we can try essentially different ones. For example, is a growth process linear, or exponential, or logarithmic? Without knowing the alternatives we might fail to structure the situation successfully.

Considering alternatives is also the basis for what is termed *thought experiment*, where one analyses the consequences of certain assumptions when applied to a situation not yet structured or understood. For this one needs to have available a supply of different schematic structures or models, together with their materializations, which potentially could describe the given situation or process. Further, to perform the thought experiment one will need to carry out various operations within the chosen schema. Mathematics offers a great variety of schemas, materializations, and operations. But the learner has to experience this potential residing in mathematics; he or she has to develop an attitude or point of view which motivates him or her to explore alternative assumptions or possibilities. In school mathematics the tendency is the other way: that there is a unique way to mathematize a given situation or process and the task is to detect the mathematical structure residing in it. This corresponds to the philosophical position that mathematical concepts are gained from nature by abstraction. A counter position is that they are invented by human beings to describe our experiences in general terms, and that for this we have a range of possibilities. This brings us close to a constructivist epistemology or to what H. Vaihinger has termed an as-if attitude (see Dörfler, 1996).

The method of thought experiment is closely related to *simulation*, which nowadays is strongly supported by powerful electronic computers. Again, by supplying a wealth of formal structures and methods, mathematics provides the basis for many simulations in many different fields. Simple examples are: exponential function as a model for growth processes; combinational graphs to model traffic networks or social structures; input–output models for economic processes. In all cases, one can experiment with the model, for example, by asking 'What happens if . . . ?'. In the model one can change parameters in ways impossible in reality. A worthwhile goal of school mathematics would be to develop awareness of the simulative power of mathematical concepts and methods. In this way again students can acquire an attitude which inclines them to explore alternatives and the consequences of different points of view, and they can experience mathematics as the means to carry out this exploration.

As the examples will show, all this can happen with quite simple mathematical concepts, and these ways of thinking are accessible at all levels of mathematics.

To summarize, the following are the features of mathematics which I would propose to use much more and in a broader way to shape school mathematics in the near future:

- mathematical concepts very often present relational structures, sometimes of considerable complexity
- mathematics develops means for materializing relations and relational structures, making them visible and manipulable
- mathematical concepts present relational structures in a schematic and formal way
- mathematics offers a great repertoire of schemas
- mathematics provides powerful means for thinking of alternatives, for thought experiments, and for simulations
- mathematics offers a great repertoire of schemas which gain their essential power from the use of variables (algebraic or diagrammatic).

Remarks on Thinking

I start by admitting that I feel unable to give a definition of the term 'thinking'. Certainly, thinking refers to a human activity which is internal to the individual and not directly accessible to observation by others. All one can do is infer from external behaviour and subjective reports a possible compatible internal behaviour (thinking). In other words, I consider the notion of thinking as a theoretical construct, for example of cognitive psychology, by which we try to explain human behaviour. In this sense it is comparable to stipulated physical entities like electromagnetic fields by which we try to understand physical phenomena like light. It is in this restricted sense that the following remarks are to be understood.

My basic thesis is that thinking can best be described in terms of the means and tools that make it possible. I do not conceive of a kind of 'pure' thinking which 'expresses itself' by means of language, diagrams, gestures, etc. This for me would be like conceiving of walking without legs, feet, ground, etc. In other words, it makes no sense to separate thinking from those expressive means and tools. I thus consider such questions as whether there is thinking without language, or whether there is purely diagrammatic thinking, to be ill posed. It is up to us if we want to call the mental manipulation and use of diagrams a form of thinking, and there is absolutely no way to decide upon this by empirical investigation.

This approach, focusing on the means of thinking, has the advantage that we can study those means, and so obtain hints as to what is thinkable, provided we have them available — means for expressing or, better, for formulating and developing our thoughts. It is in this way that I have discussed above the potential impact of mathematical concepts on the thinking of learners. My suggestion is to enhance in school mathematics the role of mathematical concepts as thinking tools and as means for shaping our experiences and even our world view. Thus my position is that experience, and what can be experienced, is to a considerable extent influenced by the cognitive system, and here especially by the system of concepts and beliefs. For instance, the cognitive availability of geometric concepts (figures) will influence our recognition of corresponding shapes in our surroundings. Acquired concepts allow us to interpret perceived phenomena in a certain way.

Another powerful use of mathematical concepts is their metaphoric projection to illuminate a phenomenon, that is, the use of mathematical structures to exhibit features of special interest or to explain our observations. I think of such simple things as 'standing in a circle', 'closing a circle (of argument)', 'pyramid of income (or age)', 'volume of trade', but also of examples from science (for example, mathematical models for the structure of an atom). Intermediate examples include those cases where we use functional properties like gradient, maximum, local change, and monotonicity to describe social or economic developments. Thus we may speak of danger rising 'in a monotonic way' or of tensions 'reaching a maximum'. Of course, such phrases can also be understood without having available the corresponding mathematical concepts, but these concepts add specific meaning to the phrases. In any case, knowledge of a rich repertoire of mathematical concepts enables us to express a great variety of relationships which otherwise elude our mental grasp and social communication.

As these remarks try to show, the specific qualities of mathematical concepts already discussed meet very well the demand for cognitive tools to empower and extend our thinking and communicating. Thus the view of thinking espoused here is my motive for proposing to emphasize those qualities of mathematics in school. I do not have a related curriculum to propose, but I am convinced that there are plenty of opportunities in school for experiencing mathematics in this way. It will be helpful to discuss those opportunities, to reflect on them, and to make a point of looking for them.

Relations, Order, and Their Graphs

A basic mathematical concept with a broad range of applications is that of the partially ordered set (POS), together with its graphical materialization as a diagram (the Hasse diagram), see Figure 5.1. Notions associated with POS include: unrelated (incomparable) elements, maximal/minimal elements, chain. An extreme case is a totally ordered set.

A typical use of the POS is as a tool to think about hierarchical structures. We may do this in a purely descriptive way, to exhibit for example who is superior to whom in an enterprise. By exploiting the power of mathematics to materialize abstract relations we gain an overview of the whole hierarchy and also the possibility to alter it. We may carry out thought experiments to explore the effects of changing the hierarchy. We may then go on to think of organizational experiments which otherwise might not have occurred to us. By offering us the repertoire of all possible POS mathematical theory enhances imagination and social creativity.

Figure 5.1   Examples of diagrams of Partially Ordered Sets (POS)

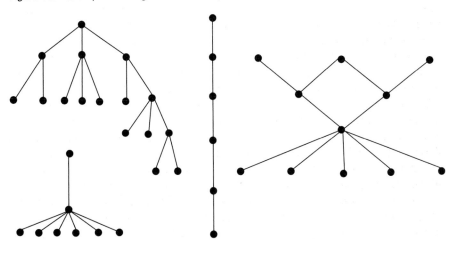

Figure 5.2   Graphs depicting friendship relations

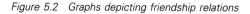

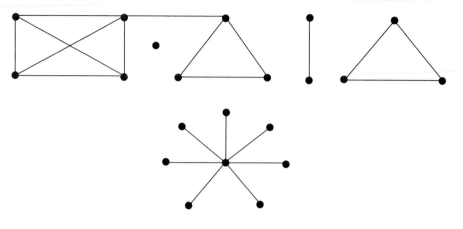

This diagrammatic presentation gives a concise description of the hierarchy and enables us to study its social consequences, for example, the distribution of power, the extent of participation in decision-making, and the extent of local autonomy. It also allows comparison of different organizational models, for example, flat structures as opposed to vertical ones. The meaning of 'superior to' can vary from case to case. The representation of a hierarchy as a POS may also exhibit practical weaknesses, for example, that somebody is exposed to instructions from different and possibly contradictory superiors.

Indeed the very idea of a POS opens up new avenues for thinking. For instance, the possibility of having incomparable elements can be very helpful when ranking things, events, or people. The result need not necessarily have a linear order: one element can be comparable to two others which are not comparable with one another. Thus, the abstract schema POS widens the thinking space by pointing out what is logically possible.

Very similar considerations apply to *combinatorial graphs* when used to describe social relations in a group of people such as acquaintance, friendship, or common business. Of course, the hierarchy diagrams just discussed are a special case of these.

Each of the drawings in Figure 5.2 is the diagram of a graph depicting, for example, a friendship relation.

Beyond a merely descriptive purpose we can use such sociograms to think about group structure, to investigate ways of changing or improving it, to find out our own position in a group, and so on. We may use them constructively, for example, to choose people to have a specific group structure with respect to a given social relationship. Here it might be found that within certain limits different diagrammatic descriptions are admissible, that there is no unique way of ascribing 'group structure' to a set of people. Again, this thinking tool may point to possible phenomena which otherwise might be overlooked: isolated elements, clusters of elements, disjoint or only loosely related subgroups. Generally speaking, it provides us with an overview of what is in principle conceivable.

In the same vein, just knowing about *equivalence relations* and their basic properties may be of great advantage whenever a set is to be partitioned into disjoint classes of mutually 'indistinguishable' elements. Examples abound within mathematics, of course: for instance, congruence relations like whole numbers having the same remainder on division by, say, 5. In geometry, congruence of figures results in a classification as does similarity. The general notion of equivalence as a kind of generalized equality helps, perhaps, understand the importance of those and other geometrical transformations for classifying figures or bodies. In everyday life equivalence is mostly indicated by having a specific value of some property (number, colour, shape, etc.). All these examples can be grasped by the same general though simple schema.

I assert that it is much easier to think about such a situation by using the schematic description than in the concrete terms of the situation itself. Mathematical schemas also help to distinguish equivalence from similarity, which in general lacks transitivity. Similarity relations and their graphs offer a perspective on the everyday notion of similarity which explains how non-similar things can be connected by chains of pair-wise similar elements. Wittgenstein has pointed out that often one conceives of objects which are 'only' similar to some other object in a given class: they do not share one defining property and cannot be called equivalent. The prominent example from Wittgenstein is the notion of game and he speaks in this connection of *family resemblance*. Similarity graphs can shed light on these ideas of Wittgenstein by making visible the abstract relationships.

The list of examples of mathematical relations and their graphs could be continued for some time. Here are just a few more, together with some of the areas where they can be used as thinking tools for description, investigation, thought experiment, simulation, and communication: *networks* (information, transport), *tree diagrams* (descendence, listing and counting possibilities), *bipartite graphs* (correspondences of all kinds between two disjoint sets).

I want to emphasize that the usual notion of *application* of mathematics to an experiential situation does not quite comprise what I mean by 'thinking tool'. As with common tools, thinking tools interact with the material to which they are applied: they are used to shape that material (given by experience) and to impose a structure which is compatible with the tools themselves. Without the tools the material remains inaccessible and cannot be operated on. On the other hand, every tool by its properties excludes certain possibilities and sets a framework for acting or thinking. Therefore it is advisable to have available as large a repertoire of tools as possible. A goal of mathematics education would thus be to develop a toolkit of mathematical notions, together with a positive attitude to looking for help in it and trying different tools from it. Education towards such a goal should repeatedly be asking questions like: How can we describe that? What alternatives do we have? What consequences do we get? What can be changed? Such a use of mathematical notions will, in general, be more qualitative than quantitative.

Functions and Functional Properties

Very much has been said about the teaching and learning of the concept of *function* and its properties. I will focus here on those aspects which are in accord with my introductory remarks on mathematics and thinking: functions, together with their materializations, as a thinking tool. Again the qualitative, descriptive, constructive, and simulative features will be in the foreground. Numerical properties and calculations are of less importance here (these receive ample treatment in school in any case).

To view something as a function is a demanding cognitive step and the ability to do so has to be developed out of a great variety of adequate experiences. This development can be supported by paradigmatic examples of functions and by exposure to their various representations. It is important to build up a comprehensive inventory of functions and their graphs. All this will contribute to an awareness that a given process, situation, or structure can be treated as a function. Such a treatment has a strongly constructive character and leads to a holistic view of the process or situation. This view is supported by the Cartesian graph which materializes the function as a whole, and thus can be used as a thinking tool for mentally creating this whole.

The effective and efficient use of every tool has to be learned and exercised. Viewing mathematical notions like that of function as thinking tools makes clear that in their intelligent use much effort and exercise has to be invested. Much of what is currently done in school is not of this quality: there, the tool character of a function is demonstrated chiefly by a few initial applications which have the purpose of motivating the ensuing lessons. The term 'functional thinking' comes close to what I have in mind. But functional thinking needs the appropriate tools and a broad experience of their use which is not developed by a purely mathematical treatment.

What I want to promote is that a notion like function in its mathematical sense should become part of everyday language whenever that is appropriate and sensible. Of course such use will not be technical, but a use to grasp experience, to discuss issues with others, to argue about phenomena, to think about a process, etc. Essentially these are roles played by all concepts, for cognition by the individual and communication within social groups. Needless to say, to attain this goal dramatic changes in classroom culture will have to occur.

The same holds for *functional properties* of all kinds and their use as cognitive tools. The essential features of notions like monotonic growth, periodic process, constant function, step function, oscillation, asymptotic behaviour, and so on are exhibited by appropriate graphs. These, together with an inventory of types of function, span a realm of possibilities of what we can expect when viewing something as a function. We are then in a position to scan the conceivable alternative ways of doing this, and we find that usually there is not just one unique way. It is a most valuable experience when we realize that it is we who do the viewing and treating: the functional structure does not reside in the phenomenon being studied, but is imposed on it or read into it. The mathematical notion once again serves to materialize abstract relations which have been inferred from experience, and makes those relations thinkable.

Many other mathematical schemas, based on the function concept, can serve as thinking tools in non-mathematical situations. The notion of *change* is of special relevance and importance and is met very often in everyday life in different guises, for example inflation rates, increase of income or temperature, etc. Measures of change of all kinds — total, relative, average, local, instantaneous — are paradigms of the relational and schematic character of mathematical concepts. By means of formulae or diagrams, relational schemas such as $\dfrac{f(b) - f(a)}{b - a}$, or $\dfrac{f(b) - f(a)}{f(a)}$ become materialized, and with suitable interpretation can be used to think with, to express a view, to argue, to simulate, etc. Different schemas offer different ways to think about change according to our interest and aims, for example they allow us to evaluate a change, to judge if it is important or negligible, etc. The experiential world becomes in a way wider and richer if these relational schemas are available for organizing and structuring it. Thinking about change also presupposes relating two states which are separated, in time or place or otherwise. In this sense the conception of change depends on memory and needs some recording of the values of the magnitude of interest. This illustrates the extent to which relations are inferred and constructed by the observer, and mathematics provides tools for these cognitive processes.

If the values of a given measure of change are viewed as the values of an appropriate function, the change of the change (acceleration) can be considered. I believe that without the algebraic and diagrammatic tools of mathematics such second-order relations, or relations of relations, are very difficult to grasp and use in thinking. The main contribution of mathematics here is to materialize the first-order relations so that the second-order relations take on a first-order character. The Cartesian graph (convex or concave) can be helpful too in understanding second-order change, as can difference tables.

This example seems to me to show very convincingly the extent to which thinking depends on, and is determined by, the available tools of presentation, visualization, and materialization, and that it does not make sense to separate thinking, or cognition generally, from its means and tools. But again, to become a cognitive tool a concept must be used actively and repeatedly in all its presentations: it is not enough merely to know it passively.

Similar remarks apply to other functional properties which can be viewed as higher-order relations — a property which may indeed contribute to difficulties with learning and using them. They apply with still greater force to the concept of derivative, or instantaneous change. This concept is possibly too technical to be integrated into everyday discourse, though whether this is so is an empirical question of great interest. In general, however, so-called higher mathematical concepts are applied more to other scientific fields than to situations of everyday life. Though they share the characteristics of mathematical concepts already discussed, the relations which they schematize are themselves already products of research: the tools, in short, are more specialized.

Miscellaneous Examples

I now give a series of minor examples each of which exhibits some of the features discussed in the two introductory sections. Some of these examples may appear trivial. But I assert that they only appear to be so to those who are already well acquainted with the corresponding mathematical concepts. At this stage of cognitive development it may be difficult or even impossible to imagine how one's thinking worked without these tools.

Like those already discussed these tools can, I believe, considerably enhance the precision and expressive power of discourse about situations and phenomena to which they can be applied. I am also convinced that it will be fairly easy to organize mathematics classes in an appropriate way to foster active experience in their use.

Sets and Set Operations

The notions of subset, complement, union, intersection, and difference provide schemas which are very helpful in expressing relations between collections in everyday life. Consider, for example, expressions like 'those people who have property A but not property B', or 'those things that are in collection A and collection B'. A further example is the notion of symmetric difference and its logical or diagrammatic expression: those cities which have less than two million inhabitants and an underground or those cities which have more than two million people but no underground. What are the other kinds of cities? Mathematical notations and diagrams (like the Euler–Venn diagram) support our thinking about sets and collections, and allow us to carry out thought experiments, simulations, etc. Mentally forming a set out of a collection of isolated objects is itself, I believe, in need of a cognitive means, which can be supplied by the usual set diagrams. Using the tools of set theory entails an awareness of the possibility of interpreting something as a set, as a union or intersection of sets, etc., and a willingness to use such interpretations in thinking and communicating. This state can be described by saying that the set notion has become a *discursive element*. In education, to attain such a goal, students have to be introduced to participation in this kind of discourse. It is clear that this necessitates a different kind of teaching and learning, possibly similar to that used in language education.

Cartesian Product

The notion of forming pairs, triples, and generally n-tuples of elements is a very powerful thinking tool, particularly for getting an overview of all the possibilities in a given situation, and counting them. Consider the case where we have objects which enjoy two different properties (colour, weight, or whatever), each of which can assume a variety of values. Generally, we can speak of n 'dimensions' with regard to which objects, including people, may differ. The mathematical notion of *n*-dimensional space supplies a general schema for grasping these phenomena and addressing such questions as: What are the logical possibilities and which of them are realizable? How can we list all possibilities? As before, using this concept as a tool presupposes a specific attitude and relation towards it beyond just knowing about it. As an analogy, to know what a hammer is, what it looks like, and what it is for, is quite different from the skill of using a hammer: a hammer is not the same as hammering. It is a pity that we do not have in our language verbs to describe the activities of using mathematical notions!

Coordinate Systems

Related to the Cartesian product is the concept of a (multidimensional) coordinate system, which supports the activity of 'coordinating'. Here I am thinking not only of numerical or quantitative coordinate systems but also of qualitative coordinates. Generally, this concept is exploited in order to present an *n*-tuple of 'elements' of various kinds (material or ideal) as a 'point' in an *n*-dimensional 'space' spanned by the *n* coordinate axes, each axis corresponding to one type of element. Graphical sketches are of great value here and should be considered a constituent part of the tool *coordinate system*.

Fractions

The fraction concept gains its full power only when its true relational quality is understood. We use it to describe the relation of a magnitude to a fixed unity with respect to some appropriate measure. This relational schema can be expressed by the usual fraction diagrams, for example as parts of a disk or of an interval. Much has been said about this already and I only want to point out the following. For this diagram to become a cognitive tool for using the fraction concept certain elements of it have to be viewed as *variables*, to be interpreted in each concrete case. This applies to all formulae and diagrams intended to express relational schemas. In order to grasp a given relational schema, for example two-fifths of the unity, specific actions have to be carried out or imagined: in this case, dividing and combining. In this way the diagram becomes what elsewhere (Dörfler, 1996) I have called an *operative prototype*.

Diagrams intended to show properties of whole numbers such as divisibility by *m*, parity, primality, etc. have to be read in a similar way: for instance divisibility as a schema for arranging a number of objects in triples. Here we find the same ingredients: material objects to be viewed as variables and as operands in constituent operations.

Conclusion: Variables As a Powerful Tool

The previous sentence points to a very powerful method of thinking, that of generalizing and abstracting by introducing variable elements. One way to develop this is to focus attention first on relations which are inferred to hold between concrete and specific objects, and then move on to consider these objects 'only' as expressing those relations and to neglect all their other properties. This will typically produce an abstract relational schema offering great flexibility in use. Very often in mathematics such a schema is then expressed by symbolic means.

As a final example, consider $K = \{x \in S \mid d(x, M) = r\}$ as a symbolic expression of the statement 'K is a circle in S with centre M and radius r'. Each letter occurring in the expression can be viewed as a variable open to concretization. Depending on the concretization K can be a common circle, a sphere, a square or a cube (with non-Euclidean d), and many other figures for which the common circle can be used as a relational schema. I think there is a close connection between the acquisition of the variable concept and the development of such relational schemas: as one develops, so does the other. On a very general level, thinking with variables might be the most powerful cognitive tool provided by mathematics to be developed in school.

Reference

DÖRFLER, W. (1996) 'Means for meaning', in COBB, P. et al. (eds) *Proceedings of the Symposium 'Symbolizing, Communicating and Mathematizing'*, Nashville, Tennessee.

Section Two

Curriculum and Classrooms for the Future

Around the world, more and more people are being taught mathematics, and the age to which mathematics is part of the compulsory school curriculum is gradually being raised in many countries. While there seems to be agreement that for societal and other reasons more people will need to learn more mathematics, there appears at first sight to be less agreement on how to avert the consequence that more people may be required to spend time — reluctantly — on a subject they find difficult or do not enjoy. Yet, as the chapters in this section testify, there is more convergence than is at first apparent — a convergence around making mathematics visible, manipulable, and relevant through carefully designed modelling activities. Clearly computers have a fundamental role to play here, not only in developing IT skills, but as tools in the modelling process. This section discusses general issues and implications for the curriculum of the 21st century and provides us with some concrete examples of innovations in uses of technology and in classroom practices that show what may be achieved.

Considering the nature of a mathematics curriculum for all students, Margaret Brown identifies a need for flexibility and breadth of applicability. In her chapter, she argues against the idea that different curricula are needed for different groups of students, pointing to the relatively poor mathematical performance of students in countries with hierarchically differentiated curricula. Brown's discussion of the state of post-16 education in the UK provides evidence of some of the dangers of early specialization and the weaknesses inherent in a 'vocational' education that does not include explicit specialist mathematics teaching.

The theme of mathematics within vocational education is taken up by Julian Williams, Geoff Wake, and Alan Jervis, who discuss the development of a competence model for prescribing and assessing mathematics curricula for vocationally focused courses. They describe a new construct, 'general mathematical competence', and present examples of activities they are developing for a vocational Science course. They attempt to draw out the relationships between general mathematical competence and mathematical content and processes, as well as the relationship between the curriculum and vocational practice. They end by posing a new research question, concerning the relevance of general mathematical competences to actual workplaces — a question which clearly relates to chapters in the previous section.

Development of the curriculum cannot be separated from development of pedagogy and Gillian Hatch's chapter raises some pertinent questions. What should be the pedagogy for quality learning in mathematics for the third millennium? This is a crucial issue since it is in the interaction of teacher and student that a mathematical ethos is created that will sustain a child in school and beyond.

Carolyn English returns us to the importance of modelling and how it can be used in the classroom, not just for learning mathematics in the abstract but to help students understand the ways in which mathematics is used in society. She argues that the overt and covert models used in everyday life need to be made available for critique by students and illustrates her point by describing a range of fascinating modelling activities used in her secondary school.

The relationship between school mathematics and mathematics outside school is an important theme throughout this book, but there are also, of course, connections to be made with other areas of the curriculum. Daniel Sandford Smith sets out what he sees as the requirements for a curriculum for scientific literacy and goes on to describe the implications for the mathematics done in science lessons. Once again we have a convergence of argument! To become scientifically literate, students need to be able to appreciate how quantitative expressions are derived and to learn to be more active in their use of mathematics, including building, interpreting, and understanding the role of models.

The next chapter in this section, by a team of chemists and mathematicians (Templer et al.) at Imperial College, takes another look at the intersection of science and mathematics. They present a case study of how mathematicians and chemists came together to work collaboratively to 'cope' with the problem of service mathematics teaching. Modelling with a computer and the development of microworlds helped the team and the students to forge new links between mathematics and chemical knowledge.

Finally, James Kaput and Jeremy Roschelle move beyond the particularities of national or institutional mathematics education reform to gain a long-term perspective on the future of mathematics education. They chart the historical democratization of access to mathematics through the development of new technologies and argue that continuing developments in technology will continue to change what it means to do mathematics. In particular, they see the potential of new technology in helping to reconnect mathematical representations and concepts to directly perceived phenomena, so that students can grapple more effectively with powerful mathematical ideas, such as the mathematics of change and variation, the mathematics of uncertainty, the mathematics of space and dimension, and the mathematics of algorithms and processes. They illustrate their ideas with examples from their project, which uses computer-manipulable graphs to support learning about motion.

Chapter 6

One Mathematics for All?

Margaret Brown

Aims of Mathematical Education

It is customary to separate educational aims into two complementary categories:

- furthering the development of society
- furthering the development of the individual.

Further subdivisions, and in particular decisions as to differential weighting, are likely to introduce ideological biases (discussed fully, for instance, by Ernest, 1991). Nevertheless most countries find it useful to attempt some more detailed statement in order to provide a basis for discussion of the curriculum.

Some countries (for example, Norway) provide a set of general educational aims in their curriculum documents, which link with more specific mathematical aims, which in turn feed into curriculum detail. In other countries (for example, the UK) aims of education have the appearance of being a later appendage unrelated to the curricular substance.

Aims may have very different emphases in different countries. Results from the IEA Third International Mathematics and Science Survey (TIMSS) indicate that the proportions of secondary mathematics teachers who feel that mathematical success requires, for example, creative thinking, or understanding of real-world applications, range from 20 per cent in some countries to over 80 per cent in others (Beaton et al., 1996).

Similarly, as part of the Second International Mathematics Survey (SIMS) a typical set of mathematical aims was selected which teachers in different countries were asked to rank:

1 To understand the logical structure of mathematics.
2 To understand the nature of proof.
3 To become interested in mathematics.
4 To know mathematical facts, principles, and algorithms.
5 To develop an attitude of inquiry.
6 To develop an awareness of the importance of mathematics in everyday life.
7 To perform computations with speed and accuracy.

8   To develop an awareness of the importance of mathematics in the basic and applied sciences.

9   To develop a systematic approach to solving problems.

(Burstein, 1992, p. 41)

The exercise elicited significant cross-cultural differences in the relative emphases given to these mathematical aims by teachers of 13-year-olds in 1980–2. For example, where US teachers prioritized the importance of mathematics in everyday life together with knowledge, computation and problem solving, the French preferred to nurture intellectual enquiry and the understanding of proof. Howson (1991) also contrasts the rationalist-inspired aims of mathematics teaching in France with the more pedestrian aims of Northern Ireland.

Most curricula are, in practice, a compromise between competing aims within a particular society at a particular point in time. Furthermore, different priorities will be claimed even within the same society in relation to students of different ages, different perceived mathematical abilities, and different career aspirations. Covertly, different priorities within the various aims are likely to be attached to students of different class, culture and gender backgrounds.

The question to be addressed in this chapter is whether the priorities within a developed post-millennial society should differ sufficiently for different students to require the provision of different curricula. In many ways it follows on from an excellent discussion of the situation over 10 years ago (Howson and Wilson, 1986).

Differentiated Aims and Curricula

Some western societies have traditionally differentiated strongly between the kinds of mathematical education which they have provided for different pupils. For example, most German pupils are directed at age 11 into one of three types of school, each providing different types of mathematics curriculum: the *Gymnasium* for intending graduates and professionals, the *Realschule* for skilled technical workers, and the *Hauptschule* for the remainder. Other European countries like France and the Netherlands have directed students to different types of school at older ages. Although in other countries such stark divisions between schools have been abandoned and the overwhelming majority of students are in comprehensive secondary schools, they may still be differentiated within the school. The US has had an elective system of differentiation via 'tracking', with students progressively dropping out of specialist mathematics courses into 'general mathematics' options, while in the UK almost all students are in differentiated sets for mathematics by age 12, with some elementary schools 'setting' at age 7.

The mathematical aims for the *highest groups* have traditionally emphasized concepts and techniques of use in the physical sciences and engineering (aim 8 in the list above) for example, trigonometry, functions; together with these there have been varying levels of introduction to pure mathematical notions such as structure and proof (aims 1 and 2). For the *middle groups*, technical mathematics at a reduced level such as simple algebra and mensuration formulae have predominated, while the *lower groups*, expecting to enter unskilled occupations at best, have concentrated on computations (aim 7) and the use of mathematics in everyday life (aim 6). Such curricular differences have been associated with a relatively stable occupational structure linked to social hierarchies, which in practice reflected divisions based mainly on class, race, and gender.

However, the results of IEA surveys (Postlethwaite, 1967; Robitaille and Garden, 1989; Beaton et al., 1996) have highlighted the fact that the mathematical 'yield' from such western countries is poor in overall terms in comparison with eastern Europe and the Far East. Although in western countries a small élite have a high mathematical attainment on leaving school, the vast majority of the population have a comparatively rather low attainment, either leaving school after following an unambitious curriculum, or staying on at school or college but studying little mathematics. This varies from countries with a strong vocational/technical tradition like Germany, in which mathematics is taken seriously in the courses of most students, to those like the UK where most students cease any study of mathematics after the age of 16. In communist (and newly ex-communist) countries and in the new 'Asian Tiger' economies the emphasis given to mathematics, combined with the decision to educate all to the highest possible level, produce a higher overall 'yield'.

Common Aims and Curricula (Up to Age 16)

More recently the rigid hierarchical structure underpinning education and, in turn, mathematical curricula in the West has been undermined owing to:

- radical changes in the nature of work, with a disappearance of unskilled jobs, more temporary and part-time posts, and more self-employment
- the prevalence of technology, with many jobs requiring computer skills, including use of spreadsheets, data bases, and statistical representation
- equal opportunities legislation and awareness, leading to greater aspirations among wider groups
- widening access to higher education, for example, in the UK, university entry moving from 6 per cent to over 30 per cent.

In spite of attempts by some governments to introduce or maintain selective schooling or early vocational differentiation, it seems likely that the long-term trends favour a more open and egalitarian curricular pattern.

The need to change the mathematics curriculum to reflect such structural changes in society started to be addressed in the UK with the Cockcroft Committee of Inquiry (DES/WO, 1982). It was agreed that it was important that all pupils should follow a broad curriculum, including mathematical investigation and real-world problem solving, and gain confidence in mathematical application. The UK National Curriculum, introduced in 1989, while still enabling curricular differentiation between pupils, at least elected to differentiate by the speed at which they followed a common curriculum rather than by allocating different pupils to distinct curricula.

The use of technology to enable wider access to mathematical ideas was acknowledged, with calculators and computer databases and spreadsheets introduced from a relatively early age. The 1995 version of the National Curriculum moves further in this direction with compulsory use of graphical calculators for all pupils and common programmes of study (although with extension material to maintain the allocation to sets based on attainment level in preparation for the differentiated three-level GCSE examination).

This type of curriculum change, favouring problem solving, application, broader content, and technology, has been introduced into many other countries, and most importantly by the National Council of Teachers of Mathematics *Standards* in the US (NCTM, 1989). The *Standards* are prefaced by aims which form a rationale for the later detail, and which reflect the underlying social and economic changes:

Needs of society:	•	an informed electorate
	•	mathematically literate workers
	•	opportunity for all students
	•	problem-solving skills that serve lifelong learning
Goals for students	•	learn to value mathematics
	•	learn to reason mathematically
	•	learn to communicate mathematically
	•	become confident of their mathematical abilities
	•	become mathematical problem solvers.

(NCTM, 1989)

The aims relating to the needs of society reflect the expectation that pupils will not be trained merely for unskilled jobs but for occupations which require mathematical and computer literacy and mathematical problem-solving skills. They also reflect equal opportunities awareness, and an expectation of frequent career change with the reference to lifelong learning.

The aims of the *Standards* are curious as there appear to be two important omissions from the goals for students. The first is that students should acquire a solid base of mathematical knowledge, concepts, and skills which is understood and can be used in appropriate circumstances. The second is that students should gain acquaintance with mainstream and/or minority cultural knowledge. Similarly de-emphasized is the corresponding *need of society* for stability, which depends on some continuity of culture and tradition. These omissions indicate, perhaps more clearly than the inclusions, the determination to break away from the past.

Post-16 Changes

The changes to widen access and to broaden the curriculum during the compulsory period of schooling are echoed also in changes post-16. In France the introduction of new, more technical/vocational baccalaureates has encouraged a significant increase in the numbers of students continuing education to 18 and at university level; in the UK the new General National Vocational Qualifications have belatedly fulfilled the same role.

At university level, wider entry and less employment security have led to new vocational courses, for example tourism, media studies, sports science. At the same time requirements for greater flexibility in employment patterns have created a demand for broader courses, modular or including combined studies, which allow students to broaden their skills profile. An example is accountancy with Spanish and management. In contrast, some students have appreciated the lessening of pressure on vocational specialization resulting from delayed career entry, and have chosen subjects like philosophy which are seen as attractive but without immediate vocational outcomes. They accept that there is likely to be a period of casual employment or travel before they settle into a more focused field, and that most occupations require generic skills such as basic literacy and numeracy, oral communication, IT skills and teamwork rather than particular advanced subject knowledge.

Such changes in curricula and in national educational systems have produced many tensions. However, because of the differences in post-16 national structures and curricula, and rapid changes in many countries, it is difficult to survey the field. The remainder of the discussion is thus based on the problems that are arising in just one country, the UK, with the hope that this may also illuminate the sources of tension in other countries.

UK Case Study: Specialist Post-16 Courses

A problem for the 16–19 age group in England and Wales has been the Conservative Government's reluctance (as of 1996) to change the highly specialized and rather demanding A-level (Advanced level) examination, which determines university entry. This examination was originally designed in the 1950s for under 10 per cent of the age group. Students traditionally studied only three, related, subjects in the post-16 period (for example, pure mathematics, applied mathematics, and physics, or English, French, and German), with the expectation that just one of these would be selected as a degree subject. However, by the early 1980s the proportion studying A-levels had increased to over 20 per cent of the age cohort, encouraged by schools allowing greater flexibility in the selection of subjects. The proportion studying mathematics remained fairly constant: although fewer students were specializing in physical sciences and fewer were choosing two mathematics A-levels, many now selected a mathematics-with-statistics option to accompany non-science subjects like history or economics.

Changes in the public examination system for age 16 (GCSE) enabled much higher numbers of students to qualify for entry to A-level study (over 40 per cent). However, the additional numbers seemed to favour the arts and humanities, a fact which may be partly explained by higher GCSE pass rates and more attractive GCSE courses, including more coursework assessment, in these subjects. Part of the explanation also may lie in more global societal trends leading to more negative attitudes to, and fewer stable career opportunities in, science and engineering. Vocational university options that expanded to satisfy demand from the new group of students staying on until 18 were thus generally in areas without a heavy reliance on mathematics (for example law and the media). Even in those with some mathematical requirement (for example business studies and computer studies) students have not generally been required to have a mathematics A-level: to have made mathematics a requirement would have prevented the rapid expansion in student numbers which was encouraged by the Government in the late 1980s and early 1990s. Equally, the growth in attractive but non-vocational courses (for example psychology and philosophy) has been largely outside mathematically dependent areas.

Hence there has been a significant drop in the proportion of post-16 students with three A-levels specializing in science and mathematics, with pupils taking only subjects in this group declining from 37 per cent of candidates in 1980 to 16 per cent in 1994. Delayed career entry and the need to keep options open has led to more students selecting a range of subjects across the arts and science boundaries, with the proportion rising from 29 per cent in 1984 to 37 per cent in 1994. This broadening trend has enabled mathematics to maintain its share of the total age cohort, with about 7 per cent of the age group attaining A-level mathematics. Nevertheless, with a drop of a quarter in the cohort size due to the falling birth-rate, the actual number of entries has declined by about a quarter. Nor has mathematics held its share of the total A-level entries, since entries for subjects such as English have expanded dramatically, by almost 200 per cent. It would also appear that although the overall proportion of the cohort entering for mathematics A-level is roughly constant, students taking mathematics are drawn from a wider range of attainment and interest than previously. To cater for this wider group, A-level mathematics courses have had to adapt, though this has happened in different ways.

To illustrate one type of approach to changing emphases, the aims of one of the newest schemes, *SMP 16–19*, which has made a conscious and successful attempt to cater for a new population, are quoted:

1   to develop positive attitudes to the learning and application of mathematics
2   to develop ability and confidence in the application of mathematics
3   to develop an appreciation of the nature of mathematics and mathematical processes
4   to develop an appreciation of how mathematical ideas help in interpreting the world in which they live
5   to develop an appreciation of aesthetic and historical aspects of mathematics
6   to develop their ability to communicate mathematical ideas both orally and in writing
7   to develop an ability to read and comprehend a piece of mathematics
8   to extend their mathematical knowledge and skills and to use these in the context of more advanced techniques
9   to acquire a sound base of the knowledge skills and attitudes required for further study in mathematics, in other subjects and in employment
10   to develop skills of modelling, generalisation and interpretation of results relevant to both applications and developments of mathematics

11   to develop learning and thinking skills of more general application, for example in decision making

12   to develop an ability in the appropriate mathematical use of calculators and microcomputers, including the use of various software packages

13   to acquire strategies for the solution of extended problems in mathematics

14   to develop an ability to argue logically and understand the nature of rigour.

(Northern Examinations and Assessment Board, 1994, p. 5)

This is a long way from the highly technical course preparing mainly physical scientists and engineers which is where A-level mathematics had started. However, it should be noted that many other mathematics courses have maintained a dull and technical emphasis, even within a modular structure. These courses have coped with the expansion in the range of students by making questions easier and even more routine; textbooks written by examiners containing long exercises of questions similar to those in the examinations have sold well. Unfortunately, such courses are popular with teachers who fear that their own knowledge is insufficient to cope with the demands entailed by aims such as those of SMP. Taverner (1996) demonstrated that only the SMP course has had the effect of changing teaching styles to include more discussion, more use of technology, and less routine practice of examination questions.

Following these various changes, there have been complaints from university mathematicians, engineers, and scientists that pupils are now less well prepared in terms of techniques than previously (for example, LMS/IMA/RSS, 1995; Sutherland and Pozzi, 1995). Such complaints relate partly to the content of the A-level courses but they may also reflect the much wider entry to the undergraduate courses. As the numbers taking A-levels in mathematics and physical sciences have fallen, the universities have increased their intakes, necessitating the acceptance of students with lower grades and in many cases with no A-levels at all but with vocational or alternative qualifications. The problems are also compounded for these university teachers by the halving in the number of students electing to follow a second mathematics A-level, again presumably in the justifiable interests of broadening their curriculum. There is thus a tension between the interests of those university teachers who wish for more technical and specialist mathematics course content at A-level, and schools who want courses to attract and be appropriate for the wider range of students who are keen to study mathematics. Other numerate disciplines in universities, for example geography, environmental studies, and business studies might well support the latter view as they would prefer students to enter with some further study in mathematics rather than with no post-16 mathematical study.

A recent review of international research on attitudes to mathematics (Black et al., 1996) has shown general agreement that the key factor in discouraging potential students who have previously done well in the subject from continuing to study it is that mathematics is perceived as irrelevant to students' lives, boring, hard, and badly taught. This is true for students of both sexes, but especially true for girls. This finding would seem to support the need for broader rather than more technical content if more students are to be attracted to the subject.

Other recent research in which I have been involved, the project 'Effective Teachers in Numeracy' supported by the UK Teacher Training Authority, has also revealed the shortcomings of the more procedural A-level mathematics courses. Primary school teachers who had studied A-level mathematics, many of them with high grades and a few even with mathematics degrees as well, not only had often developed a negative attitude to the subject, but also sometimes lacked a real understanding of basic ideas like rational numbers (Askew et al., 1997). On average, their teaching produced slightly lower average pupil gains in numeracy than teachers in the same schools with no advanced mathematics qualifications.

My own view is, therefore, that if the UK Government is reluctant to follow the example of almost all other countries in imposing further study of mathematics on students post–16, the priority must be to attract a wide group of students into A-level, or at least into the first year of an A-level course (AS-level) in mathematics. This requires the maintenance of a course which has a broad appeal, on grounds of its interest, relevance, and approachability. There should be very little optional content, so as to enable the course to cover a wide range of both pure mathematics and application, including statistics and calculus for kinematics and other applications. The course should in particular provide an introduction to the nature, development, and applications of the subject, since this is essential for specialists and can be attractive to a broad range of students. This recommendation goes against that of others who want more specialist mathematics options at 16–19 for students with different combinations of A-level subjects. I believe it is not only the logistics of teaching different courses that militate against this: most students at 16 have very little idea of what subjects they want to study at university, let alone career intentions, and hence it would be wrong to close down options by introducing specialization at too early a stage.

Nor should we necessarily design options simply in accordance with university course requirements. Lord et al. (1995) catalogue a variety of mathematical requirements across different subjects and within different university departments in the same subject. However, this may only reflect traditional assumptions rather than constituting a real evaluation of needs. Also, for example, university engineers may favour mechanics over statistics to ease their own teaching, but fail to recognize that statistics is as important a tool for engineers in employment as it is for other professionals in industry and commerce.

The position of mechanics warrants special attention. Although it is a valid and important application of mathematics it should appear in the A-level mathematics course only as one of many, and should not have the favoured place that it currently occupies in England and Wales (and in no other country). Mechanics should properly be part of an award in engineering or physics.

While statistics has greater breadth of application, there is also a case for trimming some of the more advanced statistics within some A-level courses. Releasing the hold of mechanics, and some statistics, should enable a balanced AS-level and A-level course which is appropriate to most departments in higher education. More specialist needs within university mathematics and physical science departments can be catered for in the new structure by requiring such students to take an AS level additional to their mathematics A-level in more technical mathematics, which would be a compromise between one and two mathematical A-level subjects. Alternatively, they could be provided for in preliminary courses in universities.

As in the case of A-level mathematics, for many students across the attainment spectrum university mathematics courses have not fulfilled expectations of either interest or enhancing competence: many students complete mathematics degree courses with their confidence sapped and with declining enthusiasm for the subject. As has already happened in some universities, we should redesign mathematics courses around the varying needs and attainments of the students. Continuing reductions in numbers opting for mathematics degrees, if nothing else, should act as a stimulus to such changes. We should not adopt the alternative course of requiring schools to distort the curricula for a wide range of students in order to create products which will fit in more readily to inappropriate university courses, often designed around the needs of a handful of future PhDs rather than for the majority of undergraduate students. Nevertheless, as recommended previously, there should be more incentive for high-attaining students to complete an additional mathematics course in the form of a second AS, prior to university entry, if necessary mainly by self-study or group-study.

UK Case Study: Non-specialist Post-16 Courses

Those students in education and training in England and Wales, but not following a specialist A-level or AS-level in mathematics, fall mainly into three groups:

- those following general vocational courses (GNVQs) in schools and colleges
- those following vocational courses (NVQs) in workplaces and colleges
- those following A-level courses in a range of subjects other than mathematics.

The advanced level GNVQ courses in subjects like leisure and tourism, health and social care, and construction and the built environment were created to fill a vacuum post-16 between narrow vocational courses and A-level courses. They were intended to be of the same demand as academic A-level courses but to be taught in an integrated thematic way, and were built round a set of units with a method of assessment that combined multiple choice unit tests as low hurdles with integrated portfolio assessment. Good grades were intended to be, and generally are, acceptable as qualifications for entry to higher education in lieu of A-levels. (Additional detail is given by Williams, Wake and Jervis in Chapter 7.)

Although a few GNVQ courses (for example, engineering) have a mathematics unit as a compulsory part of the qualification itself, all those doing GNVQ courses are required to continue the development of their mathematics through the *core skill* 'Application of Number'. While the content of this is intended to be applicable rather than pure, it becomes very difficult to differentiate the content and aims from those of 'mathematics' curricula at the same level. For example engineers and designers need geometrical and algebraic language, knowledge, and skills, and computing specialists need logic and algebra. Williams, Wake and Jervis come to essentially the same conclusion in their identification of general mathematical competences as a link between the mathematics classroom and the workplace. Assessment of mathematical competence has taken place through the vocational portfolio: students are required to reach a specific criterion-referenced level which relates to the level of their GNVQ. The problems of this type of assessment are well described by Williams, Wake and Jervis.

Wolf and Griffiths (1996) note that the requirements of GNVQ have led to a variety of provision, with some colleges leaving tuition, if any, to occur through the vocational course, using teachers who in terms of mathematics are poorly qualified non-specialists. Other schools and colleges are laying on specialist mathematics provision at varying levels of formality. The standard of the criteria for demonstrating competence in 'Applications of Number' has been pitched low since success is obligatory for all students. Thus there may be little incentive for a student who is able in mathematics to continue progressing. There is also a lack of rigour in assessment, although there are proposals to introduce external tests in order to improve this. Although some students on narrowly vocational NVQ courses may follow a similar core skills course, most have no mathematics teaching at all. Similarly it is unlikely at present that students following non-mathematics A-levels will continue with mathematics.

To solve these various problems, there have been proposals that all advanced GNVQ students, and also if possible NVQ students, be required to continue their study of mathematics, aiming for a free-standing mathematics qualification which is assessed by a combination of external test and individual investigative coursework related to their other studies. This would also be appropriate for non-specialist A-level students. The qualification would be available at a number of levels, but the level a student enters should be dependent on their prior mathematical attainment rather than on what level of other courses they are taking. The set of qualifications should at the lower end be roughly parallel in terms of mathematical demand to lower levels in the public examination at 16 plus (GCSE), and lead up to the first year of the specialist A-level (AS-level) at the top end. My view is that most, if not all, of the material in the syllabus for each level should be common to all students whatever their programme. It should include a strong IT focus but have elements of the philosophy, history, culture, and application of mathematics alongside problem solving, technical competence, and conceptual development.

The provision of such a set of linked qualifications would go a long way to ensuring that all students continue with a rigorous study of mathematics as they do in nearly all other countries. It further allows the teaching to be efficient while still related to the student's main areas of specialism via a coursework element. It is not, however, what is proposed at the moment, which allows for a multiplicity of mathematical modules from which students will be able to select only a small number, thus omitting important aspects and again causing problems for teachers at the next level.

Conclusion

The changed and fluid situation in employment requires all members of society to continue their study of mathematics to the highest possible level, during their schooling and in their later lifelong learning. This is also in each country's own national interest in order to improve mathematical 'yield'. To maintain flexibility a broad curriculum is required, which is related to a wide range of applications and to the current state of technology; there is little point in maintaining courses aimed at specific needs of particular subjects or careers at particular points in time.

This requires within each country a single ladder of coherent and rigorous qualifications, where differentiation is only by level of knowledge, understanding and competence and is not determined by the other courses a student is following (except in that entry to a course of study may specify a minimum prior mathematical level). The content could well be specified in terms of 'general mathematical competences' such as those identified by Williams, Wake and Jervis in Chapter 7. The ladder should include what are presently thought of as 'specialist' as well as 'non-specialist' mathematics courses. Links to vocational or academic specialisms should occur only via contextual problems and coursework projects, which should have a significant weighting, with the remainder of the assessment covered by a common test (which may be available on computer). Such a framework is an essential step in levering up standards of achievement and attitudes to mathematics in society and in raising the status of mathematics in the vocational arena.

References

ASKEW, M., RHODES, V., BROWN, M., WILIAM, D. and JOHNSON, D. (1997) *Effective Teachers of Numeracy*, London: King's College, London for the Teacher Training Agency.

BEATON, A.E., MULLIS, I.V.S., MARTIN, M.O., GONZALEZ, E.J., KELLY, D.L. and SMITH, T.A. (1996) *Mathematics Achievement in the Middle School Years: IEA's Third Mathematics and Science Study*, Chestnut Hill, Massachusetts: Boston College.

BLACK, P., BOALER, J., BROWN, M., MURRAY, R. and RHODES, V. (1996) *Survey of Existing Research into Attitudes to Mathematics and Related Areas* (Report for the School Curriculum and Assessment Authority), London: King's College, London.

BURSTEIN, L. (1992) *The IEA Study of Mathematics III: Student Growth and Classroom Processes*, Oxford: Pergamon Press.

DES/WO, COMMITTEE OF INQUIRY INTO THE TEACHING OF MATHEMATICS IN SCHOOLS (1982) *Mathematics Counts* ('The Cockcroft Report'), London: HMSO.

ERNEST, P. (1991) *The Philosophy of Mathematics Education*, Basingstoke: Falmer Press.

HOWSON, G. (1991) *National Curricula in Mathematics*, Leicester: The Mathematical Association.

HOWSON, G. and WILSON, B. (1986) *School Mathematics in the 1990s* (ICMI Study Series), Cambridge: Cambridge University Press.

LMS/IMA/RSS (1995) *Tackling the Mathematics Problem*, London: London Mathematical Society/Institute for Mathematics and its Applications/Royal Statistical Society.

LORD, K., WAKE, G. and WILLIAMS, J. (1995) *Mathematics for Progression from Advanced GNVQ to Higher Education*, Manchester: Mechanics in Action Project.

NATIONAL COUNCIL OF TEACHERS OF MATHEMATICS (1989) *Curriculum and Evaluation Standards for School Mathematics*, Reston, Virginia: NCTM.

NORTHERN EXAMINATIONS AND ASSESSMENT BOARD (1994) *Syllabuses for 1996: Mathematics (SMP 16–19)*. Manchester: NEAB.

POSTLETHWAITE, N. (1967) 'School organisation and student achievement: A study based on achievement in twelve countries,' *Stockholm Studies in Educational Psychology*, **15**, Stockholm: Almquist and Wiksell.

ROBITAILLE, D. and GARDEN, R. (1989) *The IEA Study of Mathematics II: Contexts and Outcomes of School Mathematics*, Oxford: Pergamon Press.

SUTHERLAND, R. and POZZI, S. (1995) *The Changing Mathematical Background of Undergraduate Engineers*, London: The Engineering Council.

TAVERNER, S. (1996) 'A review of modular A-level mathematics,' Paper presented at the British Educational Research Association Conference, Lancaster, September, 1996.

WOLF, A. and GRIFFITHS, G. (1996) *Improving the Delivery of Mathematics for Post-16 Vocational Students* (Paper for SCAA), London: SCAA.

Chapter 7

General Mathematical Competence: A New Way of Describing and Assessing a Mathematics Curriculum

Julian Williams, Geoff Wake and Alan Jervis

In developing a post-16 curriculum in the United Kingdom that appeals to a wider cross-section of the population as we approach the new millennium, a range of general vocational qualifications has been developed. These attempt to motivate students by being vocationally focused, although they are used in the main by those still involved in full-time education. Mathematics is part of these courses in that it is there to underpin study both as a general key skill and with a more specialist focus in appropriate courses. Students following these courses have not opted to study mathematics in its own right but see its value as being of service to their chosen domain of study. This means that the role of mathematics will be very different from that in their pre-16 curriculum where it had a place of its own.

The new general vocational qualifications are distinctively different from other full-time post-16 courses in that they have been specified using a model developed for qualifications based on competency in the workplace. This development has led to considerable problems in defining mathematics curricula appropriate to courses with particular vocational foci, whilst also providing the coherent programmes of mathematics which are essential for progression to further and higher education.

Here we outline our attempts to describe and assess a mathematics curriculum within a competence-based qualification in the area of science. We contend that our model, which attempts to define general mathematical competences, has validity across vocationally focused domains, particularly those with technology as a basis. We suggest that further work needs to be carried out to assess whether the model can be extended, to a greater or lesser degree, across all post-16 courses where mathematics is not studied as a discipline in its own right.

The Assessment of Competence in Mathematics

We identify four categories of mathematics which seem relevant to post-16 study:

- study of mathematics as an academic discipline
- mathematics required to underpin and illuminate other courses of study

- key numeracy skills required for life and further study
- mathematics required to function effectively in the workplace

Our work is grounded in describing appropriate mathematics curricula which are a synthesis of the latter three categories. However, the first category has a dominant influence in that it has traditionally defined the background expected of students progressing to work and higher education from this level of qualification.

Many students following the new vocationally focused courses see the qualification as a route to higher education rather than immediately to the job market. Here is one source of the problem: the qualification is aimed at two conflicting 'consumers', who have different needs, emphases and even languages (see Blum and Strasser, 1992). On the whole, the one speaks of content, and sometimes process, where the other speaks of competence in practical situations.

The framework of the new vocational qualifications and its specification borrows heavily from the competency model drawn from vocational training (Jessup, 1991). Yet there are major academic components, especially the mathematics and science in some courses. So far, attempts to describe the mathematics curriculum in terms of competence have met with little success (though one must allow for many other problematic factors in a situation where major innovations are introduced very rapidly with limited resources into an institutional framework already in the throes of major change). First attempts have resulted mainly in defining a large number of discrete competences associated with particular elements of content. This has had the effect of making implementation in ways which are meaningful to students very difficult. The resultant confusion has had severe implications for assessment, both in the assessment by coursework assignments, which is over-elaborate and time-consuming (see Capey, 1996) and in the external tests, where in some cases almost entire cohorts of students have failed mathematics!

In our analysis of these tests and their role, we find a confusion between competence in a setting, where the performance can benefit from significant support from tacit knowledge of the setting and high standards of success might be expected, and an academic test of mathematics which purports to be contextually applied, and which leads to predictably lower success rates (Carraher et al., 1985). Even learning to be competent in vocations like medicine and teaching is now believed to be largely tacit (Reber, 1989).

The problem in the coursework assignments has more to do with the mass of atoms of competence, each of which must be checked off. We believe that competence in practice is not reducible to such a set of discrete elements. In mathematical coursework, effective assessment of competence requires a holistic view of the work. This may be informed by consideration of a profile of elements, but these must be limited in number (see Kitchen and Williams, 1994). One cannot overemphasize the damage to mathematics education of a piecemeal approach to learning, where students rote-learn and check off a long list of ill digested skills, applied to a few stereotyped examples (Clegg, 1992).

This chapter reports our recent work on this problem. We attempt to synthesize the two perspectives for mathematics through a new construct, *general mathematical competence*, which can bridge the two worlds. The two concepts which it draws upon are mathematical modelling (in the sense of Blum, 1992), and mathematical competence in vocational tasks.

General Mathematical Competence

A general mathematical competence is the ability to perform a general mathematical skill across a range of vocational applications with a specific, coherent body of mathematical knowledge, skills and models.

The following principles define the general mathematical competence construct:

1   It is immediately obvious that the competence applies in many situations in the field of interest and is sufficiently general to be useful. This will involve the student in repeatedly using the competence; this is why a particular competence has been recognised and defined, though there may be adaptations involved. This arouses motivation through empowerment.
2   It organises a substantial, coherent body of essential mathematical knowledge (concepts, skills, and models), which is understood, practised, and assessed through performance in substantial vocationally focused tasks.
3   It emphasizes the mathematical models involved, evaluation of their underlying assumptions, and the limits of their validity. This gives emphasis to metacognitive processes which we hope will increase learning and transferability. See the work of Feuerstein, evaluated by Blagg (1991), and recent developments in accelerated cognition in science and mathematics (Shayer, 1994).

Each general mathematical competence recognizes the importance of basic techniques but also takes account of the fact that these form only part of problem-solving capabilities. For example, ideas of proportion are used when tackling many different problems: when students search for linear laws or models in science, or when they represent situations by scale drawings. Although some of the underlying mathematics of these two activities is the same it may not be recognized as such by students or workers because the two problem-solving strategies are so different and obscure this. We hope that by situating the basic mathematical techniques within problem-solving strategies commonly needed by students, they will learn how to apply them, value their usefulness, and from this position be able to develop a more general understanding.

The paradigm for us was 'Handling experimental data graphically', an obviously relevant and powerful general competence in vocationally focused science and engineering courses, which involves the organization and representation of data so as to explore a relationship between two variables measured in experiments. Students and teachers immediately see the purpose of this in the vocational context, and can see it repeatedly practised in the students' assignments.

Figure 7.1   *The growth of yeast cells*

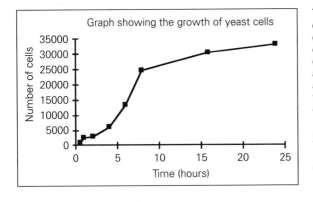

The graph shows the results of a laboratory experiment to examine the growth of yeast cells. The number of cells per cubic millimetre was estimated after counting those visible in a volume of only $2.5*10^{-4}mm^3$ for cultures at different stages of growth. This was done using a special microscope slide – a haemocytometer. The graph shows the average number of cells present after taking a large number of readings at each stage of development.

Figure 7.1 shows one of the four graphs we took from the science course materials to introduce a unit which teaches this competence. It contrasts starkly with the clean data usually to be found in maths texts which tackle this topic.

Competence in producing graphs of this type clearly involves the student's mastering a substantial body of mathematical content, including systematic tabulation, scaling, plotting and modelling with linear functions, and calculation and interpretation of the gradient. Indeed there is a potential for the growth of content to go well beyond the contents of our unit, to include non-linear functions, logarithmic scales, regions, and the introduction of calculus.

It is important that the competence is substantial in two senses. First, it has substantial importance to competence in the vocational field, it is repeated often and must be done well mathematically to be effective scientifically. Second, it may involve a substantial body of mathematical learning and practice, so it is significant for the mathematics curriculum. It is also important that there should be a limited number of large competences, so that students (and their teachers) may come to be familiar with the list. We would like them to recognize these competences when they are carried out effectively and diagnose the errors when they are defective.

Our methodology for developing a list of general mathematical competences was to ask the question 'What mathematics do effective students use and how do they use it?' In addition to talking to teachers and curriculum developers, we studied the work of students on their science assignments. In the following two examples, errors were overlooked by their teacher (indeed they were referred to us as good, mathematically successful students).

In the first (Figure 7.2), the student has taken the data at increasing time intervals and has used a spreadsheet to plot the points with the result that a non-linear scale has been produced. (There is no evidence that the student was attempting to choose a logarithmic scale here; the markings on the axis came simply from the table of values.) The student obtains the gradient of two linear fits without noticing this.

In the second (Figure 7.3), the student has done an effective job of handling the data and representing it graphically. There is even evidence of appreciation of the

Figure 7.2   Rate of reaction

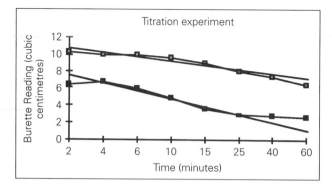

Figure 7.3   Resistance directly proportional to length

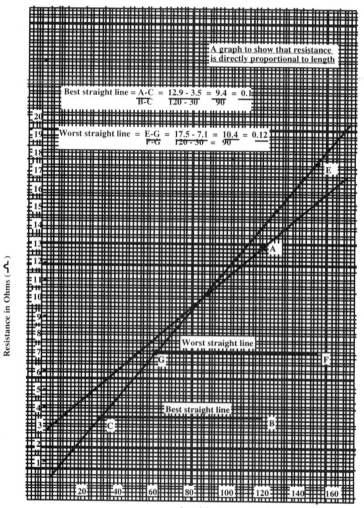

fitted lines as models of the relationship and evaluation of them as such. The result is only spoiled by an error in the calculation of one of the gradients. The expressions stated for the calculation of the gradients are incorrect, though the actual calculation has been performed correctly. We suspect these errors were missed because they had little effect on the outcome:

In both cases it seems that the defective mathematics was simply overlooked because the assignment was set for the purposes of meeting the science objectives. This highlights a problem with curriculum implementation where substantial work with mathematics is undertaken by students although the fundamental focus is not mathematics. We are asking teachers and students to break down barriers that their previous experience of school and college curriculum has erected. If there were a limited number of mathematical competences to be assessed through the assignments, handling the experimental data graphically would certainly have been on the checklist for this assignment, and the student and teacher might well have given it greater attention. Is it possible, then, to organize the content of the mathematics curriculum around a few powerful general mathematical competences which connect the mathematics to the vocational applications?

The Relationship of General Mathematical Competence with Content

In the case of science we identified seven general mathematical competences which seemed to be significant:

- handling experimental data graphically
- using models of direct and inverse proportion
- interpreting large data sets
- using formulae
- measuring in science
- using mathematical diagrams
- costing a project.

Between them these more than cover the content of the core mathematics course currently required at this level, and indicate the need for some extra mathematics content which is not explicitly stated in the curriculum.

Our evaluation of these seven general mathematical competences is still unfinished, however. We are concerned about the mathematical coherence of 'using mathematical diagrams', which includes disparate elements such as vector diagrams and scale drawings of plans and elevations (quite unconnected mathematically).

We were aware of the need to 'cover' a syllabus with dubious intellectual justification, for pragmatic reasons in mapping a curriculum for the colleges to use now. We therefore expect the further development and evaluation of this list of competences to lead to reform of the content of the mathematics curriculum for different vocational courses as well as pressure to rewrite the specifications in general mathematical competence format.

But here is a problem of interpretation. What is 'essential' to the general mathematical competence depends very much on the range of chosen applications and assignments. These are not precisely prescribed in the course specifications and we have some evidence from interviewing college staff that interpretations vary dramatically. In one case for instance a College of Building interprets a requirement for 'Tests for water samples using pH etc.' as involving an understanding of pH in terms of a logarithmic scale of hydrogen ion concentrations with the associated complex calculations. A college a few miles away interprets the same requirement as knowledge of pH as a simple 14-point scale — with no logarithmic calculations and no negative exponents!

General Mathematical Competences and Complexity of Mathematical Process

We now explore the relationship of the general mathematical competence to the process aspects of the curriculum. As a research exercise for the government agency responsible for implementation of the vocational curriculum we have developed a means of interpreting degrees of complexity of performance in the mathematics and science involved in the intended curriculum. The aim is to be able to describe and compare the content and process demands of different qualifications.

The methodology is based on that developed by Coles and Matthews (1996) using Bloom's (1956) taxonomy of learning objectives. Where Coles used six foci of performance, we preferred to simplify to four, which we call foci of activity or level of complexity of performance (see Wake and Jervis, 1997). These allow a performance or an activity to be classified in terms of the way in which the content is or is intended to be used. This is important to some higher-education consumers of qualifications, many of whom are more concerned with the students' confidence and ability to think with the mathematics they know than with a definitive list of content they would like them to have 'met' (see Lord et al., 1995).

It is even more relevant to vocational practice. Coles and Matthews drew opinions from scientists from many industrial domains and were able to classify their view of the necessary focus of performance with content. Our work does a similar job for mathematics and science over a wider spectrum of vocations in the area of science and technology. The aim of the work is to identify and compare the mathematics and science intended in the various vocational qualifications.

The four levels of process shown in Figure 7.4 are here briefly described:

1 Knowledge and skills: activity at this level involves recall, technique and fluency (conventions, facts and algorithms)
2 Comprehension: involves the understanding needed to apply the knowledge and skills to a prescribed case or application
3 Application: involves understanding the concepts and relationships sufficiently to identify the relevant methods and hence to solve a class of problems
4 Problem solving: involves the ability to evaluate, synthesize and hence develop solutions to 'new' problems.

Figure 7.4   Representing dimensions of the mathematics curriculum

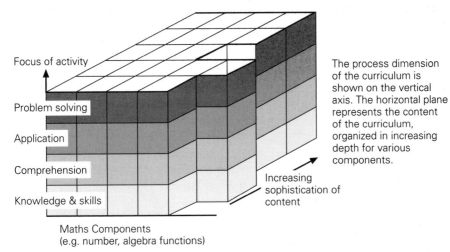

The process dimension of the curriculum is shown on the vertical axis. The horizontal plane represents the content of the curriculum, organized in increasing depth for various components.

Focus of activity

Problem solving

Application

Comprehension

Knowledge & skills

Increasing sophistication of content

Maths Components
(e.g. number, algebra functions)

With the specification of the content and the processes involved we now have what Treffers (1987) calls a two dimensional model of the curriculum. Most practitioners view basic student performance required as essentially at the first two of the four levels above.

The explicit understanding of a general mathematical competence as applicable to a class of applications involves the essence of level 3, but the development of this level of thinking takes the student through 1 and 2. Students may be involved in work at level 2 where a model is given and applies to a number of given situations. This will motivate and involve the practice of knowledge and skills, and even the development of new concepts. The development of understanding and skill in the competence in practice involves evaluation of the model's validity and of an emerging class of problems which can be solved with it. Reflection on the concepts and models involved might lead to level-4 activity. It is in principle a short step to go from the evaluation of mathematical models to the study of mathematics and problem solving itself.

Pedagogy and the General Mathematical Competence Modules

Is the general mathematical competence an instructional strategy? If the attempt to reform the curriculum with 'real' institutions and teachers is to be successful, then Treffers (1987) regards this third dimension as essential.

So far we have written materials and guides for modules based on this for the first four of the competences. This work will continue through 1997. The materials involve vocational case studies (such as the study of distribution of sludge on farmland, and the radioactivity levels found in milk) and vocational applications arising from within the vocational science units.

Figure 7.5 illustrates some examples of the following instructional modules, which are designed:

Figure 7.5   *Examples from instructional modules*

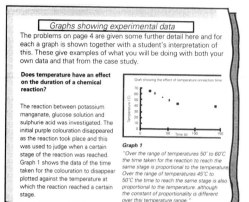

In the example module all three — case study, practical work and illustrations from all areas of science — are used to show the wide range of applications of the mathematics.

(a) Introduction

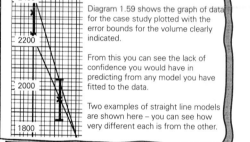

This module, for example, teaches about variables, measurement, errors, proportion, graphs and gradients. The example here shows how a graphical interpretation of error can inform model development.

Diagram 1.59 shows the graph of data for the case study plotted with the error bounds for the volume clearly indicated.

From this you can see the lack of confidence you would have in predicting from any model you have fitted to the data.

Two examples of straight line models are shown here – you can see how very different each is from the other.

(b) Teaching knowledge, skills and understanding

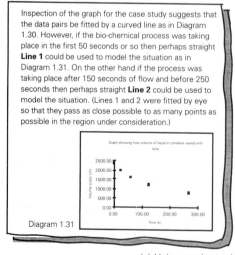

Inspection of the graph for the case study suggests that the data pairs be fitted by a curved line as in Diagram 1.30. However, if the bio-chemical process was taking place in the first 50 seconds or so then perhaps straight **Line 1** could be used to model the situation as in Diagram 1.31. On the other hand if the process was taking place after 150 seconds of flow and before 250 seconds then perhaps straight **Line 2** could be used to model the situation. (Lines 1 and 2 were fitted by eye so that they pass as close possible to as many points as possible in the region under consideration.)

Diagram 1.31

Here, for example, the idea of being able to model a restricted range of data using a straight line is introduced

(c) Using mathematics to model real situations

Figure 7.5 (cont'd)

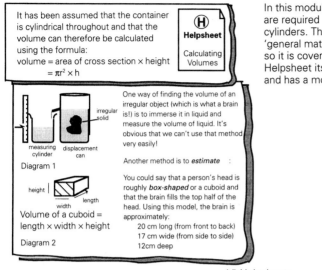

In this module, for example, students are required to find the volumes of cylinders. This is subsidiary to the 'general mathematical competence' so it is covered by a Helpsheet. The Helpsheet itself is based in science and has a modelling flavour.

(d) Helpsheets

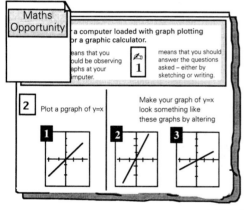

An opportunity for students to study straight lines and their equations in the form y=mx+c is developed in this unit. An accompanying activity allows students to explore this.

(e) Maths opportunities

- to have an introduction using case studies, illustrations, and/or practicals from the GNVQ Science course that can clearly be seen to be generalizable to other relevant applications
- to teach an identifiable body of mathematical knowledge (facts, concepts, and skills) from the Application of Number specifications and, where necessary, beyond
- to teach the mathematics explicitly as a set of adaptable models, wherein assumptions, interpretation, and validation issues are critical
- to identify potential points where remedial help may be needed, and cross-reference help sheets

- to identify starting points for interesting mathematical inquiries which may take the student beyond the minimal requirements of 'competence'.

Evaluation

First, there are problems connected with the teaching. Colleges adopt a wide range of styles, but the new courses encourage 'active' modes of learning which are intended to give a sense of ownership to the student. Some teachers understand by this that their teaching should be strictly limited and that students should learn independently. Mathematics courses then often reduce to drop-in workshops. On the other hand we think it is important to encourage class teaching and discussion. We designed our modules as far as possible to be useful in both situations, which led to weaknesses such as including too much written explanation.

Another problem arises from situating the mathematics across the range of science contexts. Mathematics teachers have found this daunting, especially when many of them have limited scientific backgrounds. Even science teachers often find it hard to stretch across the full range of a course which spreads beyond their specialism. We are trying to break down traditional subject barriers for the students, but we ourselves come from the old educational culture.

In the development of the competence list we found a heavy algebraic content. This may be a reflection of what is thought to be needed and what is thought to be weak in students' preparation for the vocationally focused science course. It does suggest, however, that this body of content might need quite separate teaching. We wish to make a disclaimer: we do not believe that the mathematics must always be taught 'in context' by vocational teachers or solely through the modules we have written for maths teachers to use with vocational students. There will often be cases where a substantial body of mathematics needs to be developed quite separately from the immediate application. There is a case for developing algebra through the study of general principles of number, as a pure mathematical study. Certainly the case seems very strong for teaching calculus. But we do say that students will still have to learn to be competent with the mathematics in the vocational context, in addition to studying mathematics as a separate subject, and that this is an additional, significant task.

Case Studies of Vocational Practice

It is clear that case studies are important for the pedagogy. Ideally one would wish that the students studying the module would start with their own case study, involving, for instance, work with their own experimental data. However, we are also concerned that the vocationally focused nature of the course should bring benefit to the mathematical work.

It soon became clear that the students' own practical work was not always vocationally focused, in the sense that their assignments were actually focused on their school or college labs. We therefore started to consider developing mathematics

Figure 7.6   Examples of developing mathematics from workplace settings

L Proctor and Sons is a small sheet metal fabricating works which employs four people. David Kitchen who manages the business as well as working on the shop floor has found that automation has had a large effect on the work he does. Because it is a small firm, David, who joined the firm as an apprentice at the age of sixteen over twenty years ago, needs to be able to do everything from quoting for orders, writing programs for the machinery, to actually producing the components.

A tool can be fitted in the machine in three different ways at angles of 0°, 45° or 135°. The diagram alongside shows this for a rectangle 40mm by 10mm.

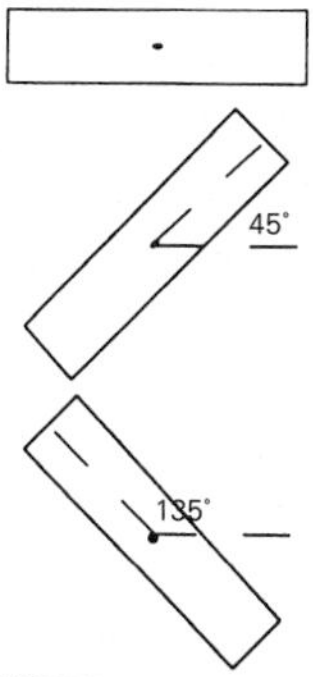

It is possible to cut out complex shapes, either by using different shaped tools or by nibbling the metal away with a circular tool. A line can be cut at an angle of 60 degrees, for example, in one of two ways. Either

(1)   a punch is used (where one side makes an angle of 60 degrees), triangular or parallelogram in form, as in the diagram below; or

(2)   a circle can be used to nibble a line by increasing the X coordinate by 1mm

ADDITIONAL DATA
Machine performance:
Repeatable accuracy better than ± 0.13 mm.
Point to point speed 57 m/min.
Punch rates up to 180 hits/min at 25 mm pitches.
Nibble rates up to 300 hits/min.
Sheet thickness up to 3.2mm.

Costs:
Each tool punch, die and stripper costs about £35.
After about 50,000 hits the tool punch must be reground at a cost of around £10.

directly from real vocational case studies. These include several original ones of our own. These allow us to consider the items of mathematical interest in the vocational science setting, rather than draw out mathematics which may be seen in the science as such. In one, for example, the item of interest was the handling of a large data set of information on the wild-life in a sanctuary. In another an engineer has to plan the coordinate geometry of a template in order to program a machine to cut a metal part (see Figure 7.6).

Mathematics in the Vocational Setting

We now ask the question: do real case studies from vocational settings show a demand for the same mathematical competences as those designed for the science curriculum? We could be preparing the students with mathematical competence for school science but these may not be so relevant to the workplace setting. Are the general mathematical competences we create for the purposes of the curriculum relevant to the workplace?

This is an interesting research question. We have made a few preliminary case studies and these have helped in our development of the general mathematical competences. Two issues immediately arise. First, if general mathematical competences which link the curriculum and the workplace can be defined, then we will bring a quite new coherence to the curriculum in pre-vocational (whether vocationally focused or not) and vocational education. This is a prize which seems well worth effort. Second, the mathematics which the practitioner in a vocational setting recognizes is well known to be relatively limited, if not non-existent. The situated mathematics is, as it were, frozen. Yet, for a non-expert, coming to understand what the practitioner does so effortlessly may be very demanding mathematically! We are, therefore, bound to make a distinction between what the user does, and how we can come to understand it. It is the latter which interests us, as it has a mathematical richness we can use, but also because we believe it more accurately reflects the process of learning and adaptation which the future worker must go through to be really effective.

In conclusion, we have described our efforts to build a curriculum and assessment scheme for mathematics based on 'general mathematical competence' in vocationally focused courses. The construct 'general mathematical competence' does seem to have the potential to provide a language for thinking about how mathematics is used in the courses, how it should be taught and assessed, and how it might become functional in future workplace settings.

References

BLAGG, N. (1991) *Can We Teach Intelligence*, Hillsdale, NJ: Lawrence Erlbaum.

BLOOM, B.S. (ed.) (1956) *Taxonomy of Educational Objectives — Book 1 — Cognitive Domain*, Michegan: Longman.

BLUM, W. (1992) 'Applications and modelling in mathematics teaching', in NISS, M., BLUM, W. and HUNTLEY, I. (eds) *Teaching Mathematical Modelling and Applications*, Chichester: Ellis-Horwood, pp. 10–29.

BLUM, W. and STRASSER, R. (1992) 'Mathematics teaching in technical and vocational colleges: Professional training versus general education', *Zentralblatt fur Didaktik der Mathematik: International Reviews on Mathematical Education*, **92**, 7, pp. 92–7.

CAPEY, J. (1996) *GNVQ Assessment Review*, London: NCVQ.

CARRAHER, T.N., CARRAHER, D.W. and SCHLIEMANN, A.D. (1985) 'Mathematics in the street and in schools', *British Journal of Developmental Psychology*, **3**, pp. 21–9.

CLEGG, A. (1992) 'A case study of mathematics in A level and BTEC science and engineering', Unpublished M.Ed. Thesis, University of Manchester.

COLES, M. and MATTHEWS, A. (1996) *Fitness for Purpose: A Means of Comparing Qualifications*, London: NCVQ.

JESSUP, G. (1991) *Outcomes: NVQs and the Emerging Model of Education and Training*, London: Falmer Press.

KITCHEN, A. and WILLIAMS, J.S. (1994) 'Implementing and assessing mathematical modelling in the academic 16–19 curriculum', in BREITEIG, T., et al. (eds) *Teaching and Learning Mathematics in Context*, Chichester: Ellis-Horwood, pp. 138–50.

LORD, K., WAKE, G.D. and WILLIAMS, J.S. (1995) *Mathematics for Progression from Advanced GNVQs to Higher Education*, Cheltenham: UCAS.

REBER, A. (1989) 'Implicit learning and tacit knowledge', *Journal of Experimental Psychology: General*, **118**, pp. 219–35.

SHAYER, M. (1994) *Really Raising Standards: Cognitive, Intervention and Academic Achievement*, London: Routledge.

TREFFERS, A. (1987) *Three Dimensions: A Model of Goal and Theory Description in Mathematics Instruction*, Reidel: Dordrecht.

WAKE, G.D. and JERVIS, A. (1997) *Mathematics and Science Capabilities of Students with Technology GNVQs*, Cheltenham: UCAS.

Chapter 8

Maximizing Energy in the Learning of Mathematics

Gillian Hatch

Working Creatively

It is my belief that when they start school all children bring with them the ability to work creatively in mathematics. This paper is concerned with establishing ways in which that ability might be preserved for learners of all ages and abilities. Thinking and behaving creatively is an increasingly important skill in a world becoming ever more dominated by technology. Society needs a plentiful supply of adults who are mathematically literate and able to apply their mathematical knowledge. In the UK at present the extent of this supply is in some doubt, whether we look at the evidence from university teachers (Gardiner, 1995) or, at a lower academic level, at the results of international surveys (Lapointe et al., 1992). I suggest that this is due to the loss of children's creative energy during their mathematical schooling and hope to offer some ways of working that may prevent this.

Often the loss of a creative approach to mathematics occurs quite early in a pupil's experience of learning mathematics in the school context. I will offer an example of this from my own experience. Some years ago I spent a summer term teaching in two secondary schools and the four primary schools which fed these secondary schools. This enabled me to compare a class of high-ability 11- to 12-year-olds in one of the secondary schools with the most able pupils a year younger in their related feeder primaries. The contrast was disturbing. The younger pupils were willing and able to attack any problem I chose to set them. They assumed that if they had been offered a task, then they could make some progress with it. I prepared material for the older pupils, looking for interesting ways to approach the ideas, but each week I had to accept that my selected material was too demanding, not in terms of content but in its demands on them to be relatively autonomous learners. Sadly, I remained in conflict with the class as to what they should be able to do for the whole term. I found it impossible to accept that I could not tap back into the behaviour they would have shown only a year before. All their energy for the learning of mathematics had been sapped. I believe that this change was caused by teacher behaviour and expectation. It seemed clear that the teacher concerned had made them dependent learners, who knew, or thought they knew, that they had to be instructed in how to respond to each new kind of mathematical problem. If we are to improve the quality of learning in our classrooms then teachers have to think very clearly about the messages which their actions are giving to pupils.

> How a teacher behaves in a classroom in a mathematical situation, and the habitual interaction which takes place speaks volumes to pupils about mathematics and the possibilities in it for them. (Love and Mason, 1992)

Another perspective on this problem has emerged from those who teach mathematics to undergraduates who comment on the poor level of conceptual understanding amongst first-year students.

> Our eighteen year olds no longer have any idea that if mathematical assertions are to have any value at all, statements must be formulated carefully and manipulated in precise, reliable, strictly defensible ways. . . . In particular they have no idea that Mathematics has to be understood logically and manipulated correctly. More than ever before they long for rules and procedures. (Gardiner, 1995)

While the large increase in the percentage of young people going on to university must be a factor in this perception from the university sector, it is clear that many find the transition to university work a traumatic one and undoubtedly some of the reasons for this lie in school mathematics teaching. Mathematics graduates, when they enrol on a course of training to become teachers of mathematics, are often voluble about the difficulties they had with their courses. Anderson (1996) gives a more objective analysis of the causes of the problem while basically agreeing with the facts. I do not agree with all the arguments put forward by Gardiner and other critics. However, I fear that I do recognize some of the behaviours they describe in my experience with undergraduate students following a degree course which gives them a qualification as a mathematics teacher.

My 12-year-old pupils, described above, also longed for rules and procedures. The problem was already discernible even at that age. We need to think through very carefully the roles within the learning of mathematics of problem solving, investigating, the attainment of understanding, and the acquisition of knowledge and of appropriate fluency. The political climate in the UK could make one feel that we were alone in finding the balance of these elements difficult to get correct. It is interesting and in some ways comforting to find similar concerns elsewhere. From Japan, Fujita et al. (1995) describe their students' dislike of mathematics and their lack of problem-solving skills.

I wish to develop the idea that the aim of mathematics teaching should be to keep all pupils in a high-energy state throughout their mathematical learning careers. Pupils in such a state will confront any problem, given to them or invented for themselves, with their previous learning in mathematics in an active and accessible state and with the assumption that they have the ability to make progress. It is clear that it is not easy to achieve this state, particularly with older or less able pupils, but as is often pointed out, this is exactly the way in which pre-school children approach their learning. The priority must be to achieve a position in which pupils of all ages and abilities can justify the mathematics they are doing and put together a logical argument to support their beliefs.

Such learners can be created only by providing high-energy classrooms for them. The task is made more difficult for teachers by the fact that the majority have not themselves grown up in such classrooms either at secondary school or at university. Most teachers have, however, retained enough of their early energy to want to study mathematics to degree level even if their experience was not really of high-energy classrooms. Occasional individuals have even retained their own learning energy throughout the formalism of a university course. But in most cases there is a reawakening task to be achieved by some means. This chapter is therefore also concerned with the nature of the high-energy classroom and how it may be created by the teacher.

What Is Lacking?

First let us consider the context and the influences on teachers of mathematics in the UK which have led to classrooms showing high energy only rarely. Over the last 20 years teachers have been subjected to many studies, often conflicting with one another, and to criticisms of all kinds. Within these lies so much advice that it is unremarkable if they are bewildered and find it difficult to know which ideas to accept. I believe there have been two significant long-term results of the influential Cockcroft report (1982). The first is the 'bottom up curriculum' i.e. a curriculum designed to meet, as its priority, the needs of the average and below-average pupil. The second is the introduction into the curriculum of 'investigations'. I do not believe that either is an unqualified success. Philosophically, I agree strongly that the curriculum of the average or below-average child should not be driven by the needs of the more able child. We need teaching and learning processes which support all learners equally and enable all individuals to reach their maximum potential.

'Pace'

But it seems possible that the 'understanding of difficulty' approach has led to the loss of a sense of urgency to progress. Indeed, some Hungarian colleagues who were visiting British schools as part of a joint project with my university observed that:

> As a result of our experiences we formed the opinion that in an English school the underlying philosophy of teaching is quite different from ours . . . Not to hurt the self 'image' of children is more important than to force them to achieve better results. (Torok and Szeredi, 1992)

Lesson pace has now become an issue for teachers in the UK as a result of the framework used to inspect our schools. When I visited schools in Hungary I felt that every lesson had this element of pace, but rarely do I observe the same effect in classrooms which I visit in the UK. Pace, I believe, is not to do with the speed of movement through the curriculum but with a sort of tautness of expectation where all the pupils' energy is bent towards the learning task, whatever its nature. Pace is not to do with getting through more 'sums' per lesson but to do with the energy expended in understanding the meaning behind the sums and reflecting on the mathematics. The creation of a high-energy classroom will certainly involve the maintenance of pace.

'Know-how'

While the UK national assessment system is dominated by the techniques of mathematics there is a great temptation to teach through memory and not understanding. In doing this we fail to ensure that what our pupils acquire is 'know-hows':

> But as soon as learning is stressed, everything changes. It seems that knowledge cannot simply be entrusted to memory; everyone must produce in one's mind the equivalent of that knowledge and replace it by a know-how. . . . Only know-hows can be counted on and do endure. (Gattegno, 1982)

Only know-hows, not memorized routines, can contribute to the high-energy state.

Investigating, Conjecturing, and Proving

In many schools investigations have been, I believe, little short of a disaster. I have written about this elsewhere (Hatch, 1995). The process of investigating is central to the kind of teaching that will create energy, but it needs to be within the central learning processes of mathematics and not undertaken at a separate time of the week or term or just to satisfy the requirements of an examination. The setting of investigations as assessment tasks, completed in a certain time span, which can be reliably marked using a numerical mark scheme, misrepresents the whole process of mathematical investigation which, as any mathematical researcher will confirm, proceeds at a definitely non-linear and unpredictable rate!

If I characterize the average mathematics classroom that I visit, I would say that, although there may be elements of investigational work, these are not well integrated into the curriculum. They have little mathematical significance and often lead to poorly developed results. There is little sense that a well tested conjecture is not the end of the road, and that even if the learners cannot at this time justify their conjectures there remains a task to be undertaken before the conjecture becomes certainty. This acceptance of the truth of unproven conjectures may well be one of the root causes of the behaviour described by Gardiner. Alongside such investigational work I see much traditional chalk, talk, and practice work. As a trainer of teachers I work hard to present other models of the mathematics classroom. The problem in getting these accepted is that they are all harder to operate and student teachers often do not see them operating in schools, therefore the status quo tends to remain unchallenged.

'Struggle'

Many texts have been developed over the last 10 years aiming to make the learning of mathematics easier. Teachers have hoped that these would help pupils to enjoy mathematics more. However, when learning is broken down into minute steps the learner neither sees the overall picture nor learns to take bigger steps for himself. He retains the information less well because the deeper parts of the brain do not become engaged. To internalize a concept in mathematics we need to engage with it in some real sense, we need to articulate it and reflect upon it, to relate it to other ideas. We need to educate our pupils to know that, out of difficulties encountered and overcome, emerges real 'know-how'. The high-energy state is characterized by the excitement of having struggled but yet won through.

Challenging Some Assumptions about Teaching

Little seems to have changed as a result of the enormous volume of research and the many reports that have come out over the years. The same problems are described repeatedly. What can be said as we approach the millennium that might change what is done by teachers in classrooms? I have come to believe that there are two basic teacher assumptions which we need to question and perhaps to oppose actively in teacher training.

The Importance of Getting Right Answers

The first of these is hard to eradicate, especially in a system in which teachers and schools are judged by the performance of pupils in technique-based tests. It is that as teachers we feel happy when the pupils get the 'sums' right. We are not inclined to dig deeper and look for lack of understanding; we feel they are doing nicely and we feel good about it. Now, of course, there are times when it is appropriate to test techniques alone so that pupils can show appropriate levels of fluency. However, at other times we need to be sure that pupils are facing difficulties of interpretation, discovering that the answers do not always drop out smoothly and that they know that sometimes a struggle is essential. We need to develop strategies for helping pupils to work with difficult ideas. Our pupils need to find that there is something intellectually satisfying at an appropriate level for each of them if they are to value their progress in mathematics. Above all, we have to believe that we are not failing if our pupils are not always succeeding easily.

As teachers we need to learn to probe their understanding, to uncover lack of clarity and misconceptions even if we do not like the results. As a teacher trainer I ask student teachers and mentors in school to work with the classic conflict teaching question: 'Which is bigger: two thirds or three quarters?' The mentors are all convinced that the pupils will have so little difficulty that a lesson based on this is just not possible. They are almost always shaken by the misconceptions and failures in understanding that emerge. Conceptual problems need to be met head on rather than avoided if real understanding is to be achieved.

Teaching As Explaining

The second assumption is that one of the main tasks of a teacher is to explain mathematics clearly to the pupils so that they understand it. When applicants to train as mathematics teachers are interviewed they often suggest that they will enjoy explaining mathematics to pupils. Yet when I ask them to describe the characteristics of a good mathematics teacher they talk first about patience and humour. Only later do some speak of the ability to give multiple explanations of the same thing thereby tacitly acknowledging the fact that one explanation is rarely effective. They seem to know as learners that a lot more is involved than simple explanation. Yet as teachers they will usually feel that a major part of their job is to explain.

A useful approach to the issue of explanations is to be found in the work of Hewitt (1994). He divides mathematical knowledge into two categories. The first is that which is arbitrary, for example standard notation, definitions etc. The second is that which can be deduced from earlier knowledge or by working logically with the elements involved in the given situation. He argues strongly that to explain to pupils things which are non-arbitrary is to risk creating dependency on the teacher, to risk them ceasing to believe that they can work for themselves on the mathematics. It leads them to demand information as to how to approach the next step. Clearly the role of the teacher may nevertheless be to assist the children to achieve their own explanations but in terms of power roles nothing could be more different. Even the correct answer to a question can be an inappropriate explanation. What is more essential is for the pupil to become aware that the answer is wrong.

Smith (1986) describes 'teaching without telling' as a process in which students' contributions are all valued as they are led to ask their own questions and are helped by the teacher only by the asking of more questions. The teacher in such a situation can often assist the pupils to move forwards just by asking them to review what they have done and reflect on it. In this way the pupils retain their self-confidence and the problem they are attempting to solve remains their own.

We need to withhold explanation unless there is no way pupils can create it for themselves. We need to monitor our behaviour carefully and try to perceive how we are using our explanations. We need to research the situations in which teacher explanation is valuable and necessary and those in which it is destructive. We need to enlarge our concept of explanation beyond simple verbal action. As a trainer of teachers I have to consider these two issues of teacher behaviour very seriously and seek ways for trainees to become aware of their significance.

What is it that a teacher should be doing to improve the quality of learning in her classroom and ensure that the pupils are kept in a high-energy state? Schoenfeld

(1994) gives a challenging description of what a classroom needs to be like to remain true to the nature of mathematics:

> If we believe that doing mathematics is an act of sense making; if we believe that mathematics is often a hands on empirical activity; if we believe that mathematical communication is important; if we believe that the mathematical community grapples with serious mathematical problems collaboratively, making tentative explanations of these phenomena, and then cycling back through these explanations (including definitions and postulates); if we believe that learning mathematics is empowering and that there is a mathematical way of thinking that has value and power, then our classroom practices must reflect those beliefs.

A Mathematical Ethos

In the recent review of research, Askew and Wiliam (1996), in summarizing the most recent international survey, speak of a 'mathematical ethos' in schools as linking with high achievement. This idea appears to connect strongly to the Schoenfeld description of high-quality learning. So our high-energy classroom needs to have such an ethos.

What might constitute a mathematical ethos in the classroom? I shall consider the areas of learning, reflection, practice and fluency, conjecturing, and memory, and the contribution which each of these can make to making our classrooms fit Schoenfeld's description.

Learning Takes Time

First of all we must convince teachers that one can never teach anyone anything: all one can do is to create a situation in which pupils may learn. The description given by Griffin (1989) of the need to allow time for learning to take place always catches the sympathy of classroom teachers, especially since I usually give it to them during a course which requires them to learn mathematics themselves. They recognize their need for that time to come to terms with the ideas and can relate this to children's needs.

> So what is the relationship between teaching and learning? I am drawn back to the conjecture behind 'teaching takes place in time, learning takes place over time' that learning is a process of maturation in the learner. The teacher cannot perform this process for the learner nor can the teacher force it upon the learner. Rather, it is the atmosphere and environment created in the classroom by the actions of the teacher which can raise the awareness of the learner and shift attention in such a way as to stimulate this process of maturation in the learner. (Griffin, 1989)

So we need to offer to pupils the chance to mature their understanding of a topic so that it will become part of their thinking and remain available to them.

Reflection

Maturation and reflection go hand in hand. A useful definition of reflection is given by Billington (1992):

> Reflection is the process by which one re-enters and focuses on a previous experi-
> ence and as a result of that focusing confirms or makes changes to ideas previously
> held.

Davis (1988) relates reflection to the linking of significant moments and sharp experiences which can be held on to mentally and referred back to when a similar context occurs. So we need to give time to helping our pupils trace ideas back, to link them to previous experiences and draw out the commonalities. This is, in some sense, the reverse process to that in which pupils build up their own explanations. The rehearsal of the relation between new ideas and old supports the building of secure conceptual networks and implicitly suggests the idea of back-tracking to firm ground if any ideas have become hazy. In the idea of reflection we can identify a resonance with Schoenfeld's phrase, 'cycling back through these explanations'. The purpose of reflection can thus be seen as that of making sense of what has been done, linking it to previous ideas. It can also include, in a classroom situation, sorting out differences of understanding between individuals.

Fluency and Practice

The relationship between understanding and fluency is a complex one. A failure of fluency can cause much loss of energy. For example it can cause such a delay in progress that the thread of the piece of work is lost. Able 13-year-old pupils who work out $18 + 5$ on their fingers or who are held up for perceptible amounts of time while they struggle to recall their tables are liable to lose impetus in any work which requires a higher level of reasoning. I have watched pupils in the early stages of a sixth-form course, 17-year-olds who have chosen to study mathematics further, struggle with algebra and experience a feeling of total inadequacy. Yet they often need only to increase their algebraic fluency by doing some practice from a conventional algebra textbook to regain their energy. Bruce (1994), in a case study of three pupils from age 15 to age 18, concludes that the student who progressed effortlessly to the higher level of mathematics was the one who not only showed robust concepts but had well developed skills in several key areas. The pupil who had not been given the time to achieve this mastery struggled and needed extra support to succeed. The most able pupil also had the capacity to refer back to internalized explanations of the automatic skills he had developed. These were certainly 'know-hows' as described by Gattegno.

Watching pupils play games as part of a recent research project, I have become aware of the power of games to create what I would wish to call 'an unreasonable amount of practice', i.e. an amount of practice which would never be tolerated if pupil attention was on the practice rather than on the game. When applied to algebraic skills, for example, this kind of activity seems to lead pupils to learn to handle immensely complicated algebraic expressions apparently almost without noticing the complexity. The attention of the pupils is switched to the game not the difficulty of the algebra, and this appears to cause a subordination of learning of algebra to the excitement of the game. Hewitt (1994) gives an account of a similar, almost game-like activity, which results in comparable effects. He speaks of: 'a functioning — something which the learner knows so well that they hardly have to give it any conscious thought'.

In our high-energy classrooms we will need to help pupils become aware of the need to practise and achieve fluency. Pimm (1995) raises the issue of the awareness of the pupils of what they are doing:

> Children are very good at practising certain things until they have mastered them — they are willing, it seems, to pay the necessary attention. . . . It crucially matters how pupils approach practice in terms of what they get from it.

In any classroom which can be characterized as having a 'mathematical ethos' it seems that pupils should be expected to understand that fluency is in their own interests. We need to share this expectation with them and offer them ways to work at their perceived needs, perhaps in a semi-autonomous way. We need to help them to see that fluency can involve more than the mindless uncritical solution of routine problems. The ability to classify routine problems, to stand back and identify what types of problem are involved and discern what kind of approach is needed for each, creates a form of reflection on fluency within the context concerned. As Pimm (1995) says:

> One key point is that if I approach a series of exercises with my eye out for the general, for what there is in common across all these activities, then I am better mathematically attuned to what is of importance. If I go through the exercises one after another, as something to get through, then my attention is crucially missing from the central focus, from the point of view of teaching. Sets of exercises where there is no connection between one and the next destroy the possibility of such focused practice.

As teachers we need to be sure that the tasks that we set for our pupils allow them to search for general structure within the particular exercises. We need to induct them into this process by discussing which problems are similar and which different.

Tasks of this kind can lead to the identification of general principles which might otherwise remain implicit. Within my work on algebraic games I became concerned as to whether the pupils thought that the rules for algebraic language changed with the letter used. I prepared a set of cards each of which had on it a linear equation. The pack contained sets of three cards which contained essentially the same equation but each card used a different letter for the variable. Overall I used a wide variety of letters, both lower and upper case. I asked a group of six to sort these cards into piles which had the same solution. Soon someone was saying that they had just solved this one and in response to my query I was told that it was just the letters that were different. When all the cards were in piles, I was able to tell them that it could not be correct as there should be the same number of cards in each pile. A quick re-examination led to the statement that 'it's the ones that are the same that should be in the same pile' and the cards were rapidly sorted by 'sameness'. There was a great air of satisfaction and energy when this task was complete, yet it held within it quite a lot of routine practice, at least if your pedagogic philosophy allows you to accept the mental solution of simple equations! The same kind of activity could be presented in a more formal way.

Another possible way to create 'thoughtful practice' is to ask students, as a group, to set their own homework problems to practise something they have just learnt. This has two outcomes: it is possible to learn whether they have internalized the ideas sufficiently to be able to do this and in the next session the ones that were 'wrong' can be discussed, allowing further reflection on the task.

Conjecturing

Another element essential to this mathematical ethos is what has become known as 'conjecturing', that is the willingness to venture to state, for response by others in the group, a conjecture which is in the process of development. It invites comment from everyone as to its relevance, precision and truth. It involves all the pupils in the evaluation of ideas. When such an ethos has been established, the attitude of critical assessment permeates the situation:

> When a conjecturing atmosphere is established, pupils respond to exposition not as assertions to be 'learned' but as a stimulus to check out the ideas for themselves, to make sense for themselves through exploration and through explaining to each other. (Love and Mason, 1992)

The speaking out loud of a conjecture gains in several ways. To utter it at all, the conjecturer must clarify it sufficiently to express it in words which carry meaning for other people. Once it is uttered, it becomes a more objective object he may be able to criticize for himself. It is, by articulation, placed firmly in the arena for others to comment on, to make the attempt to refine or refute it. The teacher may play a part in this refining act, but in this atmosphere it is possible for the teacher's input to be subjected to the same critical comment. This process can operate on many scales. It may be part of whole-class discussion as when the resolution of a piece of conflict teaching is in progress. Alternatively it may occur within small-group interaction, for example during a piece of investigational work or when pairs of children play as a unit in a game. It embodies the idea of justification, which is at the heart of a true mathematical ethos, but it allows for contributions from many people who can trigger insights for each other. Pupils need to be helped to achieve this level of discourse, but the very fact that it is verbal makes it easier. In such a classroom the teacher's role is not just one of referee; there is much to be done in the thoughtful framing of questions, in the stressing and ignoring of certain aspects of the discussion, in the repetition of a pupil's statement, perhaps in slightly different words to establish whether there is agreement as to its meaning. What may be the most significant contribution of all is the acceptance that everyone's ideas are of value and can be woven into the group progression in mathematics.

Watson (1994) describes how she works with the ideas that pupils offer in discussion. She believes that it is the teacher's task to be seen to value all pupils' contributions to discussion, to weave these into an account in which all the class have been involved. However, she also identifies a need to help the pupils, by her commentary on their results, to identify what is significant and the ideas which will contribute to the way forward in mathematics. In playing this role the teacher becomes a kind of consultant who is able to advise and comment but not take over authority over the totality of the knowledge constructed.

Know-how Versus Memorization

Gattegno distinguishes knowledge from know-how and calls attention to the fact that we have to do more with knowledge than memorize it, if it is to become functional. As a pupil at school one of my great pleasures in mathematics was that it did not involve much memory work. However it is on just this issue of memory that many pupils founder as learners of mathematics. They become teacher-dependent memorizers of what to do in an ever-increasing number of meaningless situations. Hewitt (1994) discusses this need to avoid memorization:

> Memory is an expensive way to ask people to learn. If the underlying structure can be made explicit, then a learner can be creative within that structure and generate their knowledge rather than being asked to memorise it.

The use of know-hows which can be re-accessed and recycled releases energy for intelligent action. Unless we use reflection to build such structures our pupils will not be able to retain the receptive high-energy state this paper attempts to describe. They will be using all their attention to hold on to meaningless rules, each existing independently of the others. Our high-energy pupils will need to be helped to develop links and connections whenever possible. When an automated routine suddenly comes under question they need to be able to trace it back to its roots and re-establish it. They need practice in doing this, perhaps in response to the question, 'How do you know that is correct?'

This indicates a strong relationship between the saving of memory energy and the idea of reflection. What then might help pupils to reflect and refine their understanding so that connections are made and retained? Talking mathematics both out loud and to oneself is crucial. Pimm (1987) speaks of the value of articulation:

> There is a world of difference between tacit and externalised knowledge. One force of talking aloud is that it requires the use of words, whereas merely talking to

oneself allows words to be bypassed. It may be only when you discover a difficulty in expressing what you want to say, that you realise that things are not quite as you thought. Articulation can aid the process of reflection by affording better access to the thought itself.

An Internal Monitor

As we create opportunities for pupils to discuss or reflect we must keep in the forefront of our minds the need to support the development of conceptual structures by highlighting the interconnection of ideas. In the long term every mathematics learner needs to develop his own capacity to hear ideas in his head in such a way that they feel as if they were spoken out loud. Love and Mason (1992) speak of the 'internal monitor' who supplies a commentary on the mathematics being done which all experts develop. They hold, in the tradition of Vygotsky, that pupils will only develop such a monitor by interaction with others whose own monitors are working well. It becomes, therefore, the responsibility of the teacher to seek opportunities to describe the functioning of their own monitor to help pupils to move outside their own work and criticize it. In the midst of mathematical work, experts may find themselves asking 'Am I going in the right direction?' Their internal monitors are relatively well developed. By contrast a novice, with no internal monitor with which an overall picture might be maintained, may be so deeply embedded in the calculation that he keeps on struggling, getting deeper and deeper into the mire. Vygotsky was convinced that the only way that such a monitor will develop is through social interactions with others whose monitors are active. Watson's description of her way of working seems to include the demonstration of her internal monitor. Energized pupils certainly need to have this kind of monitor when working either as individuals or in a group.

There seems to be one simple way in which we can start to work on this. My observation is that many or indeed most pupils who obtain an obviously incorrect answer, even if they know it must be nonsense, hand in the work with no comment, hoping illogically, I believe, that the teacher will not notice the error. If teachers expect pupils to annotate their work with comments as to the reasonableness of their results and demonstrate that they value an incorrect answer with a clear evaluation of why it is incorrect as highly as the correct answer, then the process is at least started. When I say this is a simple way, I mean it is simple to describe. To persuade pupils to do this will need the kind of mathematical ethos in which errors are to be examined with interest as opportunities to progress, rather than mistakes to be carefully hidden.

This leaves me with one last factor which contributes to a mathematical ethos.

Confidence and Power

We need to create pupils who have confidence in their own mathematical powers. I have for many years now watched out for the moments when a learner of any age suddenly feels powerful, though it does not happen as often as I would like. I shall give some examples drawn from a range of contexts:

Some years ago a teacher nearing the end of a full-time in-service course said to me, 'Gill, come and tell me whether this is right — no, I know it's right, but come and let me tell you about it.' For him it was a moment of breakthrough. All learners need to experience feelings of power, confidence and control over mathematical situations in which they are working.

A first-year trainee teacher, who was and in many ways remained very unsure of himself, had achieved some progress with the problem on which the group was working. I asked him to present his results to the class. Thereafter, throughout a four-year course, he remained sure that he could do mathematics and at least once referred back to this as a turning point for him.

Mark, aged 9, had found a procedure which allowed him to win a simple strategy game. He said to me with immense pride and satisfaction: 'Just think, if you put 503 sticks on the table and the rule is that I can take 1 to 9 sticks, all I have to do is take 3 sticks and I've won!' His pleasure in the generality of his solution involved an element of feeling in control of the situation. He had mastered it, he was really powerful.

Alice had discovered, in discussion, the possibility of using what she called 'take-away numbers'. She spent the rest of the afternoon creating more and more difficult examples of their use. It seemed to me like a flexing of mental muscles whose power she really enjoyed. Highly energized students can greatly enjoy this muscle-flexing process. Even the acquisition of fluency, which was what Alice was working on, can be the exercising of power over a newly acquired and well understood skill. I remember at secondary school solving pages of quadratic equations just to enjoy my newly acquired power over them. Essential, however, is the provision of activities or time for this kind of power to develop.

An Agenda for Conserving Energy

So what is the agenda for beginning to work towards the conservation of energy in mathematics learning?

Teachers need to accept two hard ideas:

- pupils need to experience challenge and struggle in their mathematics learning if they are to gain understanding
- explanation is a two-edged and too easily accepted teacher weapon.

In working as, and with, teachers we need to pay attention to the following vital issues:

- how not to tell pupils things they can work out for themselves
- how to create space for learning to mature
- how to help our pupils to become reflective

- how to avoid requiring pupils to over-use memory
- what appropriate fluency is, particularly in the era of the symbolic manipulator, but also in relation to the ordinary calculator
- how to create opportunities for pupils to talk about their mathematical ideas and develop internal monitors and rich conceptual structures
- how to help our pupils to feel powerful learners of mathematics.

References

ANDERSON, J.A. (1996) 'The place of proof in school mathematics', *Mathematics Teaching*, **155**, pp. 33–9.

ASKEW, M. and WILIAM, D. (1996) *Recent Research in Mathematics Education*, London: HMSO, pp. 5–16.

BILLINGTON, E. (1992) 'Beyond mere experience', Unpublished MPhil thesis, Open University.

BRUCE, M. (1994) 'Failing A-level mathematics from the outset', Unpublished MSc thesis, Manchester Metropolitan University.

COCKCROFT, W.H. (1982) *Mathematics Counts*, London: HMSO.

DAVIS, J. (1988) *Mathematics Update: Tutor Notes*, Milton Keynes: Open University.

FUJITA, H., ITAKA, S., UETAKE, T. and YOKOCHI, J. (1996) 'Mathematics education at risk', *Journal of the Japan Society of Mathematical Education*, reprinted in *The Mathematical Gazette*, **488**, pp. 352–5.

GARDINER, A. (1995) 'Wrong way! Go back!', *Mathematical Gazette*, **485**, pp. 335–46.

GATTEGNO, C. (1982) 'Thirty years later', *Mathematics Teaching*, **100**, pp. 42–5.

GRIFFIN, P. (1989) 'Teaching takes place in time, learning takes place over time', *Mathematics Teaching*, **126**, pp. 12–13.

HATCH, G. (1995) 'If not investigations, what?', *Mathematics Teaching*, **151**, pp. 36–9.

HEWITT, D. (1994) 'The principle of economy in the learning and teaching of mathematics', Unpublished PhD thesis, Open University.

LAPOINTE, A.E., MEAD, N.A. and ASKEW, J.M. (1992) *Learning Mathematics: Report of the Second International Assessment of Educational Progress*, Princeton NJ.

LOVE, E. and MASON, J. (1992) *Teaching Mathematics: Action and Awareness*, Milton Keynes: Open University.

MASON, J. (1994) 'Assessing what sense pupils make of mathematics', in SELLINGER, M. (ed.) *Teaching Mathematics*, London: Routledge, pp. 75–84.

PIMM, D. (1987) *Mathematics, Symbols and Meanings*, Milton Keynes: Open University.

PIMM, D. (1995) *Symbols and Meaning in School Mathematics*, London: Routledge.

SCHOENFELD, A.H. (1994) 'What do we know about mathematics curricula?', *The Journal of Mathematical Behaviour*, **13**, pp. 55–80.

SMITH, J. (1986) 'Questioning questioning', *Mathematics Teaching*, **115**, p. 47.

TOROK, J. and SZEREDI, E. (1992) 'Vade Mecum for Hungarian Students', Unpublished.

WATSON, A. (1994) 'What I do in my classroom', in SELLINGER, M. (ed.) *Teaching Mathematics*, London: Routledge, pp. 52–62.

Chapter 9

Modelling for the New Millennium

Carolyn English

In the technological society of the 21st century, mathematics is likely to become an increasingly large part of the coding, mystifying, and legitimizing language in everyday use. It is powerful because of its reputation for purity and objectivity. It follows that an important part of mathematics education should be concerned with the way mathematics is applied, encouraging in pupils an ability to decode, make sense of, and be critical of, information presented in situations that may be significant to their social or professional life.

I will later suggest a way in which pupils (aged from 11 to 16) may be introduced to applications of mathematics through modelling and show examples of how these ideas have been developed in our school.

Moving from Numeracy to Mathemacy

Much has been discussed recently about numeracy, but what exactly does it mean for a person to be numerate? Is it simply about a feel for number, an ability to carry out arithmetic operations without the use of a calculator, or a familiarity with the formal language of mathematics? Perhaps we need to include pupils' abilities to apply their mathematics to the world which they find themselves in. They will more likely need to recognize and interpret mathematics in its many guises out of school, than have to carry out an algorithm for long division or adding fractions.

Research has indicated (Lave, 1984; Spradberry, 1976; Carraher, 1991) that school mathematics is not often seen as part of the toolbox of methodologies people might use in everyday problems, and, when it is used, it is often not recognized as a method learned at school. Maybe there is a need to look at the perhaps less obvious way mathematics is used in and by society. One way of approaching this may be to view the application of mathematics as a means of interpretation and critique of the social situations in which pupils may find themselves.

To enable pupils to apply their mathematics in this way they need to become aware that if mathematics has been used to represent a situation then some mathematical model will have been constructed. I am suggesting that the application of mathematics should include a critique of this often hidden stage of the mathematical process. Among the skills we may want pupils to bring to society from the mathematics classroom could be the ability, firstly, to recognize the 'invisible' mathematics that may lie beneath any statement or decision that is made and, secondly, to interpret and critique the underlying model in tension with the effect it may have on themselves and the society of which they are a part.

Could then the notion of numeracy be expanded to include an ability not only to manipulate and interpret the formal language of mathematics, but also to identify the overt and covert uses of mathematics in the world? By looking at a notion of literacy developed through the work of Freire and Giroux amongst others, we can begin to look at ideas of 'critical citizenship' and develop some understandings of how this may relate to mathematics education.

Paulo Freire (1972) argues for people to be encouraged to develop their power to perceive critically the way they exist in the world, with which and in which they find themselves. To achieve this he argues for a 'problem posing education' calling for teachers to reject the banking theory of education and to adopt a concept of their pupils as conscious, thinking beings. He develops a concept of literacy as becoming conscious of and engaging with the relationship between ourselves and the world. Giroux, looking at Freire's model of emancipatory literacy, writes:

> Freire teaches people how to read so they can decode and demythologise both their own cultural traditions as well as those that structure and legitimate the wider social order. (Giroux, 1989, p. 153)

Aronowitz (1970) says (as with Freire's work) that to be functionally literate may have little to do with reading and writing.

> The real issue for the functionally literate is whether they can decode the messages of the media culture, counter official interpretation of social, economic, and political reality; whether they feel capable of critically evaluating events or, indeed, of intervening in them. (Aronowitz, 1970)

Presumably, then, a literate person would have both the skills and an awareness of the effects of structures in society to enable them to play an active part in the transformation of themselves and the society in which they live.

Skovsmose (1994) has concerned himself with looking at the possibility that mathematics might play a similar role, asking 'could the term mathemacy be substituted for literacy?' In trying to answer this question we may need to consider whether mathematics is viewed as an abstract subject, or whether it is as much a part of our lived experience as literacy. It would seem that mathematics is an important part of today's language, particularly in view of its strong links with technology.

Skovsmose writes about the formatting power of mathematics. He sees mathematical language as powerful, being able to actually create a reality:

> mathematics produces new inventions in reality, not only in the sense that new insights may change interpretations, but also in the sense that mathematics colonises part of reality and re-orders it. (Skovsmose, 1994, p. 42)

If mathematics is such an important part of today's language, as educators we should want pupils to be familiar with this language, and to recognize its presence and the way it may be used in situations they may find themselves in. Also the use of mathematics in many political and social activities today creates an opportunity for pupils to explore in depth many cross-curricular issues concerning 'citizenship'. Mathematics is used by people to exert power: for example, government statistics concerning unemployment, inflation, public services etc. can give an illusion to the electorate. Yet the mathematical models used to generate these figures are open to manipulation and bias. How many people have felt disempowered when faced with complex statistical facts and figures? Strong phenomenological arguments can crumble in the face of numerical 'evidence'. Although mathematically correct, models often mask hidden agendas, about which it may be helpful to be aware. I would suggest that through mathematics education we can encourage pupils to be critical of information they are presented with, and perhaps to look also at the social implications beyond. In doing this we may begin to broaden the notion of numeracy to one of mathemacy, which may encompass applications of mathematics that are appropriate to all our pupils in the new millennium.

Using Mathematical Modelling As a Medium for Mathemacy

In my school we have been developing an 11–16 curriculum around the idea of modelling. The focus is for pupils to create a mathematical model that represents some reality, whilst recognizing that it is not that reality itself. In order to do this it is likely that a problem will need to be simplified and certain assumptions made. We ask pupils to be critical of the methodologies they employ and to recognize that their particular solution to a problem is one based on a particular mathematical model. This model comprises not just the final mathematical statements, but also the assumptions and simplifications that have been made in reaching this point. Pupils are encouraged to look at these critically when justifying their solutions.

I am tentatively suggesting that if pupils are encouraged to be critical of the mathematical model they have constructed to solve a problem, rather than just find 'the' solution, they may begin to develop the skills to interpret information they are presented with more critically, recognize the hidden model and question the assumptions made and the possibility of bias in the interpretation.

> Structures of interests, power and theories (or prejudices) make up the background for the modelling process, and the first task of reflective knowing can be described by the principle: Try to make explicit the preconditions of a modelling process which become hidden when mathematical language gives it a neutral cover. (Skovsmose, 1994)

Figure 9.1   The modelling process

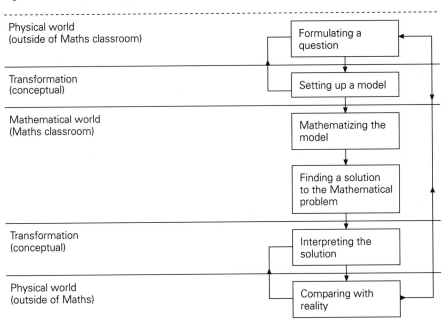

Figure 9.1 shows a framework for a modelling process not dissimilar to those found in many texts in schools (for example SMP 16–19, 1985; Open University, 1981). My research is focusing on the points of transformation, the place where the problem is brought into the mathematics classroom from elsewhere. As mathematics teachers we tend to cast our mathematical gaze over these contexts and unproblematically recontextualize a situation, presenting it to pupils ready for mathematizing. I am concerned with developing this conceptual stage with pupils; I am suggesting it is this stage that makes the difference between 'learning TO model and learning A model' (Mason, 1988). As well as looking at the possibility of pupils' becoming modellers, using mathematics as a methodology, I also hope to show that the focus on transformation would encourage pupils to be more able to interpret and critique models that they meet outside the classroom.

We have found that concentrating on the transformation stage of the modelling process seems to help pupils keep the initial problem in sight. They are given time to make a mental image of the situation, through the discussion and description it takes to recontextualize the problem. I would tentatively suggest engagement may be improved on account of this, as pupils are given the opportunity to take ownership of the problem they are trying to solve. Finally, some pupils have shown that the mental images they have constructed are useful tools for getting to grips with some of the 'big ideas' in mathematics. Some of the concepts that are often difficult to engage with, for example ratio, rates of change, probability, and convergence, are among those that have usefully emerged from our modelling problems.

Figure 9.2 *Modelling categories*

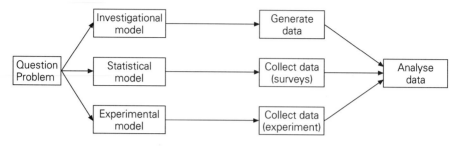

Modelling in the 11–16 Curriculum

The work on modelling has been developed in our school throughout the 11–16 age range. Pupils have been strongly encouraged to use IT as a modelling medium. We have found that spreadsheets are particularly helpful in setting up a model, as each step can be laid out separately, giving a clear view of what may be going on at each stage of the modelling process. This is useful to pupils as it gives a generic structure they can work with, which will hopefully be taken into account during the trans-formation stage of the modelling process. It gives us an opportunity as teachers to view the way our pupils are thinking, and this can promote useful discussion. The level of mathematics used has been high and pupils have shown they can engage successfully with some difficult concepts when they are used in the modelling process.

We have constructed three categories of modelling according to the way data are gathered: investigational, statistical, and experimental. I will use some examples of modelling activities we have used with pupils in school, which will explain these categories.

Investigational Models

These activities typically require an initial model to generate data which may then lead to more generalized models in an extension of the problem. Particular attention is given to the formulating of a specific question: this can be a difficult part of the process for pupils who are used to finding specific answers. 'What exactly am I trying to find out?' is a question I am often asked half-way through a modelling activity, and pupils struggle to keep sight of the wood amongst the trees. Mathematics is an axiomatic and logically structured language: relating it to a problem often requires negotiating a set of rules, assumptions, and simplifications that will be used. Time needs to be spent on this process and pupils need to get a feel for the problem. They may do this by making simple mental conjectures and deciding on important features of the problem. This valuable process can help pupils to conceptualize a problem which can initially be quite abstract.

Figure 9.3 A huddle of penguins

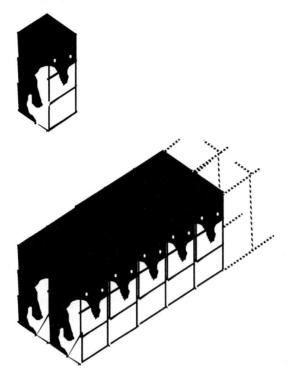

A problem we have used in this way is 'Why do penguins huddle?' It was suggested that the answer may be to do with keeping warm on the Antarctic ice-cap. There were other suggestions, but this seemed to be the most interesting and led to a more specific question concerning heat loss. The initial model was a 3×1×1 cuboid, assumed to represent a penguin (see Figure 9.3).

Assumptions were made about penguins all being the same size, standing in straight lines, having no gaps between them, losing exactly the same amount of heat through each cold surface, no stacking allowed, and so on. Using their model penguins, pupils explored different groupings and looked at the ratio of cold surface area to the volume of penguins. They developed a set of variables and relationships which could be clearly set out on a spreadsheet. Variables could be manipulated and they could examine their data for signs of convergence. There were a variety of ways to set out the model on a spreadsheet, depending on how many stages were used. Figure 9.4 shows how a pupil modelled different size rows of penguins. She gradually built up to a huddle of 100 penguins standing in 10 rows, using a similar modelling structure each time. Other pupils modelled huddles in squares of increasing size and many started off with some random huddle sizes. The resulting ratio data showed similar results for all the pupils and mathematical solutions were concluded. The notion of a variable was discussed and pupils had to decide which were 'inputs' and which were 'outputs', which were manipulable and how they related to

Figure 9.4 A pupil's model of penguin huddles

2 rows of penguins (data)

	cold heads	cold feets	cold sides	Total	Volume	Ratio
1	2	2	18	22	6	0.27272727
2	4	4	24	32	12	0.37500000
3	6	6	30	42	18	0.42857143
4	8	8	36	52	24	0.46153846
5	10	10	42	62	30	0.48387097

2 rows of penguins (mathematical model)

	cold heads	cold feets	cold sides	Total	Volume	Ratio
1	=A2*2	=B2	18	=B2+C2+D2	=A2*2*3	=F2/E2
=A2+1	=A3*2	=B3	=A3*6+12	=B3+C3+D3	=A3*2*3	=F3/E3
=A3+1	=A4*2	=B4	=A4*6+12	=B4+C4+D4	=A4*2*3	=F4/E4
=A4+1	=A5*2	=B5	=A5*6+12	=B5+C5+D5	=A5*2*3	=F5/E5
=A5+1	=A6*2	=B6	=A6*6+12	=B6+C6+D6	=A6*2*3	=F6/E6

each other. The pupils found these concepts challenging, particularly in relation to their mathematical model, which can also be seen in Figure 9.4.

In this particular problem the interpretation of their solutions was helped greatly by the fact that the pupils had created their own models and could therefore retrace their transformation of the situation. The data generated by the spreadsheet model gave them evidence that supported their conjecture and allowed them to be more specific about the best way penguins should arrange themselves in order to conserve heat. Comparison with reality was improved by watching part of a David Attenborough video. Pupils discussed the assumptions they had made and how closely they fitted with the reality they were now observing.

Modelling frameworks generally suggest a loop where the initial model is revisited several times until the modeller is satisfied with her model. There is seldom time for this in the mathematics classroom but we feel it is important that pupils are given time to interpret and critique their models in relation to their original question. They wondered how they could have made their models more accurate, possibly by using cylinders and whether it really mattered? Was there a 'best' figure for number of penguins in a huddle? The video pointed out that the penguins engaged in an intricate procedure, which led them to take it in turns being on an exposed side of the huddle. There was further discussion concerning how they managed this, was there a controller penguin in charge? Were the rules passed down through genera-tions of penguins or were they born with some instinct that told them what to do? They decided to ask their science teacher. Their results seemed to indicate penguins were engaged in an activity that would aid the survival of their species rather than survival of the fittest. Could we use other mathematical models to make similar claims for humankind?

Statistical Models

In looking at statistical modelling we have constructed two approaches. The first involves pupils' collecting their own data as part of the modelling process. The second involves the use of secondary data where the modelling process could be considered to be well under way. An important part of this approach is to deconstruct and critique the method of data collection used.

Pupils constructing their own statistical model will be required to collect their own data. The emphasis is on finding a way of selecting a sample that will give an unbiased representation of the population they are dealing with. The sample itself could be considered a variable in any statistical model and needs to be considered very carefully in terms of its size and constitution. We may advise pupils to look to other curriculum areas for a question. Sociology, geography, physical education, and personal, health, and social education (PHSE) throw up some rich issues for research, and mathematics can provide a methodology for the collection, analysis, and presentation of data. In setting up a statistical model, particularly if a questionnaire is being designed (which could be considered another manipulable variable), pupils are expected to spend some time critiquing methods of data collection and sampling. Pupils can present their hypothesis to their peers along with their questionnaire and sampling procedure. It is soon concluded that there will be many flaws, and that any data collection method will be imperfect and should always be open to criticism along with any interpretation of the results.

A question considered by two 15-year-old boys was 'Are men still sexist to women in 1995?' Their hypothesis was that men were sexist to women. They had to decide how they were going to get evidence to test their hypothesis. The first problem was the concept of sexism. It was interesting that, although both boys had met this topic in sociology, they had great difficulty in explaining what exactly would indicate that it was happening. They eventually decided negative stereotyping might count as sexism but then had to ask, What counts as negative? Is being a good cook negative? They realized their own judgments were being used to construct their indicators and spent a long time on setting up their questions. They used Likert scales to construct a scoring system that would give some indication of how strongly a person they interviewed stereotyped women (and men). Figure 9.5 shows two example questions.

Forty questionnaires were completed by male and female workers from a factory where one of the boys' fathers worked. The scores were calculated and the data were analysed and presented. The boys were confused by their results. It seemed the women had the higher scores. They checked their data but the mathematics was correct. They wrote in their report 'We found out that women were more sexist towards themselves than the men'. The class discussed the findings. The sample had been taken from the Turkish community and therefore would certainly be biased, but what did the results tell us about stereotyping? Maybe it was not so much something that happened to a person, but something that one unknowingly did to oneself, and certainly something everyone should be aware of.

Figure 9.5   Two example questions: Likert scales

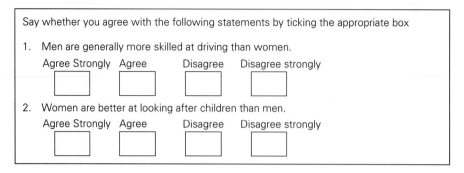

Say whether you agree with the following statements by ticking the appropriate box

1. Men are generally more skilled at driving than women.
    Agree Strongly   Agree   Disagree   Disagree strongly

2. Women are better at looking after children than men.
    Agree Strongly   Agree   Disagree   Disagree strongly

Questions for statistical models can also be drawn from the media. 'Black boys underachieve at school' was a provocative headline that interested another 15-year-old. It also linked with some of the ideas she had engaged with in sociology lessons. Formulating a precise question involved her identifying and defining some key concepts that were not clear in the statement. Firstly, what precisely is under-achievement and what would count as evidence that a pupil had underachieved? GCSE results appeared to be the measurement used by the newspaper to make the statement. She had to consider carefully whether she felt these data would be sufficient to evidence the concept of underachievement. Secondly, what counts as black? There was no information to help her answer this question in the article, so the question was left open for the time being. She wrote to the local education authority and asked for a set of the previous year's exam data and any classification used that would distinguish between different groups of students by race or gender. She found the information given did not differentiate between pupils born here and those who had immigrated. It took no account of first or second languages. She felt it was likely that these factors would skew the results of her data set unfairly. How-ever, the data as they were, when analysed, gave evidence to support the statement in the newspaper. The possible effects of that headline on pupils, teachers, and parents were discussed and there was concern from all pupils that a flawed model had been used to describe a situation.

By approaching data handling in this way we hope to bring to mathematics a healthy scepticism that may lead pupils to question the 'official' facts and figures they may be presented with in their lives. They may start to question decisions that are made on the basis of a model that has become a 'reality' to be used as a representation of the physical world, and they may come to reflect upon the effect of such decisions on themselves and the society in which they live.

Experimental Models

In this case the initial model tends to be built from observed data. A series of readings can be made and a line (or curve) of best fit can be constructed to describe

Figure 9.6   A model of pizza cooling

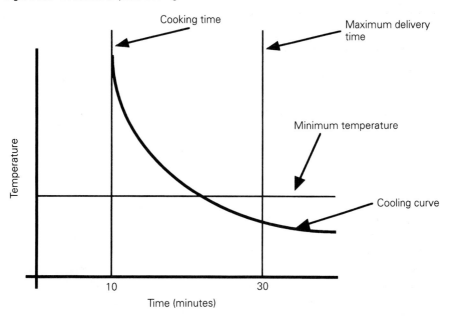

the results. This type of modelling lends itself to cross-curricular links, particu-larly with science, in which sensors and data-logging equipment may be used. In a recent project pupils engaged with problems from local pizza delivery companies. A specific question formulated by pupils was one involving packaging, looking at which type would keep a pizza the warmest. An experiment was set up in science where pupils measured the rate of heat loss using different packaging materials: polystyrene, aluminium foil, and corrugated cardboard. The pizza was modelled by boiling water in a petri-dish, and the data were collected using temperature probes linked to a computer. Results were graphed and finally saved in spreadsheet format. Rates of heat loss were discussed, which involved pupils' engaging with calculations of gradient, and the mathematical problem was solved. However, the classroom experiment involved errors in measurement and the effects of the assumptions and simplifications had to be discussed. Comparison with reality led to an economics problem. Cardboard was the cheapest packaging and was adequate as an insulation material within a certain time limit. These results were compared with a real pizza delivered to school, with a sensor stuck in it whilst connected to a laptop computer. Pupils could discuss the differences in rate of heat loss, between water and pizza dough and used a linear programming approach to address a further problem which looked at the delivery time available for a local pizza firm.

Figure 9.6 shows the time limits: 30 minutes for the maximum delivery time promised by the firm on ordering, and an allowance of 10 minutes' cooking time. A further limiting factor is the minimum acceptable temperature at delivery. The actual available delivery time can be deduced from the graph. Clearly, different cooling curves will affect the available delivery time.

Conclusion

In the first part of this chapter I suggested that pupils in the mathematics classroom be given the opportunity to develop some understandings of how mathematics may be used outside the classroom — more specifically, the processes by which mathematics is applied to social situations. I have defined a process of mathematical modelling that focuses attention on the transformation of a situation from outside the classroom to inside the classroom. In critiquing this stage of the modelling process, I hope to raise questions with pupils concerning the underlying assumptions and simplifications that exist in any mathematical model. Pupils may come to recognize that decisions are often made on the basis of an assumed model: perhaps part of their mathematics education should involve making these models more explicit.

> Once the mathematical model is assumed, the answer is straightforward. However, the models must be at the core of social negotiations and do not have to be taken for granted. (Nunes, Schliemann and Carraher, 1993)

In the second part of the chapter I have given a selection of examples showing the way we are developing the notion of modelling in our school. We have begun to look at modelling as a strand of mathematics which we should like to incorporate into all our units of work. In doing this we hope to broaden and develop the mathematical experiences of our pupils and to begin to develop a notion of a critical mathematics education in practice.

Acknowledgments

The work on modelling has been developed at Crofton School by Jeremy Burke and the author over a period of two years. I would also like to thank Jeremy for his interest and support in the writing of this chapter.

References

ARONOWITZ, S. (May 1985) 'Why should Johnny read?' *The Village Voice Lit. Sup.*

CARRAHER, D. (1991) 'Mathematics in and out of school: A selection review of studies from Brazil', in HARRIS, M. (ed.) *School Mathematics and Work*, Basingstoke: Falmer Press.

FREIRE, P. (1972) *Pedagogy of the Oppressed*, New York: Penguin.

GIROUX, H.A. (1989) *Schooling for Democracy*, Minnesota: Routledge.

LAVE, J. (1984) *Mind Mathematics and Culture in Everyday Life*, Cambridge: Cambridge University Press.

MASON, J. (1988) 'Modelling: What do we really want pupils to learn', in PIMM, D. *Mathematics Teachers and Children*, London: The Open University.

NUNES, T., SCHLIEMANN, A. and CARRAHER, D. (1993) *Street Mathematics and School Mathematics*, Cambridge, MA: Cambridge University Press.

OPEN UNIVERSITY (1981) *MST204, Project Guide for Mathematical Modelling Methods*, Milton Keynes: Open University.

SKOVSMOSE, O. (1994) *Towards a Philosophy of Critical Mathematics Education*, Netherlands: Kluwer Academic Publishers.

SMP 16–19 (1970) *Problem Solving*, Cambridge: Cambridge University Press.

SPRADBERRY, J. (1976) 'Conservative pupils? Pupil resistance to curriculum innovation', in WHITTY, G. and YOUNG, M. (eds) *Explorations in the Politics of School Knowledge*, Drifield: Nafferton.

Chapter 10

Mathematics and Scientific Literacy

Daniel Sandford Smith

The National Curriculum in Science for England and Wales (DfE, 1995) does not, I believe, promote scientific literacy for the majority. In this chapter I give my reasons for this belief and outline a different kind of curriculum for students up to age 16 years which in my view would be preferable. I go on to describe the kinds of mathematical activity that might form part of such a curriculum, and contrast these with current practice. The chapter ends with some examples.

Scientific Literacy

Richard Dawkins (1996) recently stated one of his hopes for the next millennium in this way:

> that by whatever medium . . . the publishing of material on astrology, and other mystical pseudo-science, will wither away and be replaced by astronomy and other genuine sciences.

The evidence from British television, where the popularity of programmes about the paranormal is rising, suggests that that hope is unlikely to be fulfilled in the near future. The increase in the amount of, and numbers doing, science in classrooms in England and Wales seems to have had little effect on what people think outside the classroom. This seems to me to be symptomatic of a more general malaise in science education in those countries.

The malaise is a consequence of making everyone study science up to age 16 when there is not a clear match between the intentions of science for all and the content of the National Curriculum. The present science curriculum echoes earlier curricula that were designed with a minority of students in mind, namely those who would go on to become scientists. The curriculum is composed of the facts and theories that it is thought such students should know before they move on to the next stage of their training. The traditional sciences physics, chemistry, and biology have been put together with earth science without taking much of the traditional content away, leaving the student with too much content to absorb and not enough time to do it. Little account seems to have been taken of the majority who will not reach the next stage of training, and aspects of science that might be more relevant to them have been neglected.

I think that for most people the science education they receive has little effect on the way they think about the world. When people were trying to decide which set of experts to believe during the recent BSE crisis, did the science they had learnt in school help them? The National Curriculum states that it is important for students to know about science, but in practice this knowledge is largely confined to the skills of experimenting. There is little teaching about the history, philosophy, and sociology of science.

Nor are students enabled to apply the science they have learnt in practical ways. To some extent this is a problem with the real world: the scope and breadth of science and technology which people meet in their everyday lives could never be covered entirely in school. Nevertheless, in my experience, most people like to know how things work, and this aspect of science, the underpinning of technology, is neglected in schools. Too often the applied science that is taught stems from the theory that is to be taught rather than from the interest of the student. Consider the case of electricity. Here the main aim of teaching seems to be to promote an understanding of Ohm's law and an ability to analyse circuits. There is very little about how houses are wired. In practice, people use electricity in their everyday lives without understanding the theoretical models that scientists use.

What is required for the compulsory phase of education in science is, I suggest, a curriculum that is designed to promote scientific literacy for all. Originally the term *scientific literacy* was associated with science courses that were about science and its social implications. Jenkins (1994) criticized the term because too often it meant 'understanding science on the scientists' terms'. Some of the early courses in scientific literacy do now seem rather naive, but I think the term is due for a revival. A curriculum for scientific literacy should leave students with a feeling for why the scientific approach has been so successful and the ability to understand and be critical of the scientific process.

At present a student is expected to be acquainted with so much scientific content that understanding is neglected. I doubt, for example, that most students distinguish in importance between the germ theory of disease and knowing the names of different bacteria. The content of a curriculum for scientific literacy should be chosen to reflect the important ideas in science. Recently Millar (1996) has suggested two aims for the content of a science curriculum 'for public understanding':

> to help students become more capable in their interactions with the material world, by emphasising a practically useful, technological way-of-knowing;

> gradually to develop students' understandings of a small number of powerful 'mental models' (or 'stories') about the behaviour of the natural world.

He offered the following as a possible list of mental models:

- the atomic/molecular model of matter (emphasizing the scientific understanding of chemical reactions as rearrangements of matter)

- models of the Earth–Moon and Earth–Sun systems, of the solar system, and of the universe
- the source–radiation–receiver model of interactions at a distance (leading to a ray model of light and of vision)
- the field model of interactions at a distance (gravitation, magnetism, electric fields)
- the 'germ' theory of disease
- the gene model of inheritance
- Darwin's theory of evolution of species
- models of the evolution of the Earth's surface (rock formation, plate tectonics)

All of these models could be considered as cultural milestones to compare with any work of literature or art. They illustrate the fundamental importance of science in shaping the way that we understand ourselves as humans. They also form a sound broad foundation on which a student could build deeper knowledge later on. Notwithstanding the omissions (and Millar admits that electric circuits and the Newtonian model of motion, among other models, might find a place, though with a more technological emphasis) I believe that the list above is a good starting point for a curriculum for scientific literacy in the sense I have outlined.

Mathematics in Science Lessons

In this section I consider how a curriculum for scientific literacy might affect the mathematics done in science lessons. It will be helpful first to outline the current situation. I think most science teachers in English secondary schools believe that students should arrive at their classroom equipped with enough mathematical knowledge and skill to do what is asked. Perhaps the most obvious example is that these teachers expect their students to be confident in both forming and solving equations — despite all the evidence of the difficulty that students have in transferring skills from one context to another. This delegation of responsibility to the mathematics department leads to a situation, described by Monk (1994), in which formulae are introduced with little or no preamble to show how the qualitative features of a theory lead to its quantitative ones. Stenhouse (1985) describes the overall effect as one where:

> What is inculcated in a great deal of science education is . . . not understanding but rather a sort of recipe book acquaintance with a number of mathematical techniques which tend often to be used on an ad-hoc basis without any proper understanding either of the mathematical theory and assumptions on which the techniques are based, or of the subject matter to which they are applied.

The situation is made worse by current methods of assessment. When I started teaching, physics students were supplied with a list of formulae: now the majority of the formulae to be used in the final exam have to be learnt. A typical question at GCSE now would be to calculate the resistance of a component given the voltage across the component and the current flowing through it. This type of question, involving recall and substitution, seems to me to tell us very little about students' understanding of science, and little about their ability to use mathematics in science. It leads to an impoverished view of the role of mathematics in science.

Crucial to any understanding of science is the concept of a model. For a science teacher a model is a way of thinking about or explaining the world that has some actual counterpart in reality. An entity evoked in such a model may be real, such as the germ, or it may be an analogue to help students to understand, as when an electric current is likened to the flow of water. Science teachers commonly use conceptual models like this that are analogous to situations familiar to the student. One of the major difficulties that science teachers face is to persuade students to start using more conceptually sophisticated and precisely defined models, when the relatively simple models they already use often provide sufficient explanatory power for their everyday experiences. Some failure in the simple model is necessary, and to be convinced of this the student needs to develop the skill to formalize the model in order to make predictions.

De Berg (1995) has suggested an interesting approach through the history of science. He has used this approach to the pressure–volume law to illustrate how studying the emergence of a mathematical law can help a student to 'appreciate the complexity of the relationship between theory and experiment'. He suggests that to discourage blind substitution into equations students should be taught to consider the origins of mathematical expressions, and he offers the following categories:

1 Definition based
   for example, Resistance = Voltage/Current
2 Mathematically based — derived from other expressions using mathematical laws
   for example, Power = Voltage × Current
3 Empirically based
   for example, students' own equations based on data they have collected.

I suggest that students would gain far more, scientifically and mathematically, from considering a small number of quantitative expressions (including graphical representations) in more detail. The scientifically literate person should be able to understand how quantitative expressions are derived from theories such as those in Millar's list, and with a curriculum less dominated by the need to learn formulae it ought to be possible for students to produce their own quantitative expressions. Trying to explain how these expressions are derived, and how they can be verified, not only encourages the development of relevant mathematical skills but also teaches why it is that scientists make so much use of mathematics.

If it is argued that much of this is too difficult for the less able student it should be remembered that the mathematical content of existing science courses already represents an insurmountable barrier to many less able students. This does

Figure 10.1   *The relationship between science and mathematics*

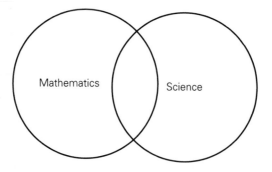

not seem to be due entirely to a lack of mathematical skill: many students do not understand why they should be 'doing maths' in a science lesson and consequently don't do it. This leads me to consider how a curriculum for scientific literacy could best be delivered. To illustrate the relationship between science and mathematics Underhill (1995) made use of a series of Venn diagrams similar to that shown in Figure 10.1.

The problem is: who is to teach the intersection? Where there is an overlap it seems common sense that mathematics and science departments should *coordinate* to tackle specific areas concurrently. But it seems that very little work has been done in this area. Perhaps more realistically, one might hope for a greater degree of *cooperation* between the two departments. But one of the overlooked consequences of the National Curriculum is that it is now harder for teachers of the 'core subjects' to teach outside them. I know far more mathematics than biology, yet I teach no mathematics (except within science lessons) and find myself teaching biology to exam classes. Similarly, there must be a considerable number of mathematics teachers who would be more comfortable teaching physics than biology teachers are.

Such rigidity in administration compounds the serious problems students have in transferring knowledge from one 'block' to another. Recently some students of mine had to interpret voltage–current data for a number of different components. They had been taught in mathematics how to draw a line of best fit but did not seem to know why one should want to do this, or how their choice of line (made by eye) might be affected by a difference in scale. They knew what a gradient was, and some even knew how to calculate it, but they had great difficulty using the term to explain the differences between graphs. A combined teaching effort across the two departments would have provided benefits for both.

Some Examples

I will now try to illustrate the role that mathematics might play in a curriculum for scientific literacy by outlining some lessons I have taught.

Figure 10.2   Scale diagrams for the pinhole camera investigation

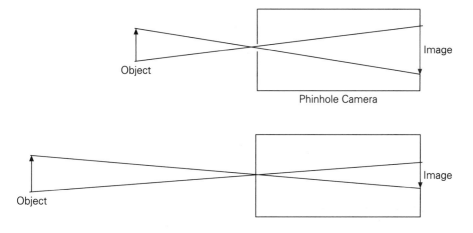

The Pinhole Camera

A class of 13-year-olds was shown a simple pinhole camera producing an image of a lamp filament. The first question was why the image was upside down. A ray model of light travelling from each part of the filament through the constricted space of the pinhole to the screen at the back of the camera leads to diagrams such as those in Figure 10.2. The students were then asked to investigate what factors would affect the size of the image, using these diagrams to explain their results.

Most students can manage to draw such diagrams to scale and use them to make qualitative predictions about how the size of the image depends on the distance of the object from the camera. They then confirm their predictions by carrying out experiments. Last year I was fortunate enough to have a more able student who, with a little help, was able to derive a formula that he could test by experiment. I think that ideally the whole class should have been able to take their results away and use mathematics to develop their models further in something like the manner described by English in Chapter 9, above. The weaker students might just use a series of scale diagrams showing the object at different distances from the camera. They could try to find a numerical relationship between the size of the image and the distance to the object. An able student should eventually see that this is an example of enlargement (dilation), with centre the pinhole and negative scale factor. He or she might then derive an expression connecting all the variables, object size, distance to camera, length of camera, and image size.

The Resistance of a Pencil Line

The next example is an investigation into the factors affecting the electrical resistance of a pencil line. This investigation was used for assessment, and is appropriate for more able students who have some degree of understanding of proportionality. Initially, pupils were asked to use their knowledge of resistance to predict what factors would affect the resistance of a pencil line. Then they were asked to carry out an investigation to check their predictions. They were encouraged to do two things, first to make practical measurements, and second to derive predictions from a model.

It was suggested that experimentally there were two ways this investigation could be carried out, one using the pencil leads themselves and the other using pencil lines drawn on to graph paper. The students carried out experiments to measure the resistance of the leads or of the lines. In the case of the lines, for example, they plotted graphs of their results to try to determine what sorts of relationship existed between resistance and length or width of line. The less able students plotted graphs of resistance against length only, and achieved fairly good straight lines. The more able students plotted graphs of resistance against width, and then with some help plotted resistance against 1/width to achieve an approximately straight line.

For the second part of the investigation, they were given the formula for the resistance of a wire: $R = \dfrac{\rho L}{A}$, where R is the resistance of the wire, L its length, A its cross-sectional area, and ρ the resistivity of the material. They were given a value for the resistivity of carbon. Those who had been measuring the resistance of pencil lines had problems measuring their cross-sectional areas. They managed to get a value for A by measuring the volume of lead deposited on the paper and using this and the length of the line to calculate the cross-sectional area. Many students succeeded in producing two sets of results, one experimental and one theoretical, that they could compare. Rather disturbingly, some of these students commented that the theoretical results gave them a much better straight-line graph of resistance against length than their experimental values, apparently unaware that this outcome was inevitable! It is true that once students start processing data they tend to lose sight of where the data came from: they need practice to become accustomed to evaluating the results of their calculations.

One student investigated the effect of the softness of the pencil on its resistance. It turned out that when he plotted resistance against hardness and softness he obtained two straight lines of differing gradients — one for H pencils and the other for B pencils as in Figure 10.3. He then got in touch with the manufacturers and found that the softness of a pencil depends on the proportion of clay in the lead, and that these straight lines reflected the fact that these proportions varied linearly.

The students found that there was a big difference between their theoretical values and their measured values. At my suggestion, they started trying to consider how close the measured and theoretical values ought to be in the light of experimental error. The results turned out to be outside the range of experimental error but, because they had got really involved in the work, they gave well thought out and cogent explanations of why the values didn't agree. For example, some of them pointed out that the paper was not perfectly smooth and this would affect the cross-sectional area 'seen' by the electrons. This investigation taught students how difficult it is to carry out an experiment: in a sense none of the experiments

Figure 10.3   The relationship between the resistance of a pencil line and the softness of the lead

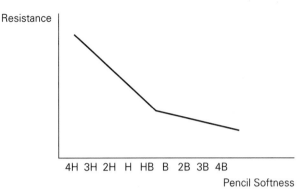

'worked'. Although the science the students were using might not be considered very exciting, they appeared to gain a good deal of satisfaction from the investigation. They produced an extended piece of work that they could take pride in, and the investigation taught them a lot about the experimental processes of science.

Horoscopes

My other example harks back to Dawkins's statement at the opening of this chapter. I initiated a debate on the validity of horoscopes and asked students if they could think of any way of testing this. I then took two magazines and read out a horoscope for each of the zodiac signs, asking them to judge how accurately their horoscope described what had happened to them the previous day. They were asked to score the horoscopes for accuracy, using a mark out of 5. What they were not told at this stage was that half the horoscopes were for the day before — 'true' horoscopes — while the other half came from a magazine some months old — 'false' horoscopes.

The trick was then explained and I drew up a table of results on the board, similar to Table 10.1. The students were asked to use the data to decide whether they should believe in horoscopes or not.

It can be seen that the scores cover a wide enough range to enable both sides to put forward arguments. The students plotted simple bar charts showing the scores for each sign, with the bars colour-coded to show which were 'true' horoscopes and which were not. They also calculated the mean scores of the 'true' and 'false' horoscopes. It would be easy to extend the mathematical scope of this investigation. Students could be asked to use the data to put forward their own belief about horoscopes, with the aim of making them think about how data can be presented to support an argument. More able students could attempt a more formal consideration of the appropriate statistical tools to analyse and present these data. The investigation has given rise to interesting discussions about how valid the experiment is and the difficulty of framing empirical tests of horoscopes. It has shown the importance

Table 10.1   Accuracy ratings for 'true' and 'false' horoscopes

Horoscope Sign	True	False
Aquarius	2 4 5	
Pisces		3
Aries		1 2
Taurus	2	
Gemini		3 2 1
Cancer	3 2	
Leo		4 5 1
Virgo	1 1 3	
Libra	2 4	
Scorpio		5 2
Sagittarius	2 3 3 2	
Capricorn		2 3

of mathematics in testing theories and has made students think about how we decide whether a prediction is scientific.

As a science teacher I am very aware of the link in students' minds between quantitative work and difficulty. The examples above show mathematics being used in science to find answers that the students want to know. They use it both to develop theories and to criticize them. This does not occur when students carry out simple substitution into formulae, which is the chief mode of mathematical activity assessed within the National Curriculum in science. A curriculum for scientific literacy (which the National Curriculum in science appears on the surface to be) requires modes of assessment that will promote more extended and less passive use of mathematics by students and teachers alike.

One of the attributes of the scientifically literate person is the ability to quantify the world around them. Students can be persuaded of the possibility, even desirability, of testing out their ideas using numbers. It will take a joint effort between mathematics and other departments to achieve this.

Acknowledgment

The author wishes to thank St Thomas More RC Comprehensive School in Wood Green, London for their support and in particular for allowing him to attend the conference Mathematics for the New Millenium when he was Head of Physics at the school.

References

AMERICAN ASSOCIATION FOR THE ADVANCEMENT OF SCIENCE, Project 2061 (1990) *Science for all Americans*, New York: Oxford University Press.
DAWKINS, R. (1996) 'The noble art of science', *The Bookseller*, 12 April 1996, pp. 15–17.

DE BERG, K.C. (1995) 'Revisiting the pressure-volume law in history — What can it teach us about the emergence of mathematical relationships in science', *Science and Education: Contributions from History, Philosophy and Sociology of Science and Mathematics*, **4**, 1, pp. 47–64.

DfE (1995) *Science in the National Curriculum*, London, HMSO.

JENKINS, E.W. (1994) 'HPS and school science education: Remediation or reconstruction?', *International Journal of Science Education*, **16**, 4, pp. 613–23.

MILLAR, R. (1996) 'Towards a science curriculum for public understanding', *School Science Review*, **77**, 280, pp. 7–18.

MONK, M. (1994) 'Mathematics in physics education: A case of more haste less speed', *Physics Education*, **29**, 4, pp. 14–19.

READ, G.A. and SMITH, T.B. (1994) 'The impact of algebraic computing on the teaching of physics and mathematics', *Physics Education*, **29**, 1, pp. 14–19.

STENHOUSE, D. (1985) *Active Philosophy in Education and Science*, London: Allen and Unwin.

UNDERHILL, R.G. (1995) 'Editorial', *School Science and Mathematics*, **95**, 5, p. 229.

Chapter 11

Mathematics Laboratories for Science Undergraduates

*Richard Templer, David Klug, Ian Gould, Phillip Kent,
Philip Ramsden and Margaret James*

This chapter describes a curriculum development project begun at Imperial College in 1994 as a collaboration between the chemistry and biochemistry departments, and a specially funded computer-based mathematics education project (then called TMP: Transitional Mathematics Project) based in the mathematics department.[1]

In many science and engineering departments, mathematics teaching is wholly in the hands of either mathematicians or, perhaps more rarely, specialists in the subjects concerned. The approach described here is an example of an alternative model, where we have set out to develop the course as a *collaboration* between scientists and mathematicians. We feel that if we have achieved anything worthwhile it is in large part due to the cooperation that exists between us and to a shared willingness to make alterations in response to educational need.

Central to our approach is the idea that the computer should be used to allow the student to explore and investigate mathematical concepts, to experiment, and to form conjectures. This is, of course, an essential part of thinking mathematically, but a part that is often marginalized in courses that are exclusively concerned with pen-and-paper algorithms.

We present this chapter in part as stories told by the scientists and the mathematicians. We hope that it will be interesting for others to see how the teams' different backgrounds meshed into a common project, and how their differing global aims and intentions developed. We have tried as much as possible to present events and decisions as they happened, without the benefit of 20:20 hindsight.

The Scientists' Story

Problems and Opportunities

The 1980s and 1990s have seen a large increase in the student populations of British universities. Many both within and outside higher education have taken the view, and some claim to have detected, that this swelling in the ranks of undergraduates has been accompanied by a gradual decrease in their mathematical abilities at the point of entry.

In the late 1970s the chemistry department had faced similar worries. At the time all teaching had been in the hands of the mathematics department, and it had been decided that the problem lay in the remoteness of the taught course from applications in chemistry. As a consequence the chemistry department had decided to take on the teaching of mathematics itself and thereby give it a clear chemical context. Within a decade it was clear that students were still poorly trained in mathematics, both before and after they had passed through our hands. Evidence for this was to be found both in examination results and in the declining standards of mathematical competency which we found within our own research groups.

By 1993 the feelings of dissatisfaction with the chemistry students' mathematical abilities (as expressed in corridor conversations by the academics in our department) had reached sufficient pitch that there was a general feeling that something should be done. The impetus to do something was enhanced by the fact that the department was gearing up to change from a three-year to a four-year degree course, presenting us with an ideal opportunity to evaluate, and possibly make radical changes to, the way in which we taught chemistry students.

The first steps towards evaluating our teaching of mathematics were hesitant. In time-honoured manner, a committee was set up to examine what the problems were and what steps we might take to improve things. The committee, on which one of us sat, was otherwise populated by those who had made the previous changes in mathematics provision. Not surprisingly re-appraisal and radical alterations were not to be on the agenda: instead, the debate took the form of an all too familiar dialogue.

— Is it surprising that our students are mathematically weak when you see how poor their school training has been?
— Not really. But those who are really struggling do get a lot of help with the remedial maths we give them — and they don't actually fail our courses, so I guess we must be repairing some of the damage.
— That's true, but it's the general level of attainment which worries me. They just don't seem to be able to do mathematics like we were able to as undergrads. The only real solution is that they need more training.
— Well that's a non-starter. We don't have the lecture slots; the Organic and Inorganic sections won't stand for any more time being spent on a subject that they think is unnecessary[2] — remember what it was like last time we got them to sacrifice lecture slots, and think of all the extra teaching time — who's going to take all that on?
— I guess in the circumstances we're doing the best we can.

With 50 per cent of our graduates going on to do PhDs at Imperial College or elsewhere this decision to do nothing did not sit well with those of us who make heavy use of mathematics in our research groups. Coincidentally, two of us had been put in charge of teaching maths to the chemists (Richard Templer) and the biochemists (David Klug) so our motivation to force through changes was double-edged. The final element was Richard's appointment to plan and coordinate the structure of the first year of the new physical chemistry course.

In analysing the structure of the old chemistry course it was clear that the aim of teaching maths in a chemical context was not being met. The delivery of mathematics lectures was not coordinated with its appearance in chemistry lectures. Mathematics was examined within one of our first-year papers, but as a single and separate question. Student failure rates on this question were very high, but this was masked by the fact that they were able to achieve good marks overall by doing well in the other questions. Parts of the maths curriculum did not even appear in any chemistry course: evidence of the gradual removal of mathematical content from courses that had taken place in response to the perceived drop in students' ability.

Of all the flaws in our mathematics training this last seemed to us to be the most dangerous and insidious, for as fast as we removed it from our courses, the need for mathematics to do real science was increasing. But what sort of mathematics? The answer to this can be seen in almost any practising scientist's laboratory. Not only do we use computer programs to process data, we also use general mathematical packages such as *Mathematica* to do our mathematics for us. It struck DRK very forcibly that mathematics courses were without exception taught by those who had enjoyed and had a high level of facility with the rigour and formality of classically taught maths. As a result they were likely to assume that this is the only way in which maths can or indeed should be taught. However, what most scientists using mathematics actually require is sufficient knowledge of mathematical concepts to fish out the appropriate mathematical tools from their software tool kit and sufficient experience to frame the scientific problem in mathematical form.

We could see that in planning and implementing the new four-year chemistry course we would be able to integrate and coordinate the mathematics teaching into the curriculum. Our colleagues were also persuaded of the need to put the mathematical content back into our courses and examine the mathematical abilities of students in the context of these courses rather than in a separate 'out of place' mathematics question. Coordinating the mathematics course to appear at the appropriate points in other courses meant that we would need to spread the internal mathematical training over three years rather than one; this we were later able to do. What we did not yet have to hand was an appropriate replacement for the mathematics course.

As is normal within a university, the chemistry department were only dimly aware of some work that was being done in the mathematics department at Imperial College on computer-based learning of maths. Those who had been involved in the earlier struggles to wrest control of mathematical training from mathematicians were not eager to form links again. In a rare and amusing moment of serendipity we were persuaded to ignore the prejudices of our elders by an article in the *Times Higher Education Supplement* (*THES*) (Kent et al., 1994) which described the work of the Transitional Mathematics Project. We were attracted by the similarity in their feelings about how maths might be taught. In particular our attention was held by the following statement:

> for those teaching and learning mathematics, computers can offer something qualitatively different, namely the experience of a 'mathematics laboratory' in which mathematical statements are active objects used to produce results . . . (Kent et al., 1994)

The idea of a mathematical laboratory in which students might explore and test mathematical approaches to solving physical problems had enormous appeal to us. It would allow us to train students in the use of mathematical tools in a realistic context. From the science student's point of view the laboratory as a training ground for experimental skills would be well understood and provide an apt contextualization for this method of mathematical training. The use of computers would also allow us to train our mathematically heterogeneous intake without running parallel courses for different abilities, since students would be able to work at their own pace. We therefore decided on the spot to go to see the TMP team.

The First Mathematical Laboratory

It only took this first meeting with Phillip Kent, Phil Ramsden and John Wood for us to decide to collaborate in running a pilot course of their 'transitional mathematics modules' in the chemistry department. What persuaded us most strongly was their fresh approach, their dedication to the exploratory approach to learning they expounded in the *THES* article and our feeling that this was a group of people with whom we could develop a working partnership.

With five months to go before the new term began we agreed to attempt to persuade the department to run the TMP courseware in a trial to take place in the Autumn term of 1994. With a background mood of somewhat despondent apathy and incipient panic over both what should be done about mathematics and the massive organizational effort the department was bracing itself against in implementing the new four-year course we decided it would not be difficult to push through changes. In fact, there was a certain degree of support within the higher levels of the department and the college.

By June of 1994 we had permission to go ahead with the course. We had managed to secure a total of 24 computers and the first six weeks of the year to present the course to 120 students. In those six weeks the students would each have a total of 14 hours of supervised time in the mathematics laboratory. The weakest students would get one hour of extra tuition per week in addition to the laboratory work. The course would cover trigonometry, fundamentals of differentiation and integration and sequences and series. We awaited the arrival of the new intake with some trepidation, but were buoyed up by the heartening endorsement of one of our colleagues who commented: 'Nothing you can do would be any worse than what we do already.'

Evaluation and Revision

In evaluating the pilot test of the maths lab we were fortunate that an independent evaluation of the progress and outcome of the course was carried out (Noss, 1995). Much of the following, however, although in accord with the evaluation report, is from our own anecdotal evidence.

We hoped that the students would pick up on the laboratory metaphor of the course and therefore take a self-taught exploratory approach to their work. They would be guided by the course material, and the staff and postgraduate demonstrators, but we also hoped that they would come to the mathematics laboratory in unscheduled periods, to spend more time on their weaker subjects. Overall, although *we* found the laboratory metaphor rather pleasing, the students just thought of the whole thing as more maths with the added disadvantage of troublesome computers thrown in on top. We were surprised to discover that the students had a tremendously wide range of computational skills and competence. They ranged from the highly computer literate to some fairly extreme cases of techno-fear.

The mathematically weakest section of the class comprised the 10 per cent who had not done A-level mathematics. It became clear early on that these were amongst the most motivated students in the class — motivated no doubt by fear — who gained the most benefit from the course. The advances these students made have not been directly measured, but we can give some indication of the changes they underwent in their attitude and approach to the use of mathematics in science in the following two stories.

A year after we had run the pilot course one of the students found herself in the physical chemistry laboratory fretting about the analysis of her experimental data. In a fairly typical student monologue she pointed out that in the experimental script the theory had not been developed to a point where she had an equation that could be used to fit the data. She was on the verge of asking one of us what to do, when she suddenly stopped talking and said 'I could do all of this using the stuff I did last year with *Mathematica* couldn't I?' and without further prompting scuttled off to do just that. A year further on and another of the supposedly weaker mathematicians was overheard explaining to some of his peers how to do a Fourier reconstruction of electron densities from X-ray diffraction data using *Mathematica*. Clearly both students show signs that they have indeed learned some mathematical techniques and know how to apply them within *Mathematica*. The most pleasing feature of these two examples is that both students had gained a remarkable degree of confidence about the use of mathematics in chemistry, which appears to be based on their experience of using *Mathematica* as a means of mathematical investigation.

At the top end of the class and amongst the computer literati the attitude to the course was also, in general, very good. These students recognized that *Mathematica* was a clever box of mathematical tricks that might allow them to do some interesting things related to chemistry. Indeed one of the students was observed to be producing three-dimensional representations of molecular orbitals on the first day of the maths lab. It would have to be said however that their attitude to the course itself was rather dismissive. As far as they were concerned the coursework was not going to be assessed, they knew the material anyway and they were therefore not going to expend much effort on it. As the chemistry course is a very tough one with an enormous work load on the students, we could hardly blame them. More importantly we wished the students themselves to regulate the amount of time that they spent on the mathematics.

What of the rump of the student year lying between these upper and lower extremes? We found that this group had a wide range of attitudes to the course, but all of them were united by their conservative attitudes to learning. Typically we found that once they had mastered the rudiments of using the *Mathematica* materials they began to hurtle through the 'work' hell-bent on finishing everything in the shortest possible time. As some problem cropped up for which our help was needed they would frequently turn to us, somewhat accusingly, and say: 'I just don't understand what I'm learning here. I mean all I have to do is ask the machine to solve the problem for me and it's done. What have I learned?' Much of our time was therefore spent attempting to convince students that although indeed the software could simply be used to solve hard problems the learning would occur only if they spent some time trying to explore and test the mathematical concepts that were being presented.

We were not entirely successful in convincing these students that this would be a good idea. In part this was because they felt that they already understood the mathematics being covered and they would not be assessed anyway. However, it became clear to us (too late) that we had not put enough effort into training either our postgraduate demonstrators, or ourselves, in the gentle arts of persuasion. Students were particularly dismissive of the abilities of the demonstrators to solve mathematical problems on the spot and clearly felt that this was their main duty. We on the other hand wanted them to coax the students into active exploration of mathematical ideas. On top of this the environment in which we had to hold the maths lab was (and still is) extremely unsatisfactory. Stuffy, small, poorly lit and unsightly environments do not assist the learning process. Our course was no exception.

The Second and Third Courses (1995–6)

By the Spring of 1995, following the pilot, we had decided on the basic pattern of mathematics training we would be giving the chemistry undergraduates. The first-year course would consist of 11 lectures introducing the basic elements of seven topics: vector algebra, basic differentiation and integration, partial differentiation, ordinary differential equations, complex numbers, and statistics and errors. These lectures would be spread over the entire academic year, at a maximum rate of one per week, and would serve as the prelude to sessions in the maths lab. In the first term these would be fully supervised, as they had been in the pilot study, but in the second and third term the students would work mostly on their own.

The lectures were introduced in response to student requests for some formal introduction to each mathematical topic. There was clearly some desire on the students' parts to return to a more traditional form of mathematical presentation. We decided that we must resist this impulse and use the hour-long lecture as a forum for the presentation of chemically relevant problems utilizing the mathematical topic of the week.

The mathematics lectures were to be timed to appear at appropriate moments with respect to core chemistry courses. We also hoped to reinforce the students' perception that their mathematics course might be of some use, by showing them examples of the use of *Mathematica* in solving pertinent chemical problems from our core course lectures. In particular we wanted to encourage the use of *Mathematica*, where doing the mathematics by hand would either be impractical or completely impossible. This attempt at close integration between the science and the maths resulted in a course structure where the chemistry lectures had to be timed in relation to the framework of the mathematics lectures — a reversal of the normal priorities that we hid from our colleagues.

If the course were successful, many students would want to approach mathematics using *Mathematica*. For this reason, we persuaded our colleagues to remove the pure mathematics questions from the first examinations. Instead it was agreed that the mathematical concepts that they had encountered would appear in questions associated with the appropriate chemistry lecture course. It was therefore important that the questions should assess a student's essential grasp of the mathematical ideas, and not simply be a check on their mathematical virtuosity.

Their mathematics itself would be assessed in a sequence of three problem sheets, and also in the physical chemistry laboratory. We had already realized that students could only be persuaded to commit time to grappling with the mathematical laboratory and the use of *Mathematica* if they felt they would get a tangible return on their efforts. The assessment is worth 10 per cent of their coursework, a unit which they must pass in order to proceed to second year. We decided that students should be allowed to attempt problems either using *Mathematica* or by hand, but that some of the problems would be sufficiently difficult that using *Mathematica* would be advantageous.

As a result of the study made on the pilot course, and our own observations of its shortcomings, two significant alterations were made to the delivery of course material in the mathematics lab. Firstly we needed to find a natural forum in which students could explore the nature of the mathematical software. In particular we wanted to make sure that they were aware of the way in which *Mathematica* worked and how the courseware was embedded within this. We therefore decided that before any mathematics was taught they would all have a three-hour introductory session to learn about *Mathematica* and acquire sufficient general computer skills to begin the course.

The most important alteration to the course came in the TMP team's redesign of the *Mathematica* materials (see below), with a complete separation between the course texts and the computational environment in which students were to do their work. We felt that it was very important for each student to feel entirely in control of the computer screen. We also felt that forcing the student to type in all input was important — it would force action on the student's part and hopefully avoid the mindless pressing of buttons with pre-entered code, which had occurred with some students during the trial. Moreover, having textual materials on paper is in some ways more convenient for the student: you can flick backwards and forwards far more easily than you can on screen.

The course began in the Autumn term of 1995 and there were clear improvements in active student participation. Indeed some students from the previous year sat in on the course, all of whom commented on the degree of improvement in the method of presentation of material.

Some chemistry lecture courses during 1995–6 did make use of *Mathematica* in the presentation of new ideas. For example in the course on molecular interactions the kinematics of an ion–ion collision are determined numerically from Newton's laws. This allowed us to show the details of the collision process, but also demonstrate the conservation of momentum. In the course on chemical kinetics the students were shown the numerical techniques for fitting decay curves directly; the use of such least squares fitting then appeared in a problem sheet from the course and reappeared in analysis of data in the physical chemistry laboratory. The number of lecturers making use of such opportunities was and remains lower than one would wish.

Students did well in their assessed work, averaging 80 per cent, and with a spread of marks that fell no lower than 40 per cent. To our surprise and delight the non A-level mathematicians did extremely well with an average around 85 per cent and with a very low spread (none dipped below 65 per cent). However, it became apparent that for many of the students there still existed a culture of indifference to the mathematical tools they were being presented with, in particular many of the students felt rather negatively about *Mathematica* as a means of solving mathematical problems.

During 1996–7 we have presented a very similar course though hopefully with a greater degree of understanding about student reaction and need. The major change to the course has been in the introduction of the book produced by TMP, *Experiments in Undergraduate Mathematics* (Kent et al., 1996). Every student was asked to purchase this book as a prerequisite for the course, since it combines the text covering mathematical background and the experiments needed to participate in the lab. The students have clearly taken this book 'seriously' in a way which they did not with loose-leaf papers. Student performance in assessed work is unchanged from 1995, but a sizeable fraction (something like a third) of the class has taken the ethos of computer-aided mathematical investigation to heart. Many have now equipped themselves with computers and *Mathematica* software and regularly use it to do mathematically related work.

Problems still remain of course. Many of those who see the power of computational mathematics and mathematical software still have difficulty getting the software to work on their particular problem. The course does not provide them with a good enough 'library' of useful *Mathematica* code which they can apply to solve new problems. Concerns have also been expressed by several of the chemistry tutors about the pressure we are putting on students who do not have A-level maths. In 1995, these students were assigned to members of staff who provided additional tutorials in maths, and naturally enough this worked well and made the students feel more relaxed and confident. Because of limits to our teaching resources a conscious decision was made in 1996 not to support this additional maths tutoring. The affected students have not been happy with this state of affairs, but we have no evidence that in fact they are doing any worse than their predecessors, although they are clearly feeling more strained under this regime.

We have realized that propagating our approach to mathematics within a science department requires that the culture of mathematical usage and presentation in the science courses themselves must have the same 'look and feel'. It has been quite difficult to persuade other lecturers to adopt this new approach. The pressures of time, and the effort required to pick up the rather unusual educational approach we have tried to build, have all militated against such direct diffusion of ideas. We have decided instead to force cohesion in mathematical approach by producing problem sheets for the mathematics course which are firmly in the scientific realm, but necessitate the use of the mathematical software to explore the science. The problems begin by (re)introducing the scientific concepts, presenting the students with *Mathematica* code which may be used to explore the problem and then launching them into a sequence of increasingly complex questions which require thought (mathematical and scientific) and creativity to solve. Since we are well aware that students are strongly driven by assessment we believe that this may be a successful way to encourage them to spend time and effort engaging with mathematical ideas and mastering the mathematical tool kit.

As a result of the promising results of the chemistry pilot course given in 1994, David Klug decided to implement a similar course in biochemistry. A short course, consisting of four one-hour lectures and four one-and-a-half-hour laboratory sessions, was given in 1995. Approximately half of the biochemistry students did not have mathematics A-level. This meant that this course would be a particularly stringent test of the flexibility of the computer-assisted approach. We had to ensure that the more mathematically able students were stretched while allowing those without A-level maths, who had not done any formal mathematics for two years, to develop some basic problem-solving and analysis skills. This meant that the lectures (largely on calculus and basic statistics) would concentrate on explaining the subject, while all techniques for solving equations would be learnt in the maths lab. The students were tested with problem sheets, included mathematical examples which would be either too difficult or too tedious to do by hand.

The response to this course over the last two years has been similar to that of the chemistry students. Those students with A-level tended to rely on the skills which they had already learnt, while those without A-level put a considerable degree of effort into the course. The students remained uncomfortable with the syntax of *Mathematica*, but they all completed the problem sheets very effectively with the average marks well above 70 per cent and no students falling below 40 per cent.

This very short course has now been extended by another four lectures. It now includes some lectures and problems on non-linear fitting, and some manipulation of data which they have collected during an experiment in their biochemistry practicals.

The Mathematicians' Story

The Transitional Mathematics Project

The Transitional Mathematics Project (TMP) began in early 1993, with three years of funding from the Teaching and Learning Technology Programme (TLTP), a large national programme aimed at developing and disseminating educational software for all university subject disciplines.

TMP's brief was to use *Mathematica* (a powerful professional program for doing mathematics) as a basis for the remedial teaching of advanced-level school mathematics to first-year undergraduates; a technology-based response to the gap that was widely seen as emerging between the mathematics being learnt at school and that expected of the average undergraduate. This gap has been much documented, see, for example LMS (1995). School mathematics in the UK has been through major curriculum reforms in the last 10 years, and whatever the value of these curriculum changes as a whole, they have certainly not served the traditional requirements of universities well. TMP's task was to be to provide materials for undergraduates to revise school mathematics as a whole, or particular topics that they had not studied. It was proposed that the materials would be made available on computer systems throughout Imperial College, for use in formal teaching and, especially, informal self-study. The idea of 'computer-based learning' materials as a basis for cheap, unsupervised 'teaching' is, of course, a pervasive one. The history of TMP's evolution away from this model is part of the story told in this chapter.

The prototype materials were paperless 'study modules' in the form of *Mathematica* 'Notebook' documents that contained explanatory text, figures, instructions for activities, and code for *Mathematica* commands to be evaluated, and adapted, by students.

The materials were trialled in the Autumn of 1993, as a part of the Imperial College Mathematics department's Preliminary Mathematics Course (PMC). This is a special 'remedial' course given at the beginning of the academic year, offering intensive individual tutoring for students identified as 'in need' by their own departments. Most students attend the course on a voluntary basis in their own time.

These first encounters highlighted important issues of (inter)activity and control which have engaged us ever since: the Notebooks appeared to work best where students were required to be active, and where they had some control over the mathematical activities they were being asked to perform. Students appeared to enjoy working with *Mathematica*, but clearly did not like reading text from a screen.

In the six months or so following the pilot use of the materials, a new design was developed in which the on-screen document associated with each module became restricted to *Mathematica* code and activity instructions, while explanatory text and figures appeared in the form of a printed document. We felt that these trials had substantially justified our belief that students could use *Mathematica* to engage with mathematics without extensive training in the former.

We were already beginning to feel a certain disquiet about the 'remedial' element of our brief, especially when tied to the idea of 'self-study' using a computer. For one thing, it seemed difficult if not impossible to rid this 'remedial' approach of stigma and of the taste of nasty medicine. For another, there was a significant tension between the 'remedial' students' supposed 'deficiency' and the fact that with the PMC their mathematical burden was increased by having to study more mathematics in their own time, in addition to regular mathematics courses.

R. Templer, D. Klug, I. Gould, P. Kent, P. Ramsden and M. James

The First Mathematical Laboratory

In the Spring of 1994, we were approached by Richard Templer and David Klug. Even at the early discussion stage it was evident that the course they were proposing was likely to differ in many ways from the PMC. The most important differences were these: the chemistry course was to be aimed at the entire class — there was to be no selection of the most 'deficient', the course was to be an integral part of the curriculum rather than an add-on, and the principal responsibility for running the course was to rest with the chemistry department, rather than with us. We had already prepared the learning modules that were to be used during the first course. We did not make any specific adjustments for a chemistry audience.

In the Summer of 1994, TLTP made some extra funding available for an external evaluation of TMP's work. We engaged the services of Richard Noss of the Institute of Education in London, to carry it out. Significantly, the decision was made, at Professor Noss's request, to focus the evaluation on the use of the materials in chemistry. This was partly a question of practicality: the PMC, based as it was on voluntary drop-in sessions aimed at a small proportion of the college's students, presented severe logistical problems, especially when one bears in mind that the evaluation aimed to study in depth the experiences of individual students. Partly, too, Professor Noss no doubt shared our suspicion that it was in chemistry that we were most likely to see genuine learning take place, and that it was therefore there that the most valuable lessons about design could be learned. This evaluation was our opportunity to subject the materials to the sternest appraisal they had ever faced, and to feed our findings back into design. We did, indeed, find that the materials were falling short of what we might desire, and in a number of ways.

We had expected to find that the syntax and notation of *Mathematica*, which differed substantially from that of traditional mathematical symbolism, would be a source of severe problems for students. We were wrong about that, or rather, we were right only in a very limited and rather surprising way. What we had not expected was that the user interface, and in particular the form of 'Notebook' documents, would prove as problematic as it did.

A *Mathematica* Notebook is a rather complex document, one whose sheer subtlety we had forgotten. To make matters worse, we had added an extra layer of complexity by placing an instructional system (of activities and exercises) on top of *Mathematica*. Many students seem not to have really grasped the nature of the documents they were working with, and some seemed unaware that *Mathematica* code could be executed in real time (as opposed, for example, to results being called up from a pre-existing databank). We began to feel that we were attempting to use *Mathematica* in two incompatible ways at the same time. Was the software an arena for the exploration of mathematical ideas, or a channel for their transmission? The presence of so much text, and perhaps too of so much pre-written code, strongly directed a student's attention to the latter.

This conflict arose even more sharply where question-and-answer *exercises* were concerned. We did not see these as central to our aims: although they were quite carefully designed we intended their role to be limited to consolidation and practice. However, we found that these exercises dominated many students' experience of the materials. We put this down partly to the rather cosily passive nature of the exercises, in which control was passed to the machine and students were relieved of the burden of exploring and being pro-active. In part, too, shift in the locus of control lent a certain air of inexorability and compulsion to the exercises. In any event, the effect was to strengthen the students' sense that *Mathematica* was an instructional device that was presenting material to be got through, rather than an environment in which they were able to take control.

Review and Revision

In response to the findings of the 1994 evaluation we began rethinking our approach. We realized that we had to worry less than we had thought about students working directly with *Mathematica*, and in fact that there might be advantages in asking them to express their mathematical ideas in this language. At the same time, we saw how important it was that the locus of control not pass from the user to the machine, and that students not be given conflicting messages about *Mathematica*.

After a great deal of debate within the group, we came up with a radical redesign, in which the 'source of instruction' was completely separated from the 'means of investigation'. Students were to approach *Mathematica* like a genuine user: there would be no pre-prepared *Mathematica* document. The instructional text was to be entirely on paper. Self-test exercises remained, but under user control; students' answers were no longer to be marked or scored.

Largely as a result of conversations with the chemistry team about their conception of the course, we hit upon the idea of the 'mathematical experiment' as a model for the computer-based activities. The idea was that students would typically find themselves being asked to make conjectures on the basis of results obtained through systematic investigation of the effect of varying one or more parameters: these conjectures could then be followed up by reading the text, by discussions with tutors and in the accompanying lectures.

The Second and Third Courses (1995–6)

The 1995 course was the first test of our materials in their revised form. It was clear that the revised module design was very much better and had fixed most of the 'global' design problems; thus we could now address problems at the level of content. We realized that our materials design put a lot of emphasis on using *Mathematica* in the specific circumstances of the mathematical experiments, but (despite good intentions to the contrary) gave students too little insight into how they could use *Mathematica* for their own purposes in chemistry. In one or two instances, though, it seemed that the students managed to overcome this limitation by themselves. We saw students using statistical functions that were part of our 'Laboratory Statistics' modules to perform non-linear fitting on data coming from the maths homeworks, and also from real lab experiments that they were doing. And our chemistry colleagues reported discussions that they were having with tutees on data fitting and error analysis that would probably not have taken place at all in the absence of the 'statistics tool kit' that the modules seemed to be providing.

We put forward an outline of another radical redesign which put 'tool kits' of *Mathematica* functions at the focus, which could then be located in activities that were more or less mathematical, and more or less chemical. This redesign was later fleshed out in the form of 'microworlds' (see below).

During the early part of 1996, we undertook a detailed reassessment of all the contents of the experimental tasks in the light of evaluation findings. Part of the impetus to do this was our agreement, made at the end of 1995, with Imperial College Press to publish our modules in book format. Thus we could produce something professional, easily available, and 'deliverable' to satisfy the terms of our original funding: the book *Experiments in Undergraduate Mathematics* appeared in September 1996.

The third course, commencing in Autumn 1996, offered essentially a rerun of 1995 for the first-year chemists, as well as a longer maths lab programme for the biochemists. Most interesting for 1996–7 was an extension of our collaboration into the second year of the chemistry course, looking at more advanced mathematical topics (groups and symmetry, ordinary differential equations, and Fourier methods), and attempting to tie in the mathematics more closely with other chemistry courses.

Future Developments

At the beginning of 1996, TLTP funding ran out and TMP mutated into the MET-RIC Project (Mathematics Education Technology-Research at Imperial College), funded directly by Imperial College for four years. The main effect of this change in status has been to free the METRIC team from the constraints of the TLTP brief, and allow us to explore a wider range of approaches to supporting the use of computers in undergraduate mathematics teaching at Imperial.

The work in chemistry seems to be developing in two main connected ways: first, the emergence of a *microworld* model for the materials, and secondly, an evolution in the way we view the relationship between mathematical and chemical knowledge. The microworlds owe their origins to the research tradition that began with microworlds based on the programming language Logo (see, for example, diSessa et al., 1995; Noss and Hoyles, 1996). We use *microworld* to mean a computational environment that represents a particular knowledge domain constructed for the purpose of learning about that domain. It contains: computational objects that embody key mathematical ideas; and activities designed so that by operating on these objects, and constructing other objects out of them, the students can encounter, recognize, and explore the mathematical ideas.

The TMP materials in their final incarnation, as they appear in Kent et al. (1996), do contain computational tools, certainly, and these tools may in some sense be said to embody mathematical ideas. But the tools tend to serve the needs of particular activities, rather than the activities guiding students to use the tools to build meanings for mathematical concepts.

The first attempts at *Mathematica*-based microworlds have a tool kit of *Mathematica* functions at their core. Paper documents contain activities related to the development of mathematical concepts and important chemical contexts in which the mathematics will be used.

The second emerging theme has to do with the relationships between mathematical and chemical knowledge and thinking. One very common account of the relationship that we rejected from the start goes roughly like this: 'Chemists use mathematics merely as a tool, a means to an end; they do not need to have any understanding of the nature of the subject.' Instead, we have worked with an account of the form: 'Chemists use mathematics as an intellectual tool in a wide variety of contexts, many (in the case of research) as yet unformulated and impossible to predict; in order to ensure that they use it appropriately, they need to have some understanding of it as it relates to their discipline.' By insisting that the mathematical tools be made at least partly transparent to students, we are allowing for the possibility of multiple links to chemistry: this is both a safeguard against inappropriate use and, one hopes, an aid to real chemical insight.

However, the use of the phrase *mathematics as tool*, though in many ways almost indispensable, covers up a number of unstated assumptions. Tools, in the ordinary way, are first made and then used. But an intellectual 'tool' is forged through use, which suggests that the traditional sequence which runs 'learn the mathematical theory, then apply it to the chemical practice' could be profitably re-examined. In our recent attempts at microworlds for chemistry we have sought to explore a more organic and reciprocal, and less strictly sequential, relationship between tool-making (that is, learning the mathematics) and tool-using (that is, putting the mathematics to work in a chemistry context). We do not intend, we should stress, to close off the route of 'making then using', which seems always to have been appropriate and helpful for some.

Acknowledgments

The mathematics team wish to acknowledge the funding of the Transitional Mathematics Project, 1993–6, by the Teaching and Learning Technology Programme, a joint funding initiative of the United Kingdom higher education funding councils. Funding for the METRIC Project, 1996–9, is being made by Imperial College of Science, Technology and Medicine.

Professor Richard Noss has remained an insightful observer of the METRIC project's work since the 1994 evaluation. We are grateful for his continuing involvement. The work on microworlds has developed in collaboration with Dr Ian Stevenson, also of the Institute of Education.

R. Templer, D. Klug, I. Gould, P. Kent, P. Ramsden and M. James

Notes

1 From 1993 to early 1996, the team members were Phillip Kent, Phil Ramsden and John Wood.
2 Chemistry is formally divided (factionalized) into three sections: physical, organic and inorganic chemistry. The physical chemists at Imperial College are charged with mathematics teaching, and part of the available time is top sliced for this part of the course.

References

DISESSA, A.A., HOYLES, C. and NOSS, R. (eds) (1995) *Computers and Exploratory Learning*, Berlin: Springer-Verlag. (NATO ASI Series F, Volume 146).

KENT, P., RAMSDEN, P. and WOOD, J. (1994) *Times Higher Educational Supplement* (London), 13 May 1994, supplement on 'Multimedia for teaching and learning', pp. x–xi.

KENT, P., RAMSDEN, P. and WOOD, J. (1996) *Experiments in Undergraduate Mathematics: A Mathematica-based Approach*, London: Imperial College Press.

LMS/IMA/RSS (1995) *Tackling the Mathematics Problem*, London: London Mathematical Society/Institute for Mathematics and its Applications/Royal Statistical Society.

NOSS, R. (1995) *Reading the Sines: Evaluation of the Transitional Mathematics / Transmath Project*, Institute of Education, University of London.

NOSS, R. and HOYLES, C. (1996) *Windows on Mathematical Meanings: Learning Cultures and Computers*, Dordrecht: Kluwer Academic.

Chapter 12

The Mathematics of Change and Variation from a Millennial Perspective: New Content, New Context

James J. Kaput and Jeremy Roschelle

In the spirit of the millennial season, this chapter steps back from the front lines of mathematics education reform and looks forward within a long-term perspective. Our perspective draws upon a historical view of the long-term evolution of representations, the transformative potential of new media, and the growing challenges of meeting societal needs. We shall see that there have been enormous changes in all these factors over the past several hundred years. Our means of expressing mathematical ideas have changed and so have our expectations regarding who can learn what mathematics and at what age. We shall examine large-scale trends in content changes and in context changes for learning and using mathematics. From this set of factors, we raise three broad questions for the present day:

1 Will the movement of mathematics from static–inert to dynamic–computational media lead to a widening of mathematical genres and forms of mathematical reasoning?
2 Will mathematical activity within computational media lead to a democratization of access to (potentially new forms of) mathematical reasoning?
3 Can these changes transform our notions of a core mathematics curriculum for all learners?

But before going further, by way of starting points we should like to give a broad view of what we take mathematics to be. *We regard mathematics as a culturally shared study of patterns and languages that is applied and extended through systematic forms of reasoning and argument.* It is both an *object* of understanding and a *means* of understanding. These patterns and languages are an essential way of understanding the worlds we experience — physical, social, and even mathematical. While our universe of experience can be apprehended and organized in many ways — through the arts, the humanities, the physical and social sciences — important aspects of our experience can be approached through systematic study of patterns. Such aspects include those that are subject to measure and quantification, that embody quantifiable change and variation, that involve specifiable uncertainty, that involve our place in space and the spatial features of the world we inhabit and construct, and that involve algorithms and more abstract structures. In addition, mathematics embodies languages for expressing, communicating, reasoning, computing, abstracting, generalizing, and formalizing — all extending the limited powers of the human mind. Finally, mathematics embodies systematic forms of reasoning and argument to help establish the certainty, generality, and reliability of our mathematical assertions. We take as a starting point that all of these aspects of mathematics change over time, and that they are especially sensitive to the media and representation systems in which they are instantiated.

A Condensed Natural History of Representation

While the evolutionary history of representational competence goes back to the beginnings of human evolution (Donald, 1991, 1993; Mithen, 1996), and can be linked to the evolution of the physiology of the brain (Bradshaw and Rogers, 1993; Calvin, 1990; Lieberman, 1991; Wills, 1993), with three exceptions this history is beyond our scope. The first is simply to recognize that representational competence, reflected in spoken and then written languages, both pictographic and phonetic, in visual representations of every sort, is a defining feature of our humanity. It is reflected in our physiology, our cultures, and our technologies, physical and cognitive.

The second exception involves the two-step evolution of writing systems from the need to create quantified records (Schmandt-Besserat, 1988, 1992). As convincingly described by Schmandt-Besserat (1980, 1981, 1985), clay tokens were first used in clay envelopes to record quantities of grain and other materials in storage and commercial and tax transactions, i.e. a given number of grain-tokens represented a certain number of bushels. Before being put inside the soft clay envelopes, these tokens were pressed into the exterior, leaving an image of the envelope's contents. Over many generations, the envelope markings replaced the tokens. The envelopes evolved into tablets, and the representations led to pictographic writing. The second step for western civilization was the invention of phonetic writing. Arbitrary characters were used to encode arbitrary sounds (phonemes), giving rise to abstract expression (Logan, 1986, 1995). This supported new written structures such as codified law, for example Hammurabic code and Moses' commandments, and, when the idea reached Greece, it enabled the expression of science, mathematics, logic, and rational philosophy (McLuhan and Logan, 1977). We draw two broad, albeit unsurprising, inferences from this history. One is that quantification — mathematics — and the functioning of human society have been inextricably linked, beginning as early as the invention of writing. The second is that representational changes in the constraints and affordances of concrete media play a critical role in how we organize our worlds (Goodman, 1978).

The third major historical event to which we direct attention is the invention of the printing press. Of special interest are three consequences. First, there was a standardization of dialects and vernaculars used in spoken language in Europe, first in England with English — as opposed to the existing standard *formal* languages, namely Latin and Greek. Second, and closely related, was the democratization of literacy (Innis, 1951; McLuhan, 1962). Up until that time, there was a small collection of written works and a tiny élite who read and commented on them. Indeed, you could fit almost all of the available written classics on to a decent sized bookshelf. Along with the democratization of literacy came a critically important third event, the dramatic widening of literary forms and the rapid proliferation of original literary material based in everyday life (as opposed to narrowly academic commentary on the classics). For example, the novel was invented. Importantly, these events occurred largely outside of, and independently of, either the universities or the monasteries. A 15th-century monk would not today recognize the 'language arts' curriculum as being about the 'literacy' which was practised and taught before the invention of the printing press. We need to remind ourselves that Shakespeare, and virtually all fiction of the 16th and 17th centuries, were regarded as 'vulgar' literature, not admitted as the subject of academic study.

More recently, we have seen the invention of dynamic visual media, film, and especially television. These have again led to a democratization of visual culture and a widening of dynamic visual forms (McLuhan, 1967). Almost from the beginning, films, for example, were not sequential representations of visual events. Film generated new art forms, much in the way that new literary art forms flourished after the development of the printing press (Arnheim, 1957). There has been a democratization of visually mediated culture (Salomon, 1979). Most people enjoy film and can understand its idioms. Most people can follow the extraordinary visual and auditory feats of contemporary television, despite the rapid sequences of images and semiotic complexity (Fiske and Hartley, 1978; Williams, 1974). This democratization of visual culture occurred without formal instruction or education, outside the academic realm. Indeed, the former masters of the visual arts had rather little ability to guide the new genres that arose in Hollywood and Madison Avenue. These genres built upon naturally occurring visual and language-interpretation capabilities widely distributed across the population.

In the same time-frame as the invention of the printing press, came the invention of manipulable formalisms, numeric and algebraic. The first of these, the Hindu-Arabic place-holder system for numbers, was intimately involved in the commercial economy of the time (Swetz, 1987). And perhaps even more important for the longer term was the rapid development of an algebraic symbol system with a syntax for manipulation. This was tied to an explosion of mathematics and science development that is continuing today and is the foundation for virtually all of the electronic, communication, transportation, and other technologies. Of critical importance, however, is that over the centuries, this mathematics and science, and the notation systems in which it was encoded, were developed by and for an intellectual élite — far less than 1 per cent of the population. As discussed below, even as late as the beginning of the 20th century it was a very tiny minority of the population who were expected to learn these symbol systems and use them productively. Another critical factor is that all of these manipulable symbol systems were instantiated in static and inert media — in pencil or pen and paper. Both of these defining constraints on the evolution of notation systems, demographic and media, changed in the last quarter of the 20th century.

We should note that each of these successive inventions, writing and the printing technology that democratized it, dynamic visual forms, and now interactive digital notations, are much more deeply embedded in ordinary life than is 'classic' school mathematics.

Dual Challenges: Much More Mathematics for Many More People

At the end of the 20th century we face a dual challenge in mathematics education at all levels, from kindergarten to adult education: we need to teach much more mathematics to many more people. Mathematics itself until recently has been increasing in abstraction and complexity, but with new, highly visual forms of mathematics appearing since the advent of the computational medium. The radical increase in the numbers of people who are expected to know and use mathematics is leading to a corresponding increase in student diversity and increases in the social cost of mathematics education — to near the limits for which societies are willing to pay. We need to achieve dramatic new efficiencies across the entire K–12 mathematics curriculum. These trends, as indicated in Figure 12.1, have been under way for centuries.

Furthermore, we have every reason to believe, as will be outlined later, that these trends will continue and may even accelerate, particularly relative to mathematical content.

To illustrate the change in content, we recall a story from Tobias Dantzig (1954):

> It appears that a [German] merchant had a son whom he desired to give an advanced commercial education. He appealed to a prominent professor of a university for advice as to where he should send his son. The reply was that if the

Figure 12.1 A long-term trend: much more maths for many more people

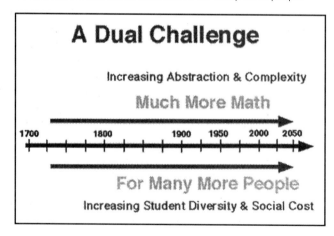

mathematical curriculum of the young man was to be confined to adding and subtracting, he perhaps could obtain the instruction in a German university; but the art of multiplying and dividing, he continued, had been greatly developed in Italy, which, in his opinion, was the only country where such advanced instruction could be obtained.

This story has been well corroborated by historians of mathematics, for example, Swetz (1987). While it concerns commercial mathematics, it makes the point that there was a time when even this mathematics was the province of an élite group of specialists. Over time, the fact that widespread acceptance of the newly available notation system had larger impact on the broader population's access to what we now term 'shopkeeper arithmetic'.

Another useful orienting statistic is derived from US Department of Education Office of Statistics data (1996). In the United States, 3.5 per cent of the 17- to 18-year-old population cohort took high school Advanced Placement Calculus (successful completion of the associated test allows them to substitute this course for a corresponding one in the university). This is almost exactly the percentage of students graduating from high school in the US a century earlier. Perhaps 2 per cent of the US population was expected to learn algebra a century ago; today in the US the slogan is 'Algebra for All'. Similar dramatic changes in expectations regarding who can or should learn mathematics have occurred internationally, throughout both the developed and developing world.

Indeed, reflecting on these longer-term trends, the question we asked about whether a democratization of mathematical reasoning would occur, now shifts from the interrogative to the imperative: we *must* teach much more mathematics to many more people. But how can we speak of much more mathematics when the curriculum is already overflowing? And for many more people when we are so unsuccessful with those we do teach?

Before replying, we ask how many people can travel 50 miles per hour? Or can fly? Or can speak and be heard a thousand miles away? Answer: most of us. Rendering much more mathematics learnable by many more people will require at least the levels of coordinated innovation standing behind the automobile, airplane or telephone. Let's step back a bit and examine these other innovations.

First note, the automobile involved considerably more than the invention of the internal combustion engine. Automobiles are embedded in a sophisticated system of interrelated innovations and practices that cover a wide range of systems, mechanical, hydraulic, electronic, as well as roadways, laws, and maps. Then there is the matter of educating and organizing the people to build, operate, and market them. Of course, jet airplanes, airports, navigation systems, worldwide communication systems, airline reservation systems, radar-based flight controllers, are at least as great a miracle. With a very occasional exception, all these staples of the late 20th century operate with extraordinary efficiency in the service of quite ordinary people — *and are expected to!*

We see parallel developments now becoming possible in educational technology. Much attention has been drawn to multimedia, with its attendant possibilities for engaging children in constructing, reasoning, and communicating across multiple representational forms. Likewise, the metaphor of the 'information superhighway', used for advances in networking, draws explicit comparisons to the universal grid of roadways and high-speed digital switches at the heart of the transportation and communication revolutions respectively. Yet new media and networking are incomplete without a third development: the possibility of mass-producing customizable educational content. Just as transportation required Henry Ford's assembly-line-produced Model T, and communications required the dial tone, educational technology needs a wave of modularization, substitutability, and combinatoric composition. This is now becoming possible under the rubric of 'component software architectures' (Cox, 1996) which allow for the mix-and-match interoperability, integration, and customization of modular functionalities: notebooks, graphs, calculators, simulations, algebraic formulae, annotation tools, etc. Component software architectures bring the possibility of constructing large complex systems through a highly distributed effort among developers, researchers, activity authors, curriculum experts, publishers, teachers, and students, among others. As we argue elsewhere (Roschelle and Kaput, 1996; Roschelle et al., in preparation), the integration of media, networks, and component architecture can begin to allow us to approach educational problems on a scale that was formerly inconceivable.

With our confidence stiffened by clear success in transportation and communication, and with an understanding that the infrastructure for similar advances in educational technology is now emerging, let us now turn to our particular interest in present day reform — democratizing access to powerful mathematics.

Mathematics of Change and Variation Through New Representational Forms

The formal algebraic symbol system evolved to serve the needs of an élite population of mathematician/scientists who used it every day over a lifetime. Today we assume that casual students by the millions must learn it for considerably more casual use in their quotidian lives. However, the mathematics of change and variation, as represented by calculus in most current curricula, is accessible only to those who have survived a long series of algebraically oriented prerequisites. The net result of this prerequisite structure is that, at least in the US, 10 per cent of the population has contact with the mathematics of change and variation, and most of those are at the college level. Moreover, most of their contact is with the *notation* of calculus rather than its conceptual core.

Educational innovators have long experimented with the construction of alternative notational systems to enable learning of mathematics and science. One well-established method is to embed mathematics in computer languages (Ayers et al., 1988; diSessa et al., 1995; Hatfield and Kieren, 1972; Noss and Hoyles, 1996; Papert, 1980; Sfard and Leron, 1996). Familiar examples could include Turtle Geometry (Abelson and diSessa, 1980), mathematical programming in ISETL (Dubinsky, 1991), and spreadsheets (Neuwirth, 1995). Another method is to embed the content in activities such as computer games (Kraus, 1982). Here we argue for a representational alternative: embedding mathematics in direct manipulation of dynamic spatial forms and conversation over those forms (Kaput, 1992). Dynamic geometry is one example of alternative notational form based upon direct manipulation of spatial forms (Jackiw, 1988–97; Goldenberg, 1997; Laborde, 1990). Direct manipulation of two-dimensional vectors is another (Roschelle, 1991). For the mathematics of change and variation, our SimCalc project has chosen to focus on directly manipulable Cartesian graphs that control the action of animations.[1]

The properties of graphs suggest interesting answers to the three major questions we posed earlier:

1   Widening of forms? Graphs already support a range of forms that is considerably wider than can be expressed in closed-form symbolic algebra (Kaput, 1994), and more specific to particular reasoning techniques. For example, as we shall describe below, graphs can easily support manipulation of piecewise defined functions, a form that is extremely cumbersome in traditional algebra.

2   Democratization of access? Graphs are already a more democratic form, appearing frequently in newspapers, television, business presentations, and even US presidential campaign speeches — at least in terms of reading and interpretation, as opposed to writing and manipulating graphs. These are all places where equations are seldom found, and indeed usually taboo. As was the case with the explosion of literary forms, graphs appear to draw upon cognitive capabilities which are more widespread or accessible than formal mathematical symbols, although not without challenges (Leinhardt et al., 1990; McDermott et al., 1987). We shall deal with the matter of writing and manipulating graphs shortly.

3   New core curriculum? Most of the basic characteristics of mathematical thinking outlined at the beginning of this chapter can be carried over to graphical representational forms, allowing students to begin grappling with powerful concepts earlier and more successfully. In the next millennium, graphical mathematics will need to be part of the basic mainstream experience for all students. But a major step in this direction will require a move from static graphs that are merely read and interpreted to dynamically manipulable graphs that can be linked to phenomena and simulations of various kinds. And this change must occur in concert with substantial changes in how the content is organized and experienced.

Our SimCalc Project is building upon the unique potential of manipulable graphs in our *MathWorlds* software, which supports learning about rates of change of objects in motion, along with many related concepts. Figure 12.2 shows a screen from an introductory activity, with a moving elevator controlled by a piecewise-defined step function for velocity. In this activity (designed by our colleague, Walter Stroup), middle-school students make velocity functions that occupy

Figure 12.2 An introductory elevators activity in SimCalc's MathWorlds software

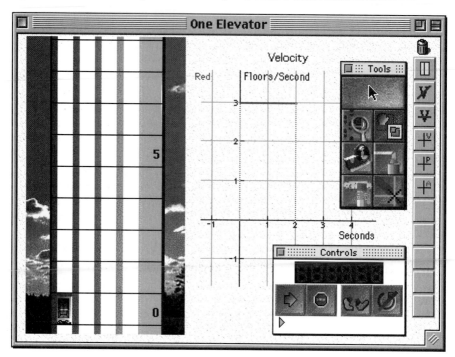

six grid squares of area. The students are asked to make as many different (positive) functions as they can, and compare similarities and differences. As mathematicians well know, all such functions will cause the elevator to move upwards six floors, but will vary in times and speeds. Pictured is a very simple one-piece velocity function. As we discuss elsewhere (Roschelle et al., in press), velocity step functions also draw upon students' prior knowledge and skills: students can compute the integral by multiplying the sides of the rectangles or simply counting squares. They can readily distinguish duration (width) from speed (height), and distance travelled (area). Questions about the meaning of negative areas (below the axis) arise naturally and their resolution can be grounded in the motion of the simulated elevator.

But now let us skip quickly ahead in our curriculum. Over many weeks with *MathWorlds*, students study the properties of velocity graphs in relation to motion, then position graphs, then relations between the two, and finally (for older students) acceleration graphs. Along the way, students also work with manipulable graphs that are piecewise linear (instead of step functions), continuous instead of discontinuous, and varying arbitrarily (not just linearly). The various representations are each dynamically linked (see Roschelle et al., in press, for further detail), so that students can directly observe the effects of changing a velocity graph upon position, or vice versa.

Kinaesthetic and Cybernetic Experience Move to the Centre

As mentioned above, the printing press led to increasing diversity of literary forms including, for example, the novel. We argued that computational representations are doing the same for mathematics, and that new forms of graphs are likely to become common tools for mathematical reasoning. Here we push our millennial comparison one step further. Among the new literary forms that emerged, the novel stands out as creating a more participatory experience for the reader; readers of novels are swept into a fully articulated world that at times seems as real as the familiar world. Indeed, the great achievement of successful authors is to relate experience in the reader's personal world to the new imaginary worlds. Moreover, novelists were now free to treat topics that were neither religious, nor mythical, nor heroic — contemporary life became the subject of literary experience. Of course, these new forms did not arrive without precedent; oral story-telling traditions paved the way; and contemporary novels are certainly no more constrained to common experience than film-makers are bound to reproducing common events.

This trend has its parallel in technology that brings motion experiences into the mathematics classroom, and thus ties the mathematics of change to its historical and familiar roots in experienced motion. Motion can be represented cybernetically (as an animation or simulation), as we described above with Elevators in *MathWorlds*. And motion can also be represented physically, in experiences of students' own body movement, or objects that they move. When desired, these physical motions can be digitised and imported as data into the computer, attached to actors, repeated, edited, and so on. Below we discuss three ways in which SimCalc is using the relationship between physical and cybernetic experience to give students new opportunities to make sense of traditionally difficult concepts such as mean value, limits, and continuity.

When using *MathWorlds* in classrooms, especially with young children, we often begin with physical motion, unconnected to the computer at all. For example, students might be asked to walk along a line, with speeds qualitatively described as 'fast', 'medium', or 'slow'. The class can then measure the time to cover a fixed distance, beginning the slow process of building and differentiating the quantities of distance, rate, and time and their relationships. Later students move to the computer and use an activity that displays a 'walking world' with animated characters whose velocities are constrained to three fixed heights, corresponding to fast, medium and slow. With the greater precision and control supported by the computer representations, students can now begin to make quantitative comparisons. Here we use the kinaesthetically rich experiences of the physical world to present difficult quantification challenges for students who have only the vaguest idea of what one might measure and why (Piaget, 1970; Thompson and Thompson, 1995). Animated clowns, on the other hand, are less grounded in real experience (indeed their gaits are cartoonish at best), but easier to control, measure, examine, and repeat. They provide pedagogically powerful intermediate idealizations of motion phenomena.

In later activities, physical and cybernetic experience can be connected directly through data. For example, in Roschelle et al. (in press), we describe an activity

Figure 12.3 Dude does Clown's mean value

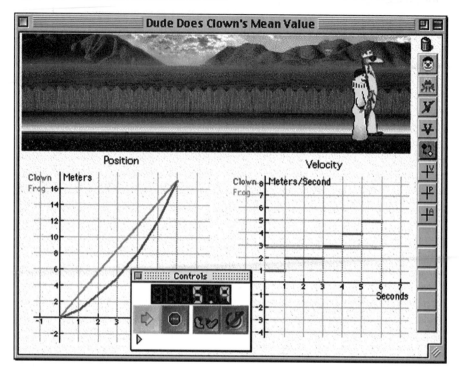

sequence in which students explore the concept of mean value, a mathematically central concept upon which much theoretical structure depends (Fleming and Kaput, 1979). Here a student's body motion is captured with a motion sensor, and input into *MathWorlds*, where it becomes replayable as the motion of the walking 'Clown' character. The motion also appears in a *MathWorlds* graph as a continuously varying velocity function (assuming the walking student varied speed). Students may now construct a second animated character ('Dude') whose motion is controlled by a single constant velocity function (see Figure 12.3). The challenge is to find the correct velocity to arrive at the same final location at exactly the same time — thus finding the mean value.

It is exciting for students to find the mean value of their own variable-velocity body motion. While a large body of research exists regarding student mathematization of motion, it focuses mainly on high school and college age students, and generally deals with 'regular' motion that is describable algebraically (McDermott et al., 1987; Thornton, 1992). In contrast, we allow students to work with highly irregular motion, generated by their own bodies, and leading towards the important technique of approximating continuous variation with piecewise linear functions.

Once students are comfortable with the concept of mean value, they can use piecewise segments to try to approximate a varying motion. In the example given above, the two motions will only intersect at one place, the final location. But in *MathWorlds* students can use two piecewise linear velocity segments (each comprising half the given interval) and thus intersect at two places, the final location and the mid-duration location. This process can be repeated with more and more (and smaller and smaller) segments, making the two characters meet 2, 4, 8, 16, 32, or more times. Of course, as the number of segments increases, the approximation between the motions becomes greater, giving students a concrete sense of taking a limit. Here students see how an idealized abstraction (a linear velocity segment) can model a continuously varying real world variable (their varying body position) with as much precision as required (see Roschelle et al., in press, for more detail).

In another class of activities, we can push the dissimilarities between physical and cybernetic motion to open further concepts for exploration. As the reader may have noticed, *MathWorlds* allows an elevator to have a discontinuous velocity graph, whereas a real elevator (and any physical object) *never* has discontinuous velocity. In our experience, students readily accept discontinuity in velocity. However, if they are eventually to learn physics, it becomes necessary to problematize the use of discontinuous functions as models of reality. Recently, we have been exploring discontinuous *position* graphs as a means to make continuity problematic for students in a series of activities we have associated with Star Trek-like 'beaming' of simulation characters to different locations. With discontinuous position graphs, students clearly recognize that the actor displays a behaviour that is impossible in the real world. Once students intuitively grasp the distinction between continuity and discontinuity (and more generally the problematic nature of the connection between simulations and physical phenomena), it is possible to raise the question with respect to velocity: is velocity in the real world continuous or discontinuous?

Explorations with the Mean Value Theorem (MVT) can provide a provocative context in which to address the continuity of velocity. Recall that the MVT states that, under certain continuity conditions on an interval, a varying rate function must intersect its mean value over that interval at least once. Students can try with their own body motion, or return to the *MathWorlds* mean value activity described above: (a) to digitize a body motion (b) to find the mean-value velocity and (c) to see if it intersects the velocity graph of the digitized walking motion. For comparison, students can try to find the mean value of a cybernetic motion consisting of a varying step function (as in the Elevators activity). Here, while there will still be a mean value, the MVT will not necessarily apply because the needed continuity has been violated: one can make an elevator trip of varying constant velocity segments (Figure 12.4), and a matching second elevator trip with constant velocity, and yet the second elevator need never go at the same speed as the first elevator. Hence students arrive experientially at the motivation for the theoretical concept of continuity over an interval, without which it becomes impossible to appreciate the preconditions for critical theorems such as the MVT.

To summarize, we see new technologies creating a possibility to reconnect mathematical representations and concepts to directly perceived phenomena. Further, we see the rich interplay between physical and cybernetic experience as pedagogically provocative in at least three ways:

Figure 12.4   Conclusions of mean value theorem fails

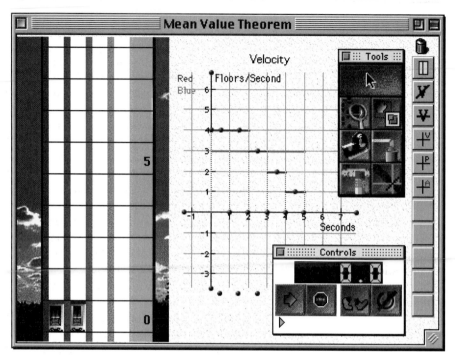

a   through juxtaposition of the different affordances of similar motions in each medium
b   through data connections that allow cybernetic models of physical motions
c   by exploiting differences in physical versus cybernetic motions to problematize critical concepts such as continuity.

Discussion: Mathematics Education at the Beginning of a New Millennium

By momentarily rising from the trenches of mathematics education reform to a larger time scale, we identified a major long-term trend: *Computational media are reshaping mathematics, both in the hands of mathematicians and in the hands of students as they explore new, more intimate connections to everyday life.* As we mentioned earlier, we can already be fairly certain this will lead to widening of mathematical forms, just as the printing press increased the range of acceptable literary forms. Already we are seeing new forms such as spreadsheets become prominent in everyday life. Computational tools are leading to new epistemological methods as professional mathematicians explore the extraordinary graphical phenomenology of dynamical systems (Stewart, 1990). Additional new forms are rapidly being invented by educators, such as mathematical programming languages and construction kits for dynamic geometry.

Based on our experiences in SimCalc, we are becoming cautiously optimistic about the second question we raised: democratic access. Some representational forms, like directly editable graphs, can make difficult concepts such as mean value, limit, and continuity in calculus newly available to ordinary middle-school (10- to 12-year-old) students. The technology's capability to provide better links between graphical representations and phenomena (physical and cybernetic) also appear essential, as this linkage grounds concepts in familiar semantic referents.

Yet as Sherin (1996) points out, new forms also lead to changes in the meaning of the concepts; in Sherin's studies, students who learned physics by programming in a computer language learned a set of physics concepts subtly different from those learned by students using traditional algebraic symbols. Indeed, in our work with SimCalc, we are currently working out the curricular bridge from editable piece-wise functions back to traditional algebra. It is by no means easy. And this is just the beginning! We want to lead students towards understandings of the larger mathematics of change and variation that includes dynamical systems because this relatively new mathematical form, with roots in Poincaré's work at the end of the previous century, is revolutionizing many sciences simultaneously as we approach the next century (Hall, 1992). However, the major long-term educational experiment with systems concepts, based in the use of *Stella*, is far from a clear success (Doerr, 1996). Other innovative approaches to systems concepts, *StarLogo* (Resnick, 1994) and *AgentSheets* (Repenning, 1994) look promising but present difficulties in linking back to commonplace notation. None the less, we believe that with time and effort, innovations in computational representations will make democratic access to systems dynamics possible.

To harness this potential fully, however, reformers will need to rise to the challenge of our third question: Can these new possibilities transform our notion of a core mathematics curriculum for all learners? The technological revolutions in transportation and communications would be meaningless or impossible if core societal institutions and infrastructures remained unchanged in their wake. Today's overnight shipments and telecommuting workers would be a shock to our forebears 100 years ago, but our curriculum would be recognized as quite familiar. If we are to overcome this stasis, we must seize the opportunities implicit in new dynamic notations to reorganize the curriculum to enable extraordinary achievement from ordinary learners.

Note

1   Funded by the NSF Applications of Advanced Technology Program, Grant #RED 9619102.

References

ABELSON, H. and DISESSA, A. (1980) *Turtle Geometry*, Cambridge, MA: MIT Press.

ARNHEIM, R. (1957) *Film As Art*, Berkeley, CA: University of California Press.

AYERS, T., DAVIS, G., DUBINSKY, E. and LEWIN, P. (1988) 'Computer experiences in learning composition of functions', *Journal for Research in Mathematics Education*, **19**, 3, pp. 246–59.

BRADSHAW, J. and ROGERS, L. (1993) *The Evolution of Lateral Asymmetries, Language, Tool-use and Intellect*, New York: Academic Press.

CALVIN, W. (1990) *The Ascent of Mind*, New York: Bantam Books.

COX, B. (1996) *Superdistribution: Objects As Property on the Electronic Frontier*, New York: Addison-Wesley.

DANTZIG, T. (1954) *Number: The Language of Science*, New York: Macmillan.

DISESSA, A., HOYLES, C. and NOSS, R. (eds) (1995) *Computers for Exploratory Learning*, New York: Springer.

DOERR, H.M. (1996) 'Stella ten years later: A review of the literature', *International Journal of Computers for Mathematical Learning*, **1**, 2, pp. 201–24.

DONALD, M. (1991) *Origins of the Modern Mind: Three Stages in the Evolution of Culture and Cognition*, Cambridge, MA: Harvard University Press.

DONALD, M. (1993) 'Precis of origins of the modern mind: Three stages in the evolution of culture and cognition', *Behavioral and Brain Sciences*, **16**, pp. 737–91.

DUBINSKY, E. (1991) 'Reflective abstraction in advanced mathematical thinking', in TALL, D. (ed.) *Advanced Mathematical Thinking*, Dordrecht, The Netherlands: Reidel, pp. 95–123.

FISKE, J. and HARTLEY, J. (1978) *Reading Television*, London: Methuen.

FLEMING, D. and KAPUT, J. (1979) *Calculus and Analytic Geometry*, New York: Harper and Row.

GOLDENBERG, E.P. (1997) 'Dynamic geometry: A new mathematical form', Manuscript available from the author, Education Development Center, Newton, MA.

GOODMAN, N. (1978) *Ways of Worldmaking*, Hassocks, Sussex: Harvester Press.

HALL, N. (1992) *Exploring Chaos: A Guide to the New Science of Disorder*, New York: Norton.

HATFIELD, L.L. and KIEREN, T.E. (1972) 'Computer-assisted problem solving in school mathematics', *Journal for Research in Mathematics Education*, **3**, 2, pp. 99–112.

INNIS, H. (1951) *The Bias of Communication*, Toronto: University of Toronto Press.

JACKIW, N. (1988–97) *The Geometer's Sketchpad* (Software; various versions), Berkeley, CA: Key Curriculum Press.

KAPUT, J. (1992) 'Technology and mathematics education', in GROUWS, D. (ed.) *Handbook on Research in Mathematics Teaching and Learning*, New York: Macmillan, pp. 515–56.

KAPUT, J. (1994) 'Democratizing access to calculus: New routes to old roots', in SCHOENFELD, A. (ed.) *Mathematical Thinking and Problem Solving*, Hillsdale, NJ: Erlbaum, pp. 77–156.

KRAUS, W.H. (1982) 'The use of problem-solving heuristics in the playing of games involving mathematics', *Journal for Research in Mathematics Education*, **13**, 3, pp. 172–82.

LABORDE, J.M. (1990) *CABRI Geometry* (Software), New York: Brooks-Cole Publishing Co.

LEINHARDT, G., ZASLAVSKY, O. and STEIN, M. (1990) 'Functions, graphs, and graphing: Tasks, learning, and teaching', *Review of Educational Research*, **60**, pp. 1–64.

LIEBERMAN, P. (1991) *The Biology and Evolution of Language*, Cambridge, MA: Harvard University Press.

LOGAN, R. (1986) *The Alphabet Effect*, New York: William Morrow.

LOGAN, R. (1995) *The Fifth Language: Learning a Living in the Computer Age*, Toronto: Stoddart.

McDERMOTT, L., ROSENQUIST, M. and ZEE, E.V. (1987) 'Student difficulties in connecting graphs and physics: Examples from kinematics', *American Journal of Physics*, **55**, 6, pp. 503–13.

McLUHAN, M. (1962) *The Gutenberg Galaxy: The Making of Typographic Man*, Toronto: University of Toronto Press.

McLUHAN, M. (1967) *The Medium Is the Massage*, New York: Bantam Books.

McLUHAN, M. and LOGAN, R.K. (1977) 'Alphabet, Mother of invention', December *Etcetera*, **34**.

MITHEN, S. (1996) *The Prehistory of the Mind: The Cognitive Origins of Art, Religion and Science*, New York: Thames and Hudson.

NEUWIRTH, E. (1995) 'Visualizing formal and structural relationships with spreadsheets', in DISESSA, A.A., HOYLES, C. and NOSS, R. (eds) *Computers and Exploratory Learning* (NATO ASI Series, Series F: Volume 146), pp. 155–73, New York: Springer-Verlag, pp. 155–74.

NOSS, R. and HOYLES, C. (1996) *Windows on Mathematical Meanings: Learning Cultures and Computers*, Dordrecht: Kluwer Academic Publishers.

PAPERT, S. (1980) *Mindstorms*, New York: Basic Books.

PIAGET, J. (1970) *The Child's Conception of Movement and Speed*, New York: Basic Books.

REPENNING, A. (1994) 'Programming substrates to create interactive learning environments', *Journal of Interactive Learning Environments*, **4**, pp. 45–74.

RESNICK, M. (1994) *Turtles, Termites, and Traffic Jams: Explorations in Massively Parallel Microworlds*, Cambridge, MA: MIT Press.

ROSCHELLE, J. (1991) 'Students' construction of qualitative physics knowledge: Learning about velocity and acceleration in a computer microworld', Unpublished doctoral dissertation, University of California, Berkeley.

ROSCHELLE, J. and KAPUT, J. (1996) 'Educational software architecture and systemic impact: The promise of component software', *Journal of Educational Computing Research*, **14**, 3, pp. 217–28.

ROSCHELLE, J., KAPUT, J. and STROUP, W. (in press) 'SimCalc: Accelerating student engagement with the mathematics of change', in JACOBSEN, M.J. and KOZMA, R.B. (eds) *Learning the Sciences of the 21st Century: Research, Design, and Implementing Advanced Technology Learning Environments*, Hillsdale, NJ: Erlbaum.

ROSCHELLE, J., KAPUT, J., STROUP, W. and KAHN, T. (in preparation) 'Scaleable integration of educational software: Exploring the promise of component architectures'.

SALOMON, G. (1979) *Interaction of Media, Cognition and Learning*, San Francisco, CA: Jossey-Bass.

SCHMANDT-BESSERAT, D. (1980) 'The envelopes that bear the first writing', *Technology and Culture*, **21**, 3.

SCHMANDT-BESSERAT, D. (1981) 'From tokens to tablets: A re-evaluation of the so-called numerical tablets', *Visible Language*, **15**.

SCHMANDT-BESSERAT, D. (1985) 'Clay symbols for data storage in the VIII Millennium BC', in *Studi di Palentologia in Onore di Salvatore M. Puglisi*, La Spaienza: Universita di Roma.

SCHMANDT-BESSERAT, D. (1988) 'Quantification and social structure', in MAINES, D.R. and COUCH, C.J. (eds) *Communication and Social Structure*, Springfield, IL: C.C. Thomas.

SCHMANDT-BESSERAT, D. (1992) *Before Writing: Vol 1. From Counting to Cuneiform*, Houston: University of Texas Press, pp. 357–85.

SFARD, A. and LERON, U. (1996) 'Just give me a computer and I will move the earth: Programming as a catalyst of a cultural revolution in the mathematics classroom', *International Journal of Computers for Mathematical Learning*, **1**, 2, pp. 189–95.

SHERIN, B. (1996) 'The symbolic basis of physical intuition: A study of two symbol systems in physics instruction', Unpublished doctoral dissertation, University of California, Berkeley.

STEWART, I. (1990) 'Change', in STEEN, L. (ed.) *On the Shoulders of Giants: New Approaches to Numeracy*, Washington, DC: National Academy Press, pp. 183–219.

SWETZ, F. (1987) *Capitalism and Arithmetic: The New Math of the 15th Century*, La Salle: Open Court.

THOMPSON, A.G. and THOMPSON, P.W. (1995) 'Talking about rates conceptually: A teacher's struggle', *Journal for Research in Mathematics Education*, **25**, pp. 279–303.

THORNTON, R. (1992) 'Enhancing and evaluating students' learning of motion concepts', in TIBERGHIEN, A. and MANDL, H. (eds) *Physics and Learning Environments*, (NATO Science Series ed.), New York: Springer-Verlag.

US DEPARTMENT OF EDUCATION (1996) *The Condition of Education 1996*, Supplemental Table 29–6, [On-line] National Center For Education Statistics, Washington, DC, Available at http://www.ed.gov/NCES/pubs/ce/c9629d06.html.

WILLIAMS, R. (1974) *Television: Technology and Cultural Form*, London: Fontana.

WILLS, C. (1993) *The Runaway Brain: The Evolution of Human Uniqueness*, New York: Basic Books.

Section Three

Thinking about Change

Many of the contributions to the conference and to this book are concerned with change — what *will* be different, what *should* be different in the future. In this section the authors examine the process of change, looking back at the history of curriculum development and looking forward to implementing visions of the curriculum of the 21st century.

However much professional mathematics educators might wish it, curriculum change is not a simple matter of proposing desirable innovations or of engaging in rational debate about the form and content of the curriculum. Although Brian Griffiths in his chapter identifies 'the principal purpose of mathematics education' to be 'rational attempts to improve mathematics teaching and learning', it is clear from his historical overview of changes in the UK that many of the changes that have taken place have been argued on a basis that falls somewhat short of this ideal of rationality. The rhetoric of power, illustrated in the 'fudge and fiddlesticks' argument quoted in the title of this chapter (and used by Heaviside in 1901), still plays an important part in the direction of curriculum reform in Britain and elsewhere. Politicians and others with vested interests make use of notions of 'common sense' that have little basis in evidence or reason. How are those of us concerned with mathematics education to find a voice in debates on changes in the curriculum? How is research in mathematics teaching and learning to have an impact on what eventually happens in classrooms? Griffiths stresses the importance of developing a language to explain and persuade — communicating not just among ourselves but also with (potentially hostile or obstructive) others, including (very importantly) teachers.

Learning from the past in order to shape the future is also a theme of William Higginson's contribution. The stories of real learners with which this chapter begins remind us of the damage that can be done to individuals, and indeed to society, in the name of mathematics education. Higginson challenges the conventional impersonal view of mathematics as he contrasts the personalities of Russell and Whitehead, deploring what he sees as the influence of Russell on the 'absolutist, axiomatic, brittle, clever, cold, disembodied, hard-edged, hierarchical, logical, precise, rational, non-visceral, non-visual, and symbolic' nature of much of mathematics, including school mathematics, in the 20th century, and arguing instead for a curriculum that, like Whitehead's mathematical world, is 'connected, organic, and active'.

The crucial role of the mathematics teacher in ensuring the quality of mathematics education and the success of proposed changes in the curriculum is a strong theme in this section, as it is in many of the other chapters of the book. As we think about how the mathematics curriculum might change, we must also think about the teachers who will participate in that change, not only as its subjects but also as its agents. For example, the chapters by both Brian Griffiths and Kenneth Ruthven recall the successes of the LAMP (Low Attainers Mathematics Project) and RAMP (Raising of Attainment in Mathematics Project) projects in the UK in the 1980s in involving and enthusing individual teachers in changing and reflecting on their practice — but the failure to disseminate the lessons learnt to other teachers who were less centrally involved. As Bernard Cornu argues, future teachers must be prepared to evolve and adapt to take into account the changes they will have to face in society, the ongoing developments in the possibilities offered by information technology, and the new knowledge provided by educational research. Cornu's description of the recent developments in France's system of initial teacher education lays great stress on the importance of educational research and a 'dynamic interplay between theory and practice'. Participants at the conference responded with interest to his contribution, recognizing the issues as internationally relevant, and finding it useful to compare their own countries' policies and practices in this area against Cornu's measures.

Cornu's chapter concludes with a call to convince the authorities and the public that educational research is essential to the 'evolution' of education. This provides a useful starting point for Ruthven's critique of the bases upon which recommendations about teachers' practice are founded. He calls for a move away from dogmatism, subjectivism, and empiricism as means of forming recommendations about practice, towards 'warranting' practice through procedures that are subjected to scrutiny. Like many of those attending the conference, Ruthven calls for a closer integration of the practice of teaching, research into teaching, and the training of teachers. His suggestions of possible ways forward may go some way towards providing an answer to Griffiths's plea for improved communication.

Chapter 13

Fudge and Fiddlesticks: A Century After

H. Brian Griffiths

An important need in the discipline of mathematics education is to find ways of expressing its conclusions effectively, either to peers or to outsiders (especially, nowadays, to politicians). To do this needs a disciplined framework and language, and a willingness to approximate and settle for the possible rather than the ideal. Thus we are talking about choosing languages for the effective achievement of an educational end in the teaching and learning of mathematics. How can we make the discipline as accepted and 'natural' as that in mathematics itself? In this chapter, I wish to recall techniques used in England to achieve various reforms in the past, and compare them with those needed today. From the successes and failures of some relevant historical examples, we might then see what we can learn for the future, for application (or modification) elsewhere — remembering that a problem occurring in both Texas and Taiwan may have a solution in the one which is not a solution in the other: this does not happen in mathematics itself. We must of course describe the examples before deriving conclusions from them; but, for brevity, we must omit much detail (which is probably well known to many readers), since it can be found in the books of Griffiths and Howson (1974), and Howson (1982).

The Perry Reform Movement

A famous example of effective communication is associated with the persuasive rhetoric used by Oliver Heaviside, when the 1901 meeting of the British Association was discussing possible changes in the mathematics curriculum:

> [Boys] have also the power of learning to work processes, long before their brains have acquired the power of understanding (more or less) the scholastic logic of what they are doing. . . . the prevalent idea of mathematical work is that you must understand the reason why first, before you proceed to practice. This is fudge and fiddlesticks . . . I know mathematical processes, that I have used with success for a very long time, of which neither I nor anyone else understands the scholastic logic. I have grown into them and so understand them in that way.

This quotation contains several interesting but debatable assertions, both mathematical and educational; and it depends for its power on rhetoric and rank. Although the hearers were often highly competent in many respects, their appreciation of the discipline of mathematics education was naive. Similar naivety continued until the 1960s, when it was still common for assertions to be made, less reasonable than Heaviside's but in similar dogmatic style, to large audiences with no prospect of any critical discussion. There were unspoken assumptions that a speaker's scientific prestige must demand respect for remarks outside his (always 'his') field, no matter how off-the-cuff they were.

Heaviside's remarks belong to the still unsettled debate on technique versus understanding, and were intended as support for the reform movement of Professor John Perry, which was gathering momentum, to change the mathematics curriculum in English secondary schools. The 'Perry' aims were clear, and not too difficult to achieve in practice if society would allow: they concerned secondary education — given to a small élite which would slowly expand through a scholarship system — and they had two prongs. One of these was for teachers to be free to teach geometry without needing to follow Euclid's exposition (contrary to the demands of the Oxbridge examiners); the other was to introduce topics that would be 'useful to a race of inventors and engineers' (as the British scientists of that time romantically saw themselves). The arguments depended partly on scientific enthusiasm, and were partly social (being based on xenophobia).

The first prong had arisen in 1871 with the founding of the Association for the Improvement of Geometry Teaching (later the Mathematical Association), but little progress had been made because the opposition depended on the authority of Arthur Cayley. I have not seen his full reasons, but the usual arguments of the period (see Richards, 1988) referred to training of the mind, tradition, and perfection of the Euclidean system. Also, among these deeply Christian mathematicians, intellectually uneasy after the effects of Darwin, such perfection had a role as an exemplar of something 'as certain as that there is a Divine Being'. But enough people eventually could separate mathematics from Divinity to overcome the opposition, by waiting until Cayley died and then cleverly timing a vote of the Cambridge MAs. This technique is inapplicable today, fortunately. The need for 'certainty' had driven people like Bertrand Russell into logic, and others (like G.H. Hardy) to the rigorous subject of analysis, then rapidly developing in continental Europe. Shortly after the anti-Euclid vote, an instructive parallel occurred when Hardy was able to persuade his peers in Cambridge to introduce Analysis into the curriculum. His arguments were hard-nosed, based on the professional requirements of research mathematicians of the time, and the textbook he later wrote was certainly not rhetorical but rather in the lofty style (as he later quoted) of 'a missionary talking down to cannibals'. But his arguments for the social aim of abolishing the Honours classification could not be in a similar terse, technical language; and even though he was a gifted writer of prose he failed in his aim, and had to settle instead for ending the numerical ordering of the Firsts and its associated mystique of the Senior Wrangler, and their pernicious effects.

With Euclid liberalized, the way was also open for Perry's second prong. Here, there was wide agreement about which mathematical topics to include (because they underlay the successful mathematical physics of the period), and about giving them a unified treatment. Disagreement about possible levels of rigour could arise, but there was trust in the ability of the schoolmasters to write suitable texts, because many were as well-qualified in mathematics as the university examiners. The reformers could achieve their aims because society had no serious political interest in obstructing them. Thus they needed to communicate only with that part of society involving teachers and examiners — professionals like themselves, with the normal human feelings (conservative and/or enthusiastic). The new curricula were widely adopted in the secondary schools (which catered for only a small minority of the population); they were taught to small classes by teachers well qualified in mathematics (though often not in teaching). Also the universities were satisfied with the preparation of the tiny proportion of pupils who went on to tertiary education, for until the 1950s their mathematics was well-matched to the tertiary syllabuses (except Analysis, which had long been a problem, though rarely acknowledged). Indeed, for many of the scientists and mathematicians produced by the new curriculum, this was a Golden Age, and they were often obstructive to later arguments for future change.

Mathematics for All

But, for a whole complex of reasons, change had to come. In the universities, courses changed to reflect the rapid progress of mathematical research; such changes were carried out in a piece-meal way, at first by enthusiasts, and soon became mismatched with the traditional preparation in secondary schools. In any case, widespread demands in all advanced countries led to plans for secondary education for *all* children, and not just an élite. This implied 'mathematics for all', and a few enthusiasts in the newly appearing comprehensive schools were beginning to look for attractive mathematics suitable for the many, rather than the few. As elsewhere, the British response led to the rise of various 'Modern Mathematics' schemes in the 1960s.

The most widespread of these was the Schools Mathematics Project (SMP), which still survives, and I want to look at its early problems of communication. Unlike the projects in most countries, it was not led by university teachers or employees of an Educational Ministry. It began around 1962, in the best 'guerrilla' tradition, with a small group of enthusiastic, well qualified schoolteachers, organized by the energy of a Professor of Mechanics, Bryan Thwaites, who knew the teachers personally from his own days as a schoolteacher. His role was largely administrative, and he had no control over the mathematical content; through his contacts, he got industrial firms to support organized preliminary conferences, to find what mathematical thinking they desired in their employees. This continued the post-Perry tradition of trying to relate mathematics to the real world, and the initiators did not follow the Bourbaki line (to emphasize structure, and give power by introducing the precise language of Set Theory) commonly chosen in other countries. Instead, the Project introduced such topics as networks, matrices, and transformation geometry, and old topics (like applied social arithmetic) treated in new ways. (At this stage they were aiming at the top academic quartile of pupils.) The writing groups decided questions of selection of material and style of presentation by the method of informal discussion in small groups, using their knowledge of pupils' language and habits to guess what might work in the classroom. Also, short conferences were held to explain matters to those practising teachers who volunteered to use the materials. Thus communication was confined, as in the Perry reform, to the most immediate and enthusiastic professionals, following the informal 'missionary' style of earlier periods of diffusion of new ideas (see Howson, 1978). A similar technique was used in the Midlands Mathematics Experiment, which was more concerned than the SMP initially with 'mathematics for all', had much less funding, and did not last as long.

In my view, the SMP material was mathematically very good, chosen with taste, soundly presented, and well designed for the originally participating schools. Their high social prestige (rather than the mathematics) was probably more responsible for the new SMP texts and examinations being rapidly adopted in schools — often by fiat of local inspectors rather than by positive choice of the teachers. The materials demanded good literary skills from pupils, so watered-down (and less satisfactory) versions were rapidly prepared for the less academic. Eventually the materials were used in about half the secondary schools in England. Often, however, through no fault of the SMP, there was inadequate in-service training for the teachers, who were generally by that time less well qualified than the original SMP team. Explicitly, the SMP put much less stress on memory and technique in favour of a questioning approach through classroom dialogue, but such an approach requires skilled, confident teachers. Instead, the hierarchy had often assigned unwilling conscripts to the guerrilla bands.

Complaints

Unlike the Perry reforms, these new ones eventually alerted many more interested parties, and hindsight tells us that explanations should have been devised for them. Here was a communication problem in mathematics education, and the Project workers had been too overworked to find simple ways of explaining its aims to people who were frequently too impatient to listen. In the universities few lecturers knew what was happening, and those who did were mainly pure mathematicians who approved the new content of the SMP course. Soon there were loud complaints, especially from academic engineers, who declared with little evidence that SMP pupils taking their courses could not do what the traditional students had always been able to do in the Golden Age; and these critics did not bother to find out what compensations there were. (Some also suffered from a limited view of what mathematics is, and perhaps were left insecure by the new material.) But the SMP had also made another mistake, in not consulting earlier such numerate colleagues as physics teachers, who also were distressed to find that pupils had not learned the mathematics they wanted at the right time. (In Perry's time, mathematics and physics teachers were often interchangeable.) The SMP did eventually publish an explanatory handbook for science teachers (see Howson, 1978, p. 138), but it was reporting a *fait accompli*.

Two further constituencies needing explanations were those of parents and employers. Pressures grew, because other agencies were by now producing new materials and approaches for widespread use in both primary and secondary schools, and there were soon protests from some mystified or hostile parents, who compared these new approaches unfavourably with their own traditional education. At least one book was written for their benefit (see Cockcroft, 1968) but, sympathetic as it was, few parents would read it if left to themselves: as soon as mathematics is 'explained', barriers of fright are erected in hearers — another communication problem!

The parental protests were reinforced by employers, who used traditional tests to select school-leavers for jobs and found the traditional skills missing. The employers forgot that the earlier 'high quality' type of applicant was now staying at school and aiming for a higher grade of job. By the mid-1970s, right-wing politicians realized that here was an issue that they could exploit especially to discredit recent progress towards comprehensive education, in ways now known to us all. But they were aided innocently by 'educated' people who did not at first see the campaign as political. Thus the 'Black Papers' were published around 1975 by the Critical Quarterly Society, containing articles by eminent contributors — headteachers, novelists, economists and the like, educated in the Golden Age, who did not attack the new mathematics alone, but the general climate of change that involved new styles of teaching the 3 Rs; and, with little mathematics, such writers would deplore such facts as that 'sticks' (i.e. Cuisenaire Rods) were being used to teach arithmetic. Their writing was astonishingly superficial, with undefined terms that made their work almost meaningless. Their Golden education had not conditioned them to apply the same critical standards as they (presumably) would use in their own specialities (see also the summary in Moon, 1986). The campaign led to the setting up of the Cockcroft Inquiry in 1978, which looked at mathematics in schools in a calm and rational manner. It met most of the ill informed criticisms, but was warmly received by teachers for its many professional recommendations for improvements.

In 1979 a right-wing Government was elected in Britain, before the Cockcroft Report was published, and the recommendations largely went unfunded. The political fuss had served its cynical purpose, although that was later revived as propaganda for a hurriedly designed National Curriculum which was later imposed with additional expensive tests and associated 'league-tables' of schools. Teachers were swamped with writing reports, to satisfy fashionable managerial modes of generating (supposedly) 'hard' information. Consequently, rational attempts to improve mathematics teaching and learning — surely the principal purpose of mathematics education — became very difficult to initiate. Effective communication with the Government ministers became impossible, since their policy was explicitly hostile to most professions, except Finance. Even left or centre opposition politicians have been infected with the imposed populist language, and although at the time of writing they have at last (1997) formed a new Government, we do not quite know how rational it will be in pursuing a populist policy on Numeracy.

Initiating Sophistication

It is interesting to wonder whether, when the storm-clouds were gathering 20 years ago, mathematics educators could have produced an effective 'sound-bites' defence against those politicians with no honest interest in rational argument, but who were then less well entrenched. It might have helped if we could have ensured that natural allies in the Establishment, other academics, the Black Paper writers, and left or centre politicians were better informed. An instructive example of how strange myths can arise among the ignorant arose in a conversation I heard at the London Mathematical Society in the mid-1980s. An eminent professor, appalled at the failings of his students, told us solemnly that it was all due to an experiment carried out in the 1960s by professors of Education! Except for fringe interest by Frank Land, I know of no Education professor who came anywhere near the English mathematics projects of the 1960s; but our professor was clearly still thinking he was working in mathematics: he had assumed the reasonable (but false) axiom that Education professors of that time did research like mathematicians, and deduced that they were bound to be involved. As a historical truth, his statement was on a par with saying that the number π is not only rational but negative; but he would have accepted a correction about mathematics ('not my field'), with far more grace than one about mathematics education. (In fact his Cambridge courses had actually taught him much about mathematics outside his field, but no mathematics education.)

One attempt at communicating with people like the professor, or rather to equip them to be more 'aware' of facts and issues, has been the holding of the annual Nottingham conferences on Undergraduate Mathematics Teaching. These began in 1976, partly owing to worries about falling numbers of applicants to university mathematics departments, and they were sponsored by the London Mathematical Society. At first eminent mathematicians came, and there was money to invite some schoolteachers; but demographic trends caused the numbers of applicants to increase again and so most of the eminent fell away — as did the money for teachers. Nevertheless, there was enough interest to enable the conferences to continue, but the participants are usually lecturers with a continuing interest in research and reflection on their teaching: the theorem-proving 'whizz-kids' most in need of treatment are relatively rare.

From the first a pattern was adopted, which has been deemed important and has been adopted with necessary variants at all International Congresses of Mathematics Education since that time. Firstly, plenary sessions are held only for imparting information or to hear of interesting work, never for debate. This helps to eliminate rhetoric and rank. Secondly, and most importantly, participants are assigned to small groups, in which they spend three days; their task is to produce a *written* reply to a 'brief' chosen by the organizing committee (which elects new members each year), then to have the reply criticized *in writing* by another of the groups, and finally to polish their reply in the light of the criticisms. The brief may be to construct a curriculum that is subject to given constraints, or to argue a case for more resources or for excluding a part of mathematics; and the completed replies are published in a volume of proceedings. The latter are of course still hasty and crude, but they help to emphasize that useful discussion must be more sophisticated than the conventional untutored coffee-table conversation in mathematics departments, that it can be intellectually appealing, and that there is a literature — we should not start from scratch in every discussion. (A selection of extracts from the collected volumes is shortly to be published.) It is interesting to watch the dynamics of the small groups, which take time to settle down and develop a common language of discourse. Some participants become surprisingly 'radical' about their own teaching, but the effect often wears off when they return home. As far as we can tell (since no relevant research has been done), a block of three days, and with no later support and feedback, is far too short to obtain truly significant effects. In a press campaign in 1995, when 'mathematics professors' were quoted as being worried about the standard of their current intakes, all were apparently unaware of a similar (but fruitless) campaign of the 1970s; but one small sign of progress appeared when two mathematicians wrote a newspaper article containing the words 'instrumental' and 'relational'. Perhaps its authors had attended a Nottingham conference in their youth.

These conferences have not devised a technical language of communication so much as a mode of formal discourse — largely between mathematicians rather than professional 'mathematics educators'. That is to be expected, since it is useless to devise a language before there is some willingness to communicate. The potential communicators find themselves involved in a situation where they feel a strong need to start talking or writing.

The LAMP and RAMP Projects

Similar effects were seen within the Projects LAMP and RAMP in the 1980s (see Ahmed and Williams, 1991). For example, the schools involved invited parents to come, but did not give them a lecture on the aims of the project; instead they were given mathematical questions to try in small groups, just as their children would experience. This technique seemed to be very popular. The 'Low Attainers Mathematics Project' (LAMP) was set up with the support of the right-wing minister Keith Joseph, after the Cockcroft Inquiry; he was concerned about the large number of low attainers among school-leavers, and the project was to develop good practice for teaching them. It generated so much interest, and doubts about what a 'Low Attainer' really is, that the Government funded a successor, the 'Raising of Attainment in Mathematics Project' (RAMP). (After that, no further funds appeared, because later ministers were out of sympathy with Joseph's ideas.) A strong feature of the two projects was the amount of time spent on a process of 'teacher-bonding', designed to get chosen groups of teachers to talk to each other frankly about their work, rather than be inhibited by talking to persons perceived to be higher in the hierarchy. This is another aspect of the 'guerrilla' approach, and seems to have had much longer lasting effects (including long friendships) than short in-service courses like the Nottingham conferences.

The two projects raised an as yet unsolved research problem: how can we generate legitimate principles from anecdotal research? A good single observation in teaching (as with a great novel) can be far more effective on a teacher's practice than a statistical survey, yet the Conservative ministers thought it clever to dismiss criticism of their policies as 'anecdotal', and to call for 'research' of a reductionist type (which they suppressed, if it was critical). Now, the evidence gained by LAMP and RAMP is usually in the form of work-sheets from teachers and pupils, from which close study allows one to make inferences about insights and progress; but it was not obvious how to summarize the enormous totality other than to pick instances that were significant to experienced teachers. The decision was therefore made to make it available in an open store for future workers, and it awaits their attention.

Designing Descriptive Languages

In many of these examples the influence of 'theorem-proving' mathematicians has been rather prominent, if not always useful. This is because — as in many countries — they have had considerable power to influence school syllabuses, while knowing little of the problems of teaching modern children. Indeed, in the Monthly Notices of the American Mathematical Society, one often sees letters openly contemptuous of 'educators' — though usually meaning PhDs with lots of education and minimal mathematics. This influence may well decline as attitudes to higher education and employment change; even mathematical research itself may decline in importance against the rise of seemingly more pressing problems in biology and economics. Young research students in mathematics will be scarcer, as employment opportunities decline. Already, many mathematicians in the former British polytechnics seem to have a different, less intellectual, attitude to mathematics than those in the traditional departments. This will affect mathematics education itself, and the attitudes to curriculum design and styles of teaching.

But in each case we have seen that when mathematics educators wish to produce a change (hopefully an improvement) in mathematics teaching, there is an immediate problem of language. This problem is one step more complicated than the 'Problem of 3 Languages' (see Griffiths, 1978), which is familiar — if not by name — to innovative text-book writers and popularizers: to invent a teaching language that forms a bridge from the sophisticated language of a part of mathematics to the naive language of the target audience. (Here, 'language' means not just vocabulary but style of thinking and expression.) As an example, it is illuminating to take a class of mathematics undergraduates through the task of devising an arithmetic curriculum for the 5- to 12-year-olds who entered British state schools after the 1870 Act made school attendance compulsory. (Historically, the curriculum evolved less abruptly.) The social constraints, unfamiliar to modern students, were that children often came from illiterate backgrounds, probably unkempt and unclean, and were assumed to have a fixed, socially static, future in the fields and factories; also taxpayers would refuse to pay for 'useless' material. It takes effort to extract any suitable topics at all, but students will eventually mention counting, tables, long division, decimals, etc. But once these are agreed, in what language should the textbooks be written? The students' derision vanishes when they find difficulty with the imposed 'English' of the 1890s best-seller *A Shilling Arithmetic* by Pendlebury. This seems to be a harder exercise for them than conventional technical problems.

As a much more complicated example, consider the task implied by the sub-title of the conference that generated the present book — 'What needs to be changed and why'. I am concerned here with the form of a possible answer, rather than attempting one of my own. Like the Perry reformers, our contemporary discussion must first clarify what is perceived to be wrong (not forgetting the 'why' of our question), otherwise proposed 'cures' may exacerbate matters. (Such clarification was missing from the superficial right-wing critiques of the 1970s.) Perry, and the reformers of the 1960s, took society and the universities as a stable background, in which to design school mathematics optimally. In our more complicated case we cannot assume such stability, and various predictions are needed. For example, we probably now know enough about the complexities to predict that the 'total' approach of the old projects will be replaced by improvement of separate fragments of the curriculum — but politicians will object to 'letting a hundred flowers bloom' (in Mao's phrase), because of cost and delay.

The discipline of mathematics education requires discussion to take place in certain styles (including the asking of awkward questions obvious to professionals), for peer criticism and possible improvement. Its connection with mathematics gives it an advantage over the general subject education, in that it already has some standards and paradigms to be measured against. If an agreed perception evolves that something really does need changing, then the next stage is to propose remedies. For the new proposals a strong view of the intended mathematical content will be essential, to meet questions like Howson's (reviewing a book so full of social philosophy that technical mathematics seemed forgotten): 'What has this to do with the 9-point circle?' Howson meant that in mathematics education it is essential to make informed decisions about including or rejecting important complexes of mathematical ideas, with specific examples that avoid airy nothings. But to refer only to mathematical content or technique (in the manner of the theorem-proving mathematicians) is mathematics, not mathematics education: proposals must also take account of time constraints and the effects on 'user' subjects; and they are useless if they ignore related aspects of teaching and learning styles and possible clashes with the larger curriculum. Once firm proposals are agreed in the appro-priate professional language, the question arises of how to put them into practice: they cannot be effective if imposed autocratically. So we need rigorous discussion of how to manage the relevant teacher training — preferably with pressure from teachers coming themselves. (This was the problem for LAMP: its concern was not to change the existing syllabuses.) After this, new languages are necessary in which, without loss of professional honesty, to 'sell' the proposals to Funding Agencies and one or more possibly obstructive groups, for example practising teachers, parents, employers, politicians. For each of these groups appropriate modes of explanation must be devised. As we have seen, such modes cannot consist only of suitably chosen words: the modes need also to be situations within which non-aggressive, rational conversation can flourish. And if the proposals are adopted it is necessary to watch out for disparities between their theory and the effects on pupils.

I am here proposing a 'dialectical' model of procedure for constructing a curriculum (for a target population), and it is clearly a long way from the Fudge and Fiddlesticks naivety of the early pioneers. It might be argued that if we use this model now any curriculum we produce will soon become obsolete in the 21st century, since most learning will be by individuals, following computer-guided programmes. But the need for other constructs will remain, and these cannot be used effectively without appropriate research carried out within a rigorous language. Even if most learning is by computer, appropriate programs will need to be written and marketed, and mathematics educators will have a duty to improve quality and sift out dross. I conclude that it will be even more necessary to heed the dialectical model because of the following pessimistic scenario. We can expect that powerful communications moguls will sell rubbish aggressively: imagine the problems of arranging honest communication about it then!

References

AHMED, A. and WILLIAMS, H. (1991) *Raising Achievement in Mathematics Project, 1986–9*, London: HMSO.

COCKCROFT, W.H. (1968) *Your Child and Mathematics*: Chambers and Murray.

GRIFFITHS, H.B. (1978) 'The structure of pure mathematics', in WAIN, G. (ed.) *Mathematical Education*, New York: Van Nostrand.

GRIFFITHS, H. and HOWSON, A.G. (1974) *Mathematics: Society and Curricula*, Cambridge: Cambridge University Press.

HOWSON, A.G. (1978) 'The diffusion of new ideas', in WAIN, G. (ed.) *Mathematical Education*, New York: Van Nostrand.

HOWSON, A.G. (1982) *A History of Mathematical Education in England*, Cambridge: Cambridge University Press.

MOON, R. (1986) *The 'New Maths' Curriculum Controversy*, Studies in Curriculum History, London: Falmer Press.

RICHARDS, J.L. (1988) *Mathematical Visions: The Pursuit of Geometry in Victorian England*, New York: Academic Press.

WAIN, G.T. (ed.) (1978) *Mathematical Education*, New York: Van Nostrand.

Chapter 14

Glimpses of the Past, Images of the Future: Moving from 20th to 21st Century Mathematics Education

William Higginson

The fact that all Mathematics is Symbolic Logic is one of the greatest discoveries of our age; and when this fact has been established, the remainder of the principles of mathematics consists in the analysis of Symbolic Logic itself. (Russell, 1903)

The conclusion is that Logic, conceived as an adequate analysis of the advance of thought, is a fake. It is a superb instrument, but it requires a background of common sense. (Whitehead, 1964)

Our set homework question, preceding the conference at which the contributions in this book were discussed, is admirably pithy, namely, 'In a new century's school mathematics: a) what ought to be different? and b) for what reasons?' In answering, the temptation is to be equally terse in turn: a) quite a lot; b) because we've botched it rather badly. Whatever virtues, such as clarity and directness, this telegraphic form might legitimately claim, problems remain. First, where it has been used before in this context it does not seem to have proved particularly helpful or effective. The most notable recent example of this minimalist style of hortation was probably the last sentence in the first paragraph of *Reshaping School Mathematics: A Philosophy and Framework for Curriculum*, a report by a blue-ribbon panel in the United States (Mathematical Sciences Education Board/National Research Council, 1990) which read: 'What is required is a complete redesign of the content of school mathematics and the way it is taught' (p. 1). Second, it makes for a rather short contribution.

But if succinctness is not a viable option here for one set of reasons, neither is an encyclopedic approach which, in a different context, the topic might well support. Hence a 'middle way' compromise, perhaps suited to an essay-length consideration of a large and complex question. I begin by stating, in summary form, 10 conclusions I have come to after reflection on the 'century problem in mathematics education'. I will then elaborate on a few of them. The conclusions, with some publications which address the themes in at least general terms, are:

- the record of mathematics education in the 20th century has largely been that of failure (Hudson, 1970; Stodolsky, 1988; Thurston, 1990)

- given the discipline's educational potential and centrality to a full understanding of, and participation in, the contemporary world, this failure can be seen as falling into the class of *corruptio optima pessima* — the corruption of the best is the worst (Papert, 1980)
- mathematics educators have, for the most part, chosen not to acknowledge the scale and the impact of their failure (Gaulin et al., 1994; Grouws, 1992)
- the effects of this failure, directly on individuals, and indirectly on societies and cultures, have been great (Gibbs et al., 1996; Lightman, 1994; Schifter, 1996; Waddington, 1977)
- the single most important reason for this failure is the implicit acceptance of a Russellian view of the nature of mathematics and the development of ways of teaching the subject which are consistent with this view (Monk, 1996; Russell, 1937, 1970)
- the best foundation, somewhat ironically, for a countervailing development in the 21st century of a healthy and appropriate mathematics education is the perspective on mathematics and its teaching articulated by Russell's one-time teacher, colleague, friend, and co-author, Whitehead (Lowe, 1985, 1990; Price, 1956; Whitehead, 1926, 1964)
- among the most prominent and numerous victims of a seemingly global reduction in support, already well under way, for publicly funded education, will be 'orthodox' mathematics teachers (Schank, 1987)
- this will be, to a great extent, an understandable reaction by many taxpayers to a set of experiences which have been largely negative and it will be one dimension of a more general 'fall' from a position of unquestioned educational and societal privilege for mathematics and science (Horgan, 1996; King, 1992)
- improvements in the power and flexibility of the various devices of new information technology will make the 'computer option' for 'orthodox' mathematics instruction not only fiscally, but also cognitively superior to conventional methods (diSessa et al., 1995; Logan, 1995; Papert, 1993)
- an approach to mathematics curriculum which builds on the deep connections the discipline has with all other forms of human activity, particularly language, the arts, and environmental concerns, will permit the development of a number of rich alternative curricula (Dissanayake, 1992; Kappraff, 1991; Noddings, 1992; Osserman, 1995; Pinker, 1995; Upitis et al., 1997; Willis, 1995).

The recent publication of the 'Centenary' issue of the *Mathematical Gazette* (July 1996) is a clear reminder that the last one hundred years has seen an ongoing consideration of a number of fundamental questions about mathematics and the ways in which it might be taught. The historical work of contemporary scholars such as Brian Griffiths (Chapter 13, above), Geoffrey Howson (1982) and Joan Richards (1988), as well as period documents by writers such as John Perry (1900, 1901), give detailed insights into the priorities and procedures of 19th- and early 20th-century mathematics education. It is, however, from biographies and autobiographies that the most vivid pictures of the ways in which mathematical ideas entered the lives of learners can be found. In the first volume of his autobiography, for instance, Bertrand Russell (1968) tells of his early infatuation with Euclid but goes on to note:

> The beginnings of Algebra I found far more difficult, perhaps as a result of bad teaching. I was made to learn by heart: 'The square of the sum of two numbers is equal to the sum of their squares increased by twice their product.' I had not the vaguest idea what this meant, and when I could not remember the words, my tutor threw a book at my head, which did not stimulate my intellect in any way. (p. 34)

In the second chapter of his autobiography, C.S. Lewis (1959) describes what he found as a 10-year-old child in his first school where 'most boys learned nothing and no boy learned much' (p. 29) . The headmaster and proprietor of the school was a man called 'Oldie' whom Lewis recalls as being 'immensely strong, physic-ally dirty' and a man whose treatment of his pupils was harshly punitive. Lewis's classmate, 'P', for making a mistake in a geometry proof was beaten by Oldie who:

> took a run of the room's length at each stroke; but P was the trained sufferer of countless thrashings and no sound escaped him until, towards the end of the torture, there came a noise quite unlike a human utterance. . . . Except at geometry (which he really liked) it might be said that Oldie did not teach at all. He called his class up and asked questions. When the replies were unsatisfactory he said in a low, calm voice. 'Bring me my cane. I see I shall need it.' . . . 'Lessons' of this sort did not take very long; what was to be done with the boys for the rest of the time? Oldie had decided that they could, with least trouble to himself, be made to do arithmetic. Accordingly, when you entered school at nine o'clock you took your slate and began doing sums. Presently you were called up to 'say a lesson'. When that was finished you went back to your place and did more sums — and so forever. (pp. 28–9)

In recent years the print and broadcast media, as well as some of our most gifted writers of fiction, such as the American Russell Banks with *Rule of the Bone* (1994), and the Australian Peter Carey with *The Tax Inspector* (1993), have made the general public much more aware of the issue of child abuse. All too often 19th-century reports of the practices of mathematics teachers have elements which are uncomfortably close to, if not identical with, such abuse. It would be comforting to think that this was only a Victorian phenomenon, perhaps not unlike certain medical practices, now transcended and best forgotten. Contemporary mathem-atics education research has, for understandable reasons, a very slim 'documentary' component. Our reports, when field-based, tend to come from carefully selected sites where the researcher is dependent on the continuing good will of the teacher. On occasion, however, the veil slips and the glimpses one gets in passing are not reassuring.

The August 19th 1996 number of *The New Yorker* magazine, for instance, contains a profile of a Nashville, Tennessee, sixth-grader, Brian Tomberlind, written by Susan Sheehan (1996). Sheehan presumably has no particular mathematics edu-cation axe to grind (the cover describes the article as 'Susan Sheehan on what it's like to be 12 and living on the margin'), so that the prominent role that 'math' (in the form of multiplication tables) plays in this boy's life is all the more sobering. A very high percentage of the interactions between Brian and his father, Nathan, recorded in the article centre on Brian's knowledge of multiplication. The first thing we hear Nathan say to Brian is, 'What about your multiplication tables?' and shortly thereafter we are told that Nathan has forbidden Brian to go out to play after school on Mondays and Wednesdays since 'Less play equals more time for homework in general and math in particular'. A few columns later we have: 'Nathan doesn't check Brian's homework, but he takes out the multiplication flash cards and asks Brian what seven times eight is. Brian hesitates, then gives an incorrect answer.' As the end of the school year grows near, we get the following interchange between Brian and his father:

> The television set is on and Nathan is watching a science program. 'What's seven times nine?' Nathan asks Brian as the show ends and a 'Columbo' rerun begins. 'Seven times nine is . . .'. It is obvious that Brian is stalling for time, but time doesn't buy him the correct answer. 'Go sharpen a pencil and write down your times tables,' Nathan says. Brian goes to the kitchen and starts opening drawers, in search of a knife. Nathan thinks that he is taking too long . . . and slaps Brian hard and noisily on the leg. . . . Back talk angers Nathan. 'I've asked you your multiplication tables for the last few months', he says . . . he sends Brian, still sobbing, off to a bedroom to write the multiplication tables.

Later Nathan tells his son, 'I'm going to ask you those multiplication tables on Monday, and if you don't know them you'll stay indoors all summer.' Brian nods.

As the profile ends, Brian, in the best Hollywood fashion, rises to the occasion at the Monday morning breakfast table:

> 'OK, Bubba,' he says as they wolf down the meal.
> 'What's seven times nine?'
> 'Seven times nine is 63,' Brian says with conviction.
> 'And six times eight?'
> '48.'
> 'What's nine times nine?'
> '81.'
> Victorious, Nathan hugs Brian. Victorious, Brian goes outside to play.

Perhaps Brian will also survive the swamp of algebra and the sea of trigonometry to achieve his goal of going to college. What might he find there? One might hope that he will fare better than the *crème-de-la-crème* of American youth at the Berkeley campus of the University of California in the late 1960s who wrote of their mathematics professor in the student 'anti-calendar':

> [his] lectures were useless and right from the book. . . . He showed no concern for the students. . . . He absolutely refuses to answer questions by completely ignoring the students. (Gibbs et al., 1996, p. 41)

Shortly thereafter, going against the advice of both the chairman and vice-chairman of one of the strongest departments in the world, the professor in question turned his back on a brilliant past and promising future in mathematics to explore other avenues. Exit Ted Kaczynski to the backwoods of Montana and later fame as the 'Unabomber' suspect.

How might we have arrived at this sorry state where candid reports of mathematics learning bring us so frequently to callousness, indifference, tears, and violence? Trying to link the nature and style of an academic discipline to the characteristics of an individual was, until fairly recently, seen as a highly dubious enterprise. The distinguished American sociologist Lewis Feuer (1974), a pioneer in this area, received very negative reviews 20 years ago for his book *Einstein and the Generations of Science*, when he attempted to interpret developments in 20th-century physics through a study of the personal, social, and cultural characteristics of individual scientists. Now, 30 years after Thomas Kuhn's revelations about the nature of scientific practice, such exercises are somewhat less likely to be dismissed out of hand. The mathematics and, to a somewhat lesser extent, the mathematics education practices of our century (think of university students encountering Bourbaki or US teenagers of the 1960s grappling with the tomes of the School Mathematics Study Group) have been absolutist, axiomatic, brittle, clever, cold, disembodied, hard-edged, hierarchical, logical, precise, rational, non-visceral, non-visual, and symbolic. Is it entirely coincidental that so many of these adjectives also fit that long-lived (1872–1970), orphaned aristocrat Bertrand Arthur William, 3rd Earl Russell (Clark, 1978; Monk, 1996; Moorehead, 1993)?

One scholar who would appear to think not is Philip Davis, the prominent applied mathematician and writer (Davis, 1997; Davis and Hersh, 1983). In a recent review (1994) of Caroline Moorehead's biography of Russell, he makes a number of observations which would be consistent with such a claim. Davis begins by noting Russell's comment to a friend that he used, when excited, to calm himself by reciting the three factors of $a^3 + b^3 + c^3 - 3abc$, which he claimed was a more effective practice than thinking of the Ice Age or the goodness of God. Davis wonders:

> ... just where Russell had picked up these factors. Was it as a young student, cramming for admission to Cambridge? I wondered whether he knew that this expression is the determinant of the 3×3 circulant matrix whose first row is [$a\ b\ c$]? And did he know that the factors, linear in a, b, c are the three eigenvalues of the matrix? Did he know that this factorization was historically the seed that, watered by Frobenius, grew into the great subject of group representation theory? ...
> I conjecture that he did not. To Russell, the algebraic expression was a mantra. He saw mathematics as the stabilizing force in the universe; it was the one place where absolute certainty reigned.

It is of interest to note the context of Russell's observation about the utility of this piece of mathematics. He was writing (Russell, 1970, p. 38) in 1941 to Lucy Donnelly to apologize for 'deafening her by shouting in her ear'. He claims to have been 'prickly' but goes on to say that 'that is no excuse for abominable behaviour'. He then reveals his secret technique for calming himself. That Davis is probably correct in suspecting that Russell had only a superficial, technical understanding of this particular algebraic expression is supported by the statement he made (Clark, 1978) about his state of mind having completed his undergraduate examinations:

> The attempt to acquire examination technique had led me to think of mathematics as consisting of artful dodges and ingenious devices and as altogether too much like a 'crossword puzzle'. . . . When I emerged from my last mathematical examination I swore that I would never look at mathematics again and sold all my mathematical books. (p. 50)

This commitment to the absolute characterized more than just Russell's conception of mathematics. Almost 40 years before Russell wrote of his calming technique, Beatrice Webb had recorded these views of her friend (in Moorehead, 1993, p. 109):

> Bertrand Russell's nature is pathetic in its subtle absoluteness: faith in an absolute ethic, absolute beauty and all of the most refined and rarified type . . . the uncompromising way in which he applies these frightens me for his future and for the future of those who love him and whom he loves. Compromise, mitigation, mixed motive, phases of health of body and mind, qualified statements, uncertain feelings, all seem unknown to him.

Davis (1994) sees Russell's influence both in an academic sense, and in more general social terms, as having been extensive:

> Russell's impact on mathematics was enormous. *Principia Mathematica*, a key technical advance between the work of Frege and Gödel, led later to much of the field of theoretical computer science, including AI. It established that most — possibly all — mathematical proofs could be expressed as the formal manipulation of symbols, verifiable, at least in theory, automatically. . . . By establishing that many mathematical concepts can be reduced to set theory, *Principia* has had a great impact on the presentation of mathematics. The tendency of mathematical writers to give definitions in the often questionable form 'a garble is a six-tuple $' is surely traceable to *Principia*. . . . from reading her book I gained confirmation of a long-held feeling that mathematics derives from specific people, and that the particular psychological flavour of a particular individual can infuse that individual's mathematical creations. . . . In the social line, Russell's so-called immoralities have regrettably become standard operating procedures in the Western world, and legal practice, at least in the U.S., has favored individual freedom at the expense of social cohesion. What with computers, social and economic algorithms, and the counterclaim that happiness comes through the lack of constraints, we are living for better or for worse, with wisdom and with folly, in a world that Russell helped make.

Given that he was, for many years, Russell's teacher, colleague, and friend at Cambridge, and the co-author of the text that Davis cites most frequently in the preceding passage, it is quite striking what a different world Alfred North Whitehead (1861–1947) went on to imagine and to help create. The publication of *Principia* coincided with the first of his two major academic moves, to London, first to University College, and then to Imperial College in 1914 as Professor of Applied Mathematics. During those years his interests broadened to include education (1929) and the philosophy of science (1926). In 1924, at 55 years of age, he accepted an invitation to become Professor of Philosophy at Harvard. One of the most accurate ways to characterize Whitehead in a number of dimensions would be to say that he was the complete opposite of Russell. Even during their years of close collaboration the two men had frequently commented on this. 'You Bertie are a nitpicker, and I am a woolgatherer', Whitehead is reputed to have said. Russell's universe, dominated from his earliest years by his desperate yearning for certainty (Monk, 1966), was one of hard edges — he saw it more 'like a heap of shot than a pot of treacle'. Treacle or not, Whitehead's worlds, including his mathematical one, were connected, organic, and active. In *Adventures of Ideas* (1967), he outlined the five prime qualities of civilization as Truth, Beauty, Art, Adventure, and Peace. Education for Whitehead was 'the acquisition of the art of the utilization of knowledge' (1967, p. 4) and knowledge itself 'kept no better than fish'. The greatest danger to true education was inert ideas — 'ideas that are merely received into the mind without being utilised or tested, or thrown into fresh combinations' (1967, p. 1).

For Whitehead, mathematics was 'essentially a study of types of order' (Price, 1956, p. 175) and pure mathematics was 'the most original creation of the human spirit', with its originality consisting in the fact that 'in mathematical science connections between things are exhibited which, apart from the agency of human reason, are extremely unobvious' (Whitehead, 1926, p. 25). He also felt that 'If civilization continues to advance, in the next two thousand years the overwhelming novelty in human thought will be the dominance of mathematical understanding' (Whitehead, 1964, p. 117).

Whitehead reflected in depth and wrote at length about education. In an essay entitled *The Rhythmic Claims of Freedom and Discipline* he wrote that 'the dominant role of education at its beginning and its end is freedom, but there is an intermediate stage of discipline with freedom in subordination' (1929, p. 31). He called these three phases the stages of Romance, Precision, and Generalization and claimed that all mental development was composed of cycles of these stages. In the stage of Romance, the key factor was the development of interest, which Whitehead saw as necessary for attention and apprehension.

In closing, let me point to three projects which, in my view, exemplify the potential of a 'Whiteheadian' perspective. The first is a 'national vision statement', the second a book based on research in a primary classroom, and the third a framework for curriculum development with a strong aesthetic dimension.

In the Summer of 1996 at the third of a series of National Mathematics Education Institutes, a group of teachers, consultants, administrators, and mathematicians undertook the task of creating a concise, well illustrated statement of purpose for Canadian mathematics education. The result of this initiative, *Tomorrow's Mathematics Classroom: A Vision of Mathematics Education for Canada* (Higginson and Flewelling, 1997), is a set of four documents, one each at the primary, junior, intermediate, and senior levels. The stated purposes of these materials are 'to clarify issues and to stimulate debate on desirable directions for curriculum reform'. Each document is a six-page brochure, in which a rich mathematical situation is articulated and developed from student and teacher perspectives. On the 'back' panel of each brochure, there is a common 'vision' of mathematics, teachers and students which reads:

In Tomorrow's Mathematics Classroom Mathematics:
— is experienced as a diverse, powerful, and evolving discipline, as a way of thinking, as a way of communicating, and as a way of perceiving the world, with significant links to all aspects of human experience;
— emerges from, and is made explicit through, exploration and interaction, using a wide range of technologies and resource materials;
— is embedded in potentially-rich learning situations that are interesting and relevant for students and enable all to participate and grow;
— plays three important roles; as a set of useful tools, as one of many disciplines which can contribute to the understanding of a situation, and as a field worthy of study for its own sake, that is, as servant, citizen and sovereign.
The Teacher:
— provides students with stimulating and well-designed learning activities to promote intellectual, emotional and social growth;
— interacts with students to encourage, inspire, challenge, discuss, share, clarify, articulate, reflect, assess, and to celebrate growth and diversity;
— shows the benefits that come from keeping abreast of developments in mathematics and mathematics education;
— acts as someone who assists, someone who confirms and directs, and someone who animates and inspires students by epitomizing the curious, enthusiastic, passionate, and risk-taking learner, that is, as informer, facilitator and artist.
The Students:
— build their own mathematical knowledge through a process of exploration, interaction, and reflection, centered on rich learning activities;
— develop and refine skills in the areas of mathematics, communications, problem-solving, logical reasoning, creative thinking, technology, independence and interdependence;
— use their skills to deal effectively, confidently, sensitively and objectively with situations involving complexity, constraints, diversity, novelty, ambiguity, uncertainty, and error;
— act as individuals who select and use existing rules, understand the principles and patterns underlying these rules, and who create new rules to deal more effectively with situations, that is, as compliers, cognizers, and creators.

A second initiative, which shares many of the Whiteheadian characteristics of the Vision project, in particular a strong social/constructive/aesthetic foundation, is a research project which has recently been published as a book (Upitis et al., 1997). Starting from the work of a researcher (Upitis) in the Vancouver classroom of a grade three–four teacher (Phillips), the text analyses the children's reactions to a set of 'mathematics projects' with strong artistic links, such as music composition, visual art based on geometric patterns, and video animation. Both the content and the form of this book are unusual but one thing which emerges with considerable clarity is the children's consistently strong mathematical insights arising naturally from these artistic tasks, which were approached very much in the spirit of Whitehead's Romance–Precision–Generalization cycle. As one perceptive 9-year-old stated with some passion early in the work on geometric pattern, when commenting on a photograph of a tiled roof that she had brought to class in response to a challenge to find examples of tessellation patterns from outside the classroom, 'no holes is even more important for a roof than a floor' (p. 28).

A third project, now in its very early stages of development, is an extension of the Vancouver experience in that it attempts to create a theoretical framework to support this sort of work. Project MASC (its logo will be the mask-like image of the Lorenz attractor from chaos theory) is an exploration of the potential of approaching mathematics and its learning (M), from a triad of aesthetic (A), social (S), and constructive (C), bases. It assumes that mathematics arises in social contexts, grows through accretive (in a Popperian sense) constructions, and has its value determined mainly by aesthetic criteria. Early investigations of a MASC unit based on the mathematics of origami have been exceptionally rich.

Finally, in a chapter that strongly recommends a reconsideration of the educational ideas of Alfred North Whitehead as a source of renewal for mathematics education as we approach a new century, it is perhaps appropriate to note the perspicacious views of that profound and stimulating thinker as he reflected on the future some seven decades ago in the Lowell Lectures at Harvard University published as *Science and the Modern World* (1926). In the powerful final chapter, entitled 'Requisites for Social Progress' he commented:

> We must expect, therefore, that the future will disclose dangers. It is the business of the future to be dangerous; and it is among the merits of science that it equips the future for its duties. The prosperous middle classes, who ruled the nineteenth century, placed an excessive value upon placidity of existence. They refused to face the necessities for social reform imposed by the new industrial system, and they are now refusing to face the necessities for intellectual reform imposed by the new knowledge. The middle class pessimism over the future of the world comes from a confusion between civilisation and security. (Whitehead, 1926, pp. 298–9)

References

BANKS, R. (1994) *The Rule of the Bone*, New York: Knopf.

CAREY, P. (1993) *The Tax Inspector*, New York: Vintage.

CLARK, R.W. (1978) *The Life of Bertrand Russell*, Harmondsworth: Penguin.

DAVIS, P.J. (1994) 'Russell's real paradox: The wise man is a fool', (A review of Moorehead, 1993), *SIAM News*, **26**, 6, July.

DAVIS, P.J. (1997) *Mathematical Encounters of the Second Kind*, Boston: Birkhauser.

DAVIS, P.J. and HERSH, R. (1983) *The Mathematical Experience*, Harmondsworth: Penguin.

DISESSA, ANDREA, A., HOYLES, C. and NOSS, R. (eds) (1995) *Computers and Exploratory Learning*, Berlin: Springer.

DISSANAYAKE, E. (1992) *Homo Aestheticus: Where Art Comes from and Why*, New York: The Free Press.

FEUER, L.S. (1974) *Einstein and the Generations of Science*, New York: Basic.

GAULIN, C., HODGSON, B.R., WHEELER, D.H. and EGSGARD, J.C. (eds) (1994) *Proceedings of the 7th International Congress on Mathematical Education*, Quebec, Laval University Press.

GIBBS, N., LACAYO, R., MORROW, L. and SMOLOWE, J. (eds) (1996) *Mad Genius: The Odyssey, Pursuit, and Capture of the Unabomber Suspect*, New York: Warner.

GROUWS, D. (ed.) (1992) *Handbook of Research on Mathematics Teaching and Learning*, New York: Macmillan (NCTM).

HIGGINSON, W. and FLEWELLING, G. (eds) (1997) 'Tomorrow's mathematic's classroom: A vision of mathematics education for Canada', MSTE Group: Faculty of Education, Queen's University, Kingston, Canada.

HORGAN, J. (1996) *The End of Science: Facing the Limits of Knowledge in the Twilight of the Scientific Age*, Reading: Addison-Wesley.

HOWSON, A.G. (1982) *A History of Mathematics Education in England*, Cambridge: Cambridge University Press.

HUDSON, L. (1970) *Frames of Mind: Ability, Perception and Self-perception in the Arts and Sciences*, Harmondsworth: Penguin.

KAPPRAFF, J. (1991) *Connections: The Geometric Bridge between Art and Science*, New York: McGraw-Hill.

KING, J.P. (1992) *The Art of Mathematics*, New York: Plenum.

LEWIS, C.S. (1959) *Surprised by Joy: The Shape of My Early Life*, London: Fontana.

LIGHTMAN, A. (1994) *Good Benito*, New York: Pantheon.

LOGAN, R. (1995) *The Fifth Language: Learning a living in the Computer Age*, Toronto: Stoddart.

LOWE, V.A.N. (1985) *Whitehead: The Man and His Work Volume 1: 1861–1910*, Baltimore: Johns Hopkins Press.

LOWE, V.A.N. (1990) *Whitehead: The Man and His Work Volume 2 1910–1947*, Baltimore: Johns Hopkins Press.

MATHEMATICAL SCIENCES EDUCATION BOARD NATIONAL RESEARCH COUNCIL (1990) *Reshaping School Mathematics: A Philosophy and Framework for Curriculum*, Washington: National Academy Press.

MONK, R. (1996) *Bertrand Russell: The Spirit of Solitude*, London: Jonathan Cape.

MOOREHEAD, C. (1993) *Bertrand Russell: A Life*, New York: Viking.

NODDINGS, N. (1992) *The Challenge to Care in Schools: An Alternative Approach to Education*, New York: Teachers College Press.

OSSERMAN, R. (1995) *Poetry of the Universe: A Mathematical Exploration of the Cosmos*, New York: Anchor.

PAPERT, S. (1980) *Mindstorms: Children, Computers, and Powerful Ideas*, New York: Basic.

PAPERT, S. (1993) *The Children's Machine: Rethinking School in the Age of the Computer*, New York: Basic.

PERRY, J. (1900) *England's Neglect of Science*, London: T. Fisher Unwin.

PERRY, J. (ed.) (1901) *Discussion on the Teaching of Mathematics*: British Association Meeting at Glasgow, 1901, London: Macmillan.

PINKER, S. (1995) *The Language Instinct: How the Mind Creates Language*, New York: Harper Perennial.

PRICE, L. (1956) *Dialogues of Alfred North Whitehead*, New York: Mentor.

RICHARDS, J.L. (1988) *Mathematical Visions: The Pursuit of Geometry in Victorian England*, New York: Academic.

RUSSELL, B. (1937) *The Principles of Mathematics*, 2nd edition, London: George Allen and Unwin.

RUSSELL, B. (1968) *The Autobiography of Bertrand Russell: 1872–1914*, London: Bantam.

RUSSELL. B. (1970) *The Autobiography of Bertrand Russell: The Final Years: 1944–1969*, London: Bantam.

SCHANK, R. (1987) 'Let's eliminate math from schools', *Whole Earth Rev.*, Summer, pp. 58–62.

SCHIFTER, D. (ed.) (1996) *What's Happening in Math Class? Volume 2: Reconstructing Professional Identities*, New York: Teachers College Press.

SHEEHAN, S. (1996) 'Kid, twelve', *The New Yorker*, August 19, pp. 50–60.

STODOLSKY, S.S. (1988) *The Subject Matters: Classroom Activity in Math and Social Studies*, Chicago: University of Chicago Press.

THURSTON, W. (1990) 'Mathematical education', *Notices of the American Mathematical Society*, **37**, 7, September, pp. 844–50.

UPITIS, R., PHILLIPS, E. and HIGGINSON, W. (1997) *Creative Mathematics: Exploring Children's Understanding*, London and New York: Routledge.

WADDINGTON, C.H. (1977) *Tools for Thought*, St Albans: Paladin.

WHITEHEAD, A.N. (1926) *Science and the Modern World*, New York: Macmillan.

WHITEHEAD, A.N. (1948) *An Introduction to Mathematics*, London: Oxford University Press.

WHITEHEAD, A.N. (1964) *Science and Philosophy*, Paterson, NJ: Littlefield, Adams.

WHITEHEAD, A.N. (1967) *Adventures of Ideas*, New York: The Free Press.

WILLIS, D. (1995) *The Sand Dollar and the Slide Rule: Drawing Blueprints from Nature*, Reading: Addison-Wesley.

Dedication

This chapter is dedicated to Dr A. John Coleman, Head of the Department of Mathematics at Queen's University (1961–1980), teacher and colleague, mentor and continuing model, exemplar and enthusiast in many fields, for intimations of wider worlds, including the writings of ANW.

Chapter 15

Training Today the Teacher of Tomorrow

Bernard Cornu

The evolution of society will have profound consequences for education and, in particular, teaching as a profession will be subject to change. But it is not easy to know exactly what this profession will be like in 10 or 20 years' time. Preparing today the teacher of tomorrow is a huge challenge for universities and colleges: they must prepare future teachers to acquire new competencies that will enable them to evolve and adapt their skills throughout their career.

Society Is Evolving

Society is evolving very rapidly, particularly under the influence of information and communication technologies. New technologies are penetrating all aspects of life, bringing new tools, new concepts, and new ways of thinking. They are becoming increasingly integrated into everyday life. Up until now, changes in society in general have been more marked than changes in education. One of the questions we must ask ourselves is how far the integration of new technologies into education must follow the changes in society, or are there alternative visions. But if the latter is the case, there is the problem of reducing the gap between what happens in society and in education.

Education Is Changing

There are many reasons why education is changing. The following three are particularly important and have consequences for teacher education.

Social and Economic Causes

Democratization of education in most countries has dramatically increased the numbers and diversity of pupils. Heterogeneity is increasing in schools and classes. Additionally, the main problems of society — and cities — are penetrating schools:

unemployment has many consequences for the way pupils live, and for the way they look at their future. Social conflicts also are penetrating schools: security and delinquency raise many questions for education institutions. Teachers therefore need to develop a diversified set of new competencies, not necessarily directly linked with knowledge and its acquisition.

Information and Communication Technologies (ICT)

New technologies influence education in many ways, the most visible being the hardware and software now available in schools, and all the activities using ICT which are now provided for pupils. But ICT has (potentially at least) a fundamental influence on school subjects themselves, on knowledge, on curricula, on the way specialists work, on the way one can teach, on the way pupils work (alone or with others) and on the way pupils learn. These influences have consequences for the competencies teachers need which in turn have implications for teacher education.

The Influence of Educational Research

Educational sciences, didactics, and pedagogy are all providing information on the routes to the acquisition of new concepts and abilities. Considerable progress is being made in educational research, which can offer insights on tools and methods for teaching. Educational research also points to how new technologies can be integrated into practice, and most of the best tools, software, and experiments using ICT in education are those where new technologies have been combined with detailed and systematic study of teaching or learning. It is not enough to be successful in one class, in one experiment: the conditions for reproducibility of situations must be clarified and analysed. Thus educational research is gaining in importance and in prestige, even though it is not in many countries accorded the same status as research in other fields.

The Role of the Teacher Is Changing

It is not easy to describe what the profession of teacher will involve in the future. The classical way teachers work (alone with the pupils in the classroom for teaching, alone at home for marking and preparing lessons) will certainly change. The way teachers work with their pupils may become more diverse — with the whole class, with a small group, with pupils individually — and the way teachers work with colleagues also is evolving, with the development of 'team working'. How teachers work in school also is changing. The school of tomorrow may be quite different from what it is now in terms of its organization of rooms, equipment, and facilities. This may help to make teaching more of a profession. Certainly the roles of the teacher and the competencies he or she needs will become more wide-ranging. They may include some or all of the following:

- A teacher must master the knowledge to be transmitted.
- A teacher must master the teaching and learning processes.
- A teacher must be able to create and develop his or her teaching; he or she must have the competency of a technician and an engineer.
- A teacher must continuously be able to build up his or her own competencies.
- A teacher must be able to use the results of educational research, and to question research.
- A teacher must transmit to pupils a love for learning and an appetite for knowledge.
- A teacher must arouse the curiosity of the pupils.
- A teacher must prepare and mould the citizens of tomorrow: their judgment, their freedom.
- A teacher must prepare the pupils to pass their examinations (a short-term objective, compared with the previous one).
- A teacher must sometimes replace the parents' authority when they fail.
- A teacher must apply and put into practice the educational policy of the Minister.
- A teacher must be the guarantor of equity and equality for all pupils.
- A teacher must transmit the fundamental values of a society.
- A teacher must be an adviser.
- A teacher must be an organizer.
- A teacher must be a leader and a manager.
- A teacher must be an evaluator.
- A teacher must be able to work alone (preparing lessons and marking work and examinations).
- A teacher must be able to work in teams with colleagues (for example, in consultation, preparation of lessons, sharing competencies, reflection on practices, and research).
- A teacher will have to work at home as well as at school.
- A teacher must be able to work in a laboratory environment, because of the need to incorporate information and communication technologies.
- A teacher must be able to work with the whole class, but also with small groups, and with individual pupils.
- A teacher must be able to evolve and adapt.
- A teacher must manage the fact that increasingly he or she will not be the only one to transmit knowledge: he or she will have to manage access to knowledge, to help pupils organize knowledge.
- A teacher has to help pupils to conceptualize, theorize, model, and build abstractions.

It is clear that acquiring such a broad set of competencies is impossible for any one individual and so the question of the relationship between individual and collective competency is raised. Do we need every teacher to be competent in everything, or do we need teams among which these competencies are shared?

Teacher Education Is Changing

As education is changing, teacher education, at least in France, is considered to be a crucially important field: it is the key point in managing the changes in education and preparing the educational system of tomorrow. Most governments are aware of the importance of teacher education and are trying to adapt it to the new needs. In France, teacher education was radically reformed in 1990.

The French System after the 1990 Reform

Before 1990, primary and secondary teachers were trained in separate institutions. Primary teachers were trained in *écoles normales*, where they received pedagogical training for two years. Écoles normales had almost no link with universities, and functioned as a 'closed world' relating only to the primary educational system. Secondary teachers, on the other hand, were trained at university, but took courses only in their subject with no professional or pedagogical preparation. After they were recruited, and during their first year of professional activity (with a timetable reduced to one third), they took one year in a pedagogical centre where they were expected mainly to attend lectures by inspectors.

The main aims of the 1990 reform were to train future teachers in a university institution, to train primary and secondary teachers in the same institution, and to give all future teachers a professional training. In 1990, new institutes were created: the IUFM (Instituts Universitaires de Formation des Maîtres: University Institutes for Teacher Education). There are 29 such institutes in France, which train all future teachers. As a consequence of the reform, the period of study to train primary teachers is of the same length as that for secondary teachers, and primary and secondary teachers are now paid the same salaries. These two changes have been crucial points in the reform, not least because they have accorded primary teachers the same status as their secondary colleagues.

In France recruitment and training are linked. Future teachers have first to complete three years at university, studying generally only one subject, where they receive a 'licence' (equivalent to a Bachelor's Degree). They then go to the IUFM for two years for their professional training. There is a selection process for entering the IUFM; in Grenoble, for instance, 7000 students applied and 1500 were admitted in the first year. At the end of the first year at IUFM, students take one of the competitive examinations organized by the state for recruiting teachers. If they succeed, they have a second year at IUFM (some students may pass the recruitment exam as 'free candidates', having prepared it on their own, not in an IUFM; they then take the second year at IUFM). Students are recruited as future teachers at the end of the first year, at which time they are awarded the status of civil servant and receive a salary. At the end of the second year, after an evaluation, they are given a post in a school.

The content of the training includes the study of an academic area, pedagogy, didactics, general tools, and personal training. It includes interaction between theory and practice, with practice periods in schools. Seminars are offered for reflection on and analysis of particular teaching situations encountered.

The first year is devoted mainly to preparation for the competitive examination. Future primary teachers have to study many different subjects, with courses orientated towards pedagogical and didactical approaches. Future secondary teachers study one subject only, usually in a highly academic way, although they too have practice periods in schools.

The second year has a more professional orientation, with students spending about one third of their time in schools, where they teach with full responsibility. They also take courses at the Institute, and one of the main issues is to link these courses with what happens in schools. They have to write a personal essay (*mémoire*), which is a research project on the problems encountered in their teaching practice. This research is seen as a key tool to develop the reflective practitioner.

The IUFM also contribute to in-service teacher training as well as participating in educational research in collaboration with universities.

Among all the issues faced by IUFM, the following are the most important:

- What weight should be attributed respectively to subject content and pedagogy in the curriculum, and what are the interactions between the two?
- What role should the human and social sciences (for example, psychology, sociology, philosophy) play in teacher education and how should they be taught?
- What role should be attributed respectively to theory (courses at the Institute) and practice (periods in schools)? What is the interplay between the two? How does theory question practice and how does practice nourish theory in a dynamic and reciprocal process?
- What roles are given respectively to staff in the Institute and tutors in schools, and what kind of collaboration between them with regard to supervising students is the most effective for teaching practice?

It is interesting to note that whilst Britain, with its pragmatic and empirical culture, is increasing still further its heavy emphasis on practical training in schools and de-emphasizing theory, France, which has an academic tradition in teacher training, is also placing more importance on developing the practical side but within a framework that favours a dynamic interplay between theory and practice.

Since they know that they will be confronted with practical teaching, future teachers' expectations prior to their first experience are for short-term inputs: they would like to be given recipes for teaching 'the' right way to teach such and such a topic. They greatly enjoy and value the practice periods in schools, but they are often disappointed by some courses at the Institute which they find too theoretical, too far from direct application. It is only one or two years later that they understand how fundamental inputs prepare them for long-term competency, and help them to reflect and to build that competency.

Mathematics and the Role of Mathematics in Society

New technologies have opened windows on new tools and ways of working. Links between mathematics and computer science have led to the development of new concepts and to the exploration of fresh fields. The possibility of experimenting, modelling, and visualizing in mathematics has changed the way mathematicians work. Mathematics teachers therefore need new competencies, linked with these social evolutions and new technologies. In France, the Ministry has recently published the competencies mathematics teachers should have at the beginning of their career. There are three main categories:

- Mathematical competencies, including mastering what happens in the class-room, such as organizing a lesson, organizing work and participation of pupils, and managing time. These competencies also include mastering the knowledge to be taught and reflecting on mathematics; ensuring a good balance between the different parts of the curriculum; emphasizing concepts, methods, and links with other disciplines; mastering the use of pedagogical tools. Little is said about new technologies although pocket calculators and computers are mentioned as pedagogical tools to be used.
- Competencies in building relationships with pupils and colleagues: organizing the work of the pupils throughout the year; evaluating; adapting the teaching to the pupils; helping pupils in their personal work; being prepared to work in a team with colleagues.
- Competencies with respect to the educational system.

There is a long tradition in France of educational research and in-service training for mathematics teachers and the IUFM, which are in charge of pre-service training, benefit from this tradition.

Future primary teachers must take courses in mathematics. They must master the mathematical knowledge necessary in order to teach mathematics at school; they must acquire the didactical competencies necessary for managing learning; and they must reflect on mathematical culture and its impact on school. Primary and secondary teachers are trained to use new technologies (computers as tools for the teacher, and as tools for mathematics; the didactical impact of new technologies; the use of the main software, for example spreadsheets, graphers, symbolic systems, and dynamic geometry software).

The competitive examination through which secondary mathematics teachers are recruited by the State is based mainly on mathematics. It includes a part where candidates work on a folder provided by the examiners, which contains a theme on which the candidate must produce examples and exercises; extracts from the curriculum; and a list of documents available during the examination. Work on this folder was intended to be the 'professional' part of the examination, but in fact it is closer to mathematics than to teaching.

Some Core Principles

- There is not just one way to be a good teacher: pedagogic styles and pedagogic strategies are diverse, and each teacher must build his or her own strategies. Therefore diversity is essential in teacher education.
- It is not possible to provide future teachers with all the competencies they need for their career, so the ability to adapt and evolve is essential. Increasingly, in-service training will be an important component of the teaching profession.
- Teachers usually reproduce the way they were taught themselves: this means that methods are as important as content in initial teacher training. For instance, one does not learn team work through courses about team work, but by actually practising team work. Similarly, actually using information and communication technologies in teacher education is more important than courses about new technologies.

Trends and Perspectives

The teaching profession is undergoing profound change, and teacher education is vital for its evolution. But there are many problems, such as how to cope with universal change (one must train not just some teachers, or the best ones, to acquire new competencies, but all teachers) and the difficulty of integrating new competencies into teacher education. Not least, the teacher trainers need these new competencies themselves.

Because of the pyramid of ages a large number of teachers will be recruited in the next 10 years in France, and the number of candidates and the competition for places for the teaching profession mean that the entry level will improve. This situation provides us with an excellent opportunity to introduce changes in education through teacher education. Thus reflection about teacher education, its contents and its methods, is very prevalent in our country.

Articulation between theory and practice in teacher education is one of the main topics discussed. Integrating information and communication technologies into teacher education also is a key point. The IUFM are elaborating a policy for this to take account of equipment, the different uses of ICT, the implementation of networks, and the development of research and production. One of the major difficulties is to help staff to achieve competence in integrating ICT into their practice. We are encountering a huge problem in the training of trainers. It is not enough to have some staff giving courses about the use and integration of ICT: we need ICT to be integrated into the whole training and we need every member of staff to undertake this integration. Teacher training in general, and ICT in particular, may break the syndrome of isolation and encourage interaction between teachers in different institutions, and even different countries — but this takes time.

Educational research is essential for the evolution of education. In France, this kind of research is not considered to be as important or as serious as research in classical subjects. We are trying to convince first the ministerial authorities, but also university staff and the general public, that educational research is *necessary* for education, and that a policy must be put in place in order to promote and develop educational research. A first step has been taken, with the creation by the Minister of Education of a National Committee for Coordination of Educational Research. It is clear that the IUFM must build up their contribution to educational research, and must ensure that most of their staff participate in this activity.

Chapter 16

Reconstructing Professional Judgment in Mathematics Education: From Good Practice to Warranted Practice

Kenneth Ruthven

The central challenge currently facing school mathematics in Britain — at both local and national levels — is to meet public expectations not just of greater pupil achievement, but of greater professional accountability. At school level, this process has been driven by open enrolment and the strengthened role of parents in school governance, fuelled by the publication of examination results and inspection reports. At national level, particular attention has been focused on mathematics, not simply because it is seen as a key factor underpinning economic performance, but because it is the subject area in which international comparisons of pupil achievement have been both extensive and unfavourable. Public discussion has all too readily attributed poor performance to features of school organization, curriculum design, technology use, or teaching method. This issue is, of course, a longstanding one. In particular, it has helped to secure sponsorship for successive attempts to revise — and revive — school mathematics, the most recent dating back to the Cockcroft Report (Cockcroft, 1982).

Cockcroft and the Construction of 'Good Practice'

Whatever view one now takes of the Cockcroft recommendations, the report remains a remarkable document, not only for the extent of the consultations and deliberations on which it drew, but for attempting to ground its conclusions in an appropriate body of systematic evidence, ideas, and argument about mathematics education. The influence of Cockcroft on the subsequent development of official policies has been considerable. In particular, it is Cockcroft's conclusions on the place of 'exposition, discussion, appropriate practical work, problem solving, investigation, consolidation, and practice' within mathematics teaching (Cockcroft, 1982, 243) which has come to be regarded as the principal Cockcroft commandment: preached by Sir Keith Joseph's 'mathematics missionaries' through the initiatives of the eighties intended to 'develop and encourage "good practice"' (Ahmed, 1987, vii); reaffirmed at the start of Kenneth Baker's great crusade by the National Curriculum Mathematics Working Group; 'The Cockcroft Report served to highlight and disseminate good practice in our schools' (DES/WO, 1988, p. 7); 'Our recommendations have been much influenced by it and we endorse and approve developments in the classroom such as practical work, problem solving and investigative work which have already taken place because of it' (DES/WO, 1988, p. 20); invoked by the inspectorial inquisition of the 1990s: 'The one over-riding feature of good practice in mathematics within a school as a whole ... was the variety of teaching approaches used and an appropriate balance within those approaches', (HMI, 1992, p. 21).

These quotations illustrate the prominence which the appeal to 'good practice' has come to play in the discourse of reform. For many teachers, this arrogation of the term is a professional impertinence. And this uncritical usage has foreclosed what Cockcroft saw as a far from clear-cut issue: 'We are aware that there are some teachers who would wish us to indicate a definitive style for the teaching of mathematics, but we do not believe that this is either desirable or possible. Approaches to the teaching of a particular piece of mathematics need to be related to the topic itself and to the abilities and experience of both teachers and pupils' (Cockcroft, 1982, p. 71).

This presumptive language has permitted a shift from argument to advocacy with the official acceptance of Cockcroft, and from advocacy to authority with the advent of the National Curriculum. As HMI (Her Majesty's Inspectors) note, with characteristically straight face: 'The introduction of the National Curriculum provided not only encouragement but also a statutory requirement for all schools to develop their curricula according to these guidelines' (HMI, 1991, p. 21). It is this predominance of advocacy and authority over argument which is the central problem of any idea of 'good practice', whether it is sanctioned by custom (how it has always been done); by convention (how everyone else does it); by canon (how Cockcroft and the National Curriculum say it should be done); or by conviction (how we believe it ought to be done).

The National Curriculum, however, brought an important innovation in the discourse of reform. Denied the opportunity to legislate directly on teaching approaches, the Mathematics Working Group insisted on a component of the curriculum which would oblige schools to attend to the reform agenda. Originally termed 'practical applications of mathematics' (DES/WO, 1988, p. 13), eventually to become 'using and applying mathematics' (DES/WO, 1991, p. 1), the Working Group were insistent that it was not only this component which 'requires a wide range of teaching and learning approaches' (DES/WO, 1988, p. 14).

Both school inspections and the official evaluation of the implementation of the National Curriculum, have established the limited impact of this reform. HMI report that, at primary level:

> Through lack of previous teaching and direct experience by primary teachers, the important issues of using and applying mathematics were underdeveloped. Many teachers assumed that they were automatically included in whatever they were doing, so coverage was superficial. (HMI, 1992, p. 18)

At secondary level:

> About a third of schools approached [the 'using and applying mathematics' com-
> ponents] as they were intended to be: as part of the whole mathematics curriculum,
> permeating each activity in some way. Another third began to address them
> through adding investigational work, problem solving and practical activities to
> their curriculum. The remainder ignored them or assumed, incorrectly, that they
> were included in whatever they were doing. (HMI, 1992, p. 19).

These outcomes are not surprising, since this reform appears to have replicated
most of the features known to undermine the successful implementation of change
in education (Gross et al., 1971): vagueness over the nature of the innovation and
its rationale; superficial guidance combined with limited opportunities for teachers
to prepare themselves; absence of readily identifiable classroom materials to support
implementation; little desire amongst teachers for the change and few incentives.

RAMP and the Promotion of 'Reflective Practice'

This attempt at reform by central regulation contrasts strikingly with the social
influence approach adopted by the major post-Cockcroft initiatives to promote
change in classroom practice. The LAMP, and then RAMP, projects were based on
the principle that:

> Improvements and change can only be sustained if teachers in the classroom
> believe in and support the developments taking place. Impositions from above are
> therefore unlikely to work. Dissemination must always be firmly rooted in the
> personal experiences of teachers in their classrooms. This is achieved through a
> constantly growing and developing network of personal contact and involvement.
> (Ahmed, 1987, pp. 81–2).

This emphasis is well grounded in what we know about creating the motivation and the means for significant change in teaching (Fullan, 1991). But it also
introduces an important epistemological commitment.

Within these projects:

> teacher-researchers explored possibilities and ideas within their own classrooms,
> involved their colleagues through discussion and collaborative teaching and kept
> personal records. An important ... strategy ... involves individuals writing and
> talking about their own situations and experiences in a personal and uninhibited
> way. These 'case studies' ... prove invaluable to other teachers. By their nature
> they are not prescriptive. Within each experience there are ingredients which other
> teachers may identify as being transferable to their own classroom. Through such
> discussion and personal experimentation the processes of questioning, experiment-
> ing, reflecting and evaluating become embedded in a teacher's practice. These
> processes become a continuous research cycle where evaluation leads to further
> questioning, which leads to further experimentation, reflection, evaluation and so
> on. This cycle is far from being a 'clinical' or 'academic' one. For teachers to

reflect so intensely on their own classroom practice, beliefs and assumptions, both individually and in working groups, involves a good deal of emotional investment. (Ahmed, 1987, p. 7)

In short, the project methodology appeals to ideas of 'action research' and 'reflective practice'.

In a generally sympathetic account, Michelle Selinger drew on her experience as a participant observer in the activities of a local RAMP group over the course of one school year. After attending a national conference she noted:

On the surface it would appear that LAMP and RAMP have successfully changed many teachers' attitudes to the way in which mathematics is taught in schools. There are teachers who are now questioning their previous practice and discussing ways in which they can evolve new strategies and attempt to help children learn mathematics more effectively and successfully. However, I would question the extent to which it has actually changed classroom practice and the depth to which the ideas have been assimilated by the teachers involved. (Selinger, 1987, p. 21)

To explore these issues more systematically, Selinger carried out case-studies of two of the teacher-researchers in the local RAMP group. From these she drew conclusions about the success of the project in effecting change in four areas:

The first was the level of professional awareness of the teacher-researchers: [they] have changed their attitudes and their perceptions. . . . [They] have examined their teaching approaches and through discussion with other members of the group have been encouraged to try ideas out in their classroom. The second area . . . was the learning environment of the classroom: [they] have to some extent improved the environment by becoming increasingly aware of the pupils' needs and the way in which they learn. . . . However . . . the third area which concerns the achievement and motivation of pupils is . . . more difficult to assess since these teacher-researchers have not sufficiently taken into account the reactions of their pupils. They are aware that some pupils have increased their motivation, but have missed the reactions of others. . . . Dissemination was the fourth area. . . . As a result of their participation in RAMP, the teacher-researchers considerably altered their perceptions of what makes inservice provision effective. . . . They had become aware that change was a slow process and that many teachers were conservative and therefore unable to change overnight. They now believe effective inservice strategies should be provided through active participation of the recipients. (Selinger, 1987, pp. 57–9)

What emerges from these observations is the central epistemological problem of 'reflective practice': while personal experience and reflection can confer an important subjective validity on ideas, how can they be triangulated with the experiences and ideas of others, and with evidence systematically collected and analysed according to explicit principles and procedures? In effect, what Selinger highlights is a limited range of triangulation within the project — predominantly through sharing ideas within the in-group of participants; and the danger that this may give rise to a corresponding tendency to discount dissonant perspectives from out-groups — in this case, pupils and other teachers.

Indicators and the Identification of 'Effective Practice'

From the dogmatism of 'good practice' and the subjectivism of 'reflective practice' the UK system now seems to be lurching towards the empiricism of 'effective practice'. Essentially, this approach emphasizes the role of performance indicators — most commonly of pupil achievement — in guiding educational practice. A weaker version of this approach is based on the view that: 'Providing clear and fair feedback to schools on their performance may be a feasible way to improve schools — letting schools improve themselves' (Fitz-Gibbon, 1992, p. 98). A stronger version seeks to derive general recommendations from the practice of particularly effective systems, schools, or teachers.

Already, the publication of school-level data on pupil performance is encouraging schools to advance their standing in National Curriculum assessment and public examinations. Popular responses are to teach increasingly to the test; to give pupils more regular practice of test-taking; and to give special attention to pupils working at those level or grade boundaries linked to critical school indicators. But how can schools move beyond these essentially cosmetic measures to bring more substantial improvement? Refinement of the performance indicators so as to present test and examination results in a form which indicates 'value added' should help to distinguish the effects of teaching from the entry characteristics of pupils. But this still begs the central question of how to improve teaching.

One prospective source is the burgeoning school effectiveness literature. To date, however, such studies have tended to focus on whole-school characteristics of leadership, organization, and ethos rather than on classroom processes and their tailoring to specific curricular areas. None the less, the accumulation of evidence that the great majority of variation between schools is due to classroom variation (Reynolds and Packer, 1992) is encouraging greater interest in classroom practice; and findings that effects are relatively strong in mathematics are focusing attention here (Mortimore et al., 1988; Fitz-Gibbon, 1992).

In the mean time, some have sought to derive recommendations for classroom practice from the findings of international studies of mathematical achievement. There has been a rash of speculative claims, usually based on uncritical comparisons between a conveniently restricted group of systems on a similarly limited set of outcomes and factors. A more fastidious IAEP study recently concluded that: 'the findings describing teaching practices . . . do not identify any particular practice that is common to all high-performing populations' (Lapointe et al., 1992, p. 51). On the contrary, it was possible to find both high- and low-achieving populations with high values on any of the classroom process factors which were examined — chiefly concerned with the frequency of exposition, practice, and testing and the use of concrete materials, calculators, and computers. Because the 'system' variable confounds a complex of educational and cultural differences, and may be associated with systematic biases in other indices, the IAEP went on to conduct within-system analyses of achievement, with hardly more conclusive findings. The SIMS project conducted a study of achievement *gains* over one school year (Schmidt and Burstein, 1993), finding notably fewer significant effects related to characteristics of classroom instruction than did the IAEP study of achievement *levels*. The two studies concur that there was no general trend linking teaching practices to pupil achievement.

There are important conceptual weaknesses in these international studies of educational achievement; weaknesses to which school effectiveness studies and educational policy discussions also are prone. First, they may focus on superficial aspects of classroom process at the expense of more important underlying factors; notably aspects not readily identifiable through the self-report questionnaires used to gather information:

> The simple characteristics of instruction have never predicted instructional effectiveness, although this is where many of our reform efforts have been centred. The issue is not individualized instruction or small-group instruction, but rather the quality of thought and effort that occur within these structures. Different classroom strategies can work; the key is quality of instruction, and to find that key we must observe classroom teaching directly. (Good and Biddle, 1988, p. 116)

Second, all the uncertainties of correlational studies remain: even where school effectiveness studies appear to highlight characteristics common to effective schools, this does not establish that other schools will become more effective by taking on these characteristics. As yet there have been few attempts, and apparently less success, in translating the findings of such research into strategies for improvement (Reynolds, 1992).

A more promising source of guidance on improving the effectiveness of teaching is research into classroom processes and their effects. Here in particular, some researchers have been able to identify core features of effective teaching, and then to test the robustness of their findings through intervention studies, leading to the identification of what can be broadly characterized as *active teaching*. (For a general overview see Scheerens, 1992; Creemers, 1994; and, for a specifically mathematics-focused account, Good and Biddle, 1988.)

> Teachers whose students made higher gains were much more active in presenting concepts, explaining the meaning of these concepts, providing appropriate practice activities, and monitoring these activities prior to assigning seatwork. (Good and Biddle, 1988, p. 130)

These conclusions, nevertheless, should not be overgeneralized:

> Some of the control teachers in our studies have obtained high levels of student achievement using instructional systems that differed from those in the program we developed. (Good and Biddle, 1988, p. 131)

One of the limitations of these studies is that they focus on generic pedagogical concepts, and so take no direct account of the subject or topic being taught. This, however, has been the focus of another developing body of research into the practice of highly effective teachers (Leinhardt, 1988). Essentially, this research starts from the finding that it is not just the substance of these teachers' didactical knowledge that is important, but the quality of its organization into coherent topic scripts which guide lesson planning and shape interaction with pupils. Expert teachers' lesson agendas are compact, coherent and complete, and locate the lesson within a topic script. Lesson agendas consist of action segments identifying what teacher and pupils should be doing at each stage of the lesson, linked to critical tests used to determine whether or not to continue from one stage to the next. Finally, expert teachers provide more coherent explanations, explicitly related to underlying mathematical principles.

Although such studies are starting to provide a valuable knowledge-base for the improvement of teaching, there are some important limitations to the construct of 'effective practice'. First, by focusing on comparisons between schools or systems, and adopting established performance indicators, effectiveness analyses restrict themselves to the known and given. At best, they can enable schools to improve within the parameters of this familiar world. Hence some of the criticisms that they are predisposed towards a conservative view of the goals and processes of schooling (Lampert, 1988). Second, there is a recurring danger that findings may prove to be artefacts of the analytical techniques and performance indicators employed. Already it has been recognized that classroom effects may be lost or overlooked in studies which focus on school effects (Dunkin and Biddle, 1974; Reynolds and Packer, 1992). Equally, where the emphasis is on broad, aggregate measures, this tends to marginalize the fine texture of subject teaching, emphasizing more global pedagogical issues over more local didactical ones.

Scrutiny and the Substantiation of 'Warranted Practice'

At the core of each of the constructs I have discussed — but largely implicit in its operation — is an epistemology of professional judgment. Each construct has important strengths as well as serious weaknesses. The strength of 'good practice' is in holding out a new vision of school mathematics; its weakness is uncritical judgment based on commitment to that vision. The strength of 'reflective practice' is in recognizing the importance of personal experience in changing practice; its weakness is untriangulated judgment on the basis of experience alone. The strength of 'effective practice' is in insisting that judgments about practice should be supported by evidence; its weakness is that such evidence and judgment may be too readily bounded by the familiar and accepted.

In my view, sustained improvement and professional accountability in school mathematics call for a reconstruction of professional judgment on a more adequate — and more explicit — epistemological base: to create what I will term 'warranted practice'. The qualifier 'warranted' carries two important senses. The first — borrowed from philosophical discourse — is of providing reasoned grounds for the practice as intended. The second — borrowed from commercial discourse — is of assuring that the practice as implemented does indeed realize its claims.

The central procedural principles for the warranting of practice might be as follows:

- articulation of a clear operational model for practice, explicitly indicating the ends to be sought and the means to be employed
- provision of a coherent rationale for the model, showing how its intended operation is well grounded in wider professional knowledge and takes account of evidence from its implementation
- monitoring of practice, based on principles of triangulation: of implementation against intention; of experience against evidence; across internal participants and against external standards
- continuing analysis and revaluation of the operational model in the light of evidence from monitoring practice, and of developments in professional knowledge
- warranting of practice at each managerial level of the educational system, in the light of circumstances at that and lower levels.

It is important to emphasize that the idea of warranted practice refers not to the particular content of practice, but to the forms of scrutiny to which it is subjected. Indeed, it is precisely to centre attention on this process of scrutiny that I will talk of the 'warranting of practice' rather than 'warranted practice'.

The most important level for the warranting of practice is that of the school. Certainly this is a corollary of a view of schools as publicly accountable, self-managing institutions. Warranting relates directly to the processes of planning, developing, monitoring, and accounting for their practice which schools are already starting to accept as their responsibility. In particular warranting links school plans and classroom practice in a recurring development and research cycle. But it calls for a far higher degree of explicitness about the intentions of practice, a greater concern for its grounding, and a deeper scrutiny of its implementation than is current. Warranting is, of course, equally applicable to the teaching of mathematics in colleges and universities and to the training of teachers. Similarly, one would expect national bodies and agencies which play a role in shaping or evaluating the practice of schools, colleges, and universities to warrant their practice — and their prescriptions for, and evaluations of, the practice of others — no less rigorously.

Clearly, the warranting of practice would benefit enormously from an appropriate research base. Mike Askew and Dylan Wiliam have recently completed a review of research into mathematics teaching, aimed at supporting teachers in pre-service and in-service training. They concentrated on studies conducted in real classrooms which have demonstrated significant impact on the quality of pupils' achievement in, or attitudes to, mathematics. In order to ensure the quality of the research selected, they confined their attention largely to work reported in refereed journals after peer review. They make two important observations:

> There have been many exciting and innovative [British] curriculum developments in mathematics . . . but, unfortunately, even where careful evaluations were carried out these were not reported in refereed journals subject to peer review.

> Most of the research cited here has been conducted in the United States — it has been a sobering experience to realise how little British research there is on important issues in teaching and learning. (Askew and Wiliam, 1995, p. 1)

Even in the United States, Jere Brophy has questioned the extent to which the predominant models of mathematics education research are capable of contributing to the improvement of practice:

> [Mathematics educators] will have to provide much more detailed guidelines about the kinds of teaching they see as optimal, as well as to amass convincing evidence in support of their ideas, if they expect the bulk of the educational community to accept them. Philosophical and theoretical exegesis is not enough. Nor is empirical research [which] focuses on student learning . . . but not on instruction itself . . . [or does] not include adequate distinctions between curriculum and instruction, adequate provisions for assessing processes and linking them to outcomes, and adequate sampling to allow the identification of principles that generalise beyond unique contexts and apply to typical classroom settings. (Brophy, 1986, p. 367)

David Hargreaves has recently compared the educational and medical professions (Hargreaves, 1996). He notes how practice in both is profoundly people-centred and often necessarily pragmatic. What is notably different is the place of research and researchers within the two professions. In medicine, much research is conducted by practitioners and is directly aimed at improving practice; other practitioners have an immediate incentive to take note of — and discuss — such research, and their familiarity with the research process helps them to extract ideas, methods, and findings and tailor them to their particular situation. In education, it is extremely rare to find this coincidence of roles and interests within what are largely distinct groups of practitioners and researchers.

Hargreaves also points to corresponding differences in professional education. Teachers — and with them teacher educators — still expect to devise or adopt much of their professional practice by personal preference and experiment, occasionally guided by the accumulated wisdom of their seniors, but not by codified records of — and commentaries on — expert practice, or a corpus of applied research addressing recurring professional problems and concerns. For hospital doctors, acquisition of professional expertise means becoming more effective not just in terms of practical skills, but also by familiarity with relevant research, through a protracted period of supervised practice during which increasingly demanding responsibilities are gradually taken on. In either profession, if practitioners are to articulate, substantiate, analyse, evaluate and improve their practice, they require a form of training which comprises more than experience and apprenticeship.

As Donald McIntyre has argued, from the start of their careers, teachers should be encouraged to engage in practical theorising about teaching:

> Initial teacher education should be concerned with the critical examination, development and experimental use of ideas from many sources, including both the elucidated practice of experienced teachers and also a diverse theoretical and research-based literature, i.e. with theorising about practice. (McIntyre, 1995a, pp. 366–7)

Indeed, for McIntyre (1995b), this provides one of the few good grounds for universities' continuing involvement in teacher education.

Towards Professional Integration and the Systematic Improvement of Practice

Essentially, these observations suggest that educational improvement is likely to depend on a much higher degree of integration between the practice of teaching, research into teaching, and the training of teachers than is found in the present system. Moreover, while private intuition and reflection may be important sources of insight in all three spheres, claims for the desirability and efficacy of particular forms of practice need to be warranted. Throughout the education system, this implies a new priority of evidence over experience, of scrutiny over sentiment, of argument over advocacy. This brings us back to the challenge of finding an appropriate transposition of the methods, evidence, and findings of research into the currently very different context of school practice.

The most immediately obvious and attractive kind of initiative would involve supporting work within schools directly aimed at the improvement of mathematics teaching through scrutinizing current practice and its outcomes, and the identification and appraisal of viable adaptations and alternatives. An initiative of this type would, however, be likely to encounter two particular obstacles. One is the currently restricted range of research tools tuned to collecting and analysing evidence about teaching and learning under typical school conditions. The other is the lack of a powerful means through which teachers can actively explore and evaluate alternative perspectives and practices in mathematics teaching.

Consequently, there is a pressing need to develop strategies aimed at helping schools to improve the quality of the evidence available to them about their classroom practice in mathematics and its outcomes. There is an extensive repertoire of approaches to collecting and analysing such evidence available within the research literature, but there has been little serious attempt to adapt these to provide accessible and viable methods by which schools can generate a richer evidence-base for management and decision-making, and incorporate such methods within their mechanisms for the assessment of pupils and the evaluation of practice.

Similarly, a promising initiative — aimed at providing a versatile resource both to inform school improvement and to support broader professional development — would be to prepare analytic case-studies of a range of teaching approaches. Such studies would be designed to make it possible to examine key features of the teaching approaches, their claimed outcomes, and the mechanisms which link these.

They ought to consist of much more than mere records of teaching to be admired. They should provide evidence from which the success of such teaching can be assessed; practitioners' accounts of the plans and principles informing it; evidence about pupils' participation in, and response to, the teaching. All this evidence ought to be presented in a form amenable both to exploration and to the presentation of structured commentaries — perhaps in multimedia format using software supporting relevant types of interaction with the resource and analysis of its content.

A recently developed resource which starts to indicate the potential of such case studies is the *Learning about Teaching* CD-ROM developed in Australia (Mousley and Sullivan, 1996). This resource documents exemplary lessons, not just through a video-record of the classroom activity, but through the teacher's lesson plan and a transcript of classroom talk, as well as pre- and post-lesson interviews with the teacher. In particular, classroom activity can be accessed not only in chronological sequence, but in terms of phases of the lesson, interactions involving particular students, and exemplifications of different components of teaching. This example shows how use of a computer-based medium makes it possible to structure interactions with naturalistic records of practice in terms of powerful analytic frameworks derived from research on teaching.

At root, however, the reconstruction of professional judgment is more a matter of cultural change than of technical innovation. In Chapter 15, Bernard Cornu outlines the ambitious new approach to teacher preparation currently being developed in France. An explicit goal of these reforms has been to escape from a view of professional knowledge as individual and invisible. In the telling account of the official evaluation of the previous school-based system:

> The great majority of mentors chosen . . . to carry out . . . the professional training
> of future teachers, 'paradoxically' do not see themselves as 'trainers' but as 'ordin-
> ary teachers entrusted with a student teacher'. . . . Deeply convinced that 'there is
> no true training' for 'the difficult job of teacher', that it must be learnt 'on the job'
> and that experience is difficult to pass on, . . . all that they consider themselves able
> to do with their students is to let them attend their classes, without either feeling
> capable of theorising their professional practice or claiming to offer a 'model' to
> imitate. (Leselbaum, 1987 pp. 59–60)

There must be some doubt, however, as to how successful the French re-forms will be in transforming this culture. Certainly, student teachers now follow university-based courses in the didactics of mathematics and in educational and professional studies. But the governing conception appears to be one of — in Bernard Cornu's words — 'theory (courses at the Institute) and practice (periods in school)', with the linking of the two dependent on the professional report prepared by the student. In an evaluation of the reforms, new teachers were questioned about different aspects of their training, after one year at work (Esquieu and Péan, 1995). In mathematics and sciences, rather less than half considered their university courses in didactics and in educational and professional studies to have been useful, and less than a quarter rated preparation of the professional report positively. To British eyes these findings are not surprising: it is precisely such considerations that have provided the major impetus to develop more strongly school-based models of teacher preparation.

Yet, it is arguable that the British reforms still do not address the root issue. If new teachers do not find their more experienced colleagues bringing theoretical perspectives to bear on their practice, or engaging in the kinds of theorizing of practice exemplified by the professional report, they are unlikely to regard these as particularly valuable parts of their training, wherever that training takes place, or whatever form it takes. Nor, as Linda Haggarty has demonstrated, do school mentors find it easy to discharge the role they are accorded within the new model:

> They appeared to adopt roles in which the complexity of the reality [of teaching] was ignored but instead they concentrated on decontextualised theory: on how teaching 'ought' to be rather than how it was. (Haggerty, 1992, pp. 360–1)

The result, as Anne Meredith has shown, is that:

> School-based learning from the trainees' perspective . . . consists of components which correspond closely to descriptions of apprenticeship, such as learning by imitation, observation and practice, together with other aspects such as learning from feedback and discussion. It also has a personalised and experimental component which involves learning by doing, by making mistakes and by seeing and finding out for oneself in a process of trial and improvement. (Meredith, 1996, p. 217)

Moreover, from this perspective:

> Learning to teach . . . has an inevitable quality; skills, ideas and judgements can be 'picked up' osmotically through mere presence in school whilst making mistakes is inescapable. [This] presumption of learning is detrimental to development, leading to the rejection of strategies such as critical questioning, action planning and the analysis of 'bad lessons'. (Meredith, 1996, p. 217)

In both Britain and France, many new teachers of mathematics will have to be recruited in the next decade to replace the disproportionate numbers now approaching retirement and to meet public aspirations for higher mathematical achievement. The French reforms recognize that these challenges cannot be met without revaluing the status of teaching, and developing the knowledge which teachers bring to their task. The British experience shows that far more is required than a simple reform of the initial preparation of teachers. Developing a systematic culture of research-based practice is likely to depend on the formation of multi-faceted partnerships, with highly permeable boundaries, between university faculties of education and groups of schools committed not just to improving their practice, but to developing a qualitatively different basis for it. Some may see this as a wild millennial vision. For, in many ways, teaching has hardly moved beyond what Daniel Bell has identified as the characteristic dependence of 19th-century enterprises on pragmatic forms of 'talented tinkering' for the generation of new ideas and the improvement of practice.

As the new century approaches, is teaching ready to embrace 'the axial principle of the post-industrial society . . . the centrality of theoretical knowledge and its new role, when codified, as the director of social change' (Bell, 1980, p. 501)?

References

AHMED, A. (1987) *Better Mathematics*, London: HMSO.

ASKEW, M. and WILIAM, D. (1995) *Recent Research in Mathematics Education: 5–16*, London: HMSO.

BELL, D. (1980) 'The social framework of the information society', in FORESTER, T. (ed.) *The Microelectronics Revolution*, Oxford: Basil Blackwell 500–549.

BROPHY, J. (1986) 'Where are the data? A reply to Comfrey', *Journal for Research in Mathematics Education*, **17**, 5, pp. 361–8.

COCKCROFT, W.H. (1982) *Mathematics Counts*, London: HMSO.

CREEMERS, B. (1994) *The Effective Classroom*, London: Cassell.

DES/WO (1988) *Mathematics for Ages 5 to 16*, London: DES/WO.

DES/WO (1991) *Mathematics for Ages 5 to 16*, London: DES/WO.

DUNKIN, M. and BIDDLE, B. (1974) *The Study of Teaching*, New York: Holt, Rinehart and Winston.

ESQUIEU, N. and PÉAN, S. (1995) *L'Opinion des Enseignants Nouvellement Recrutés sur la Formation Reçue dans les Instituts Universitaires de Formation de Maîtres*, Note d'Information 95.49, Direction de l'évaluation et de la prospective, Paris: Ministère de l'Education Nationale, de l'Enseignement Supérieur et de la Recherche.

FITZ-GIBBON, C. (1992) 'School effects at A-Level: Genesis of an information system?', in REYNOLDS, D. and CUTTANCE, P. (eds) *School Effectiveness: Research, Policy and Practice*, London: Cassell, pp. 96–120.

FULLAN, M. (1991) *The New Meaning of Educational Change*, London: Cassell.

GOOD, T. and BIDDLE, B. (1988) 'Research and the improvement of mathematics instruction: The need for observational resources', in GROUWS, D. (ed.) *Effective Mathematics Teaching*, Reston, VA: National Council of Teachers of Mathematics/Lawrence Erlbaum Associates, pp. 114–42.

GROSS, N., GIAQUINTA, J.B. and BERNSTEIN, M. (1971) *Implementing Organizational Innovations: A Sociological Analysis of Planned Educational Change*, London: Harper and Row.

HAGGARTY, L. (1992) 'Investigating a new approach to mathematics teacher education', Unpublished DPhil Dissertation, University of Oxford.

HARGREAVES, D.H. (1996) 'Teaching as a research based profession: Possibilities and prospects', Teacher Training Agency Annual Lecture.

HER MAJESTY'S INSPECTORATE (1991) *Mathematics: Key Stages 1 and 3*, London: HMSO.

HER MAJESTY'S INSPECTORATE (1992) *Mathematics: Key Stages 1, 2 and 3*, London: HMSO.

LAMPERT, M. (1988) 'What can research on teacher education tell us about improving quality in mathematics education', *Teaching and Teacher Education*, **4**, 2, pp. 157–70.

LAPOINTE, A., MEAD, N. and ASKEW, J. (1992) *Learning Mathematics*, Princeton NJ: Educational Testing Service.

LEINHARDT, G. (1998) 'Expertise in instructional lessons: An example from fractions', in GROUWS, D. (ed.) *Effective Mathematics Teaching*, Reston, VA: National Council of Teachers of Mathematics/Lawrence Erlbaum Associates, pp. 47–66.

LESELBAUM, N. (1987) 'La formation des enseignants du second degré dans les centres pédagogiques régionaux', Paris: Institut National de Recherche Pédagogique.

McINTYRE, D.I. (1995a) 'Initial teacher education as practical theorising: A response to Paul Hirst', *British Journal of Educational Studies*, **43**, 4, pp. 365–83.

McINTYRE, D.I. (1995b) 'Good and bad arguments for universities' continued involvement in initial teacher training', Unpublished lecture, University of Cambridge.

MEREDITH, A. (1996) 'The construction of knowledge for teaching through apprenticeship training', Unpublished PhD dissertation, University of Cambridge.

MORTIMORE, P., SAMMONS, P., STOLL, L., LEWIS, D. and ECOB, R. (1988) *School Matters: The Junior Years*, London: Open Books.

MOUSLEY, J. and SULLIVAN, P. (1996) *Learning about Teaching* (CD-ROM and study guide), Geelong: Deakin University.

NATIONAL CURRICULUM MATHEMATICS WORKING GROUP (1987) *Interim Report*, London: DES/WO.

REYNOLDS, D. (1992) 'School effectiveness and school improvement: An updated review of the British literature', in REYNOLDS, D. and CUTTANCE, P. (eds) *School Effectiveness: Research. Policy and Practice*, London: Cassell, pp. 1–24.

REYNOLDS, D. and PACKER, A. (1992) 'School effectiveness and school improvement in the 1990's', in REYNOLDS, D. and CUTTANCE, P. (eds) *School Effectiveness: Research, Policy and Practice*, London: Cassell, pp. 171–187.

SCHEERENS, J. (1992) *Effective Schooling: Research, Theory and Practice*, London: Cassell.

SCHMIDT, W. and BURSTEIN, L. (1993) 'Concomitants of growth in mathematics achievement during the Population A school year', in BURSTEIN, L. (ed.) *The IEA Study of Mathematics III: Student Growth and Classroom Processes*, Oxford: Pergamon, pp. 309–27.

SELINGER, M. (1987) 'Raising achievement in mathematics project (RAMP): A case study of an innovative inservice programme', Unpublished MPhil thesis, University of Cambridge.

Section Four

Learning from the Pacific Rim

Mathematics education is often said to be in a state of crisis. Those in the western world observe a 'crisis of skills' and make unflattering comparisons with the relatively high levels of computational dexterity found in school populations in the Far East. But countries of the Pacific Rim also perceive themselves to be in mathematical crisis — a 'crisis of creativity'. In the chapter from Korea, a country which scores very highly on most international comparisons of mathematics attainment, Hee-Chan Lew describes the 'total crisis' in his country and graphically illustrates how most students are quite unable to relate their well developed manipulative skills to the real world. He goes on to describe the principles of the proposed new mathematics curriculum in Korea, principles which are explicitly related to wider goals of social reform.

Fou-Lai Lin and Liang-Chi Tsao, from Taiwan, present a picture of test obsession where the college entrance exam dominates students' (and parents') lives. Both Taiwan and Korea are planning to adapt their curricula to encourage creative problem solving — in fact moving in the opposite direction to that urged by many commentators in Britain! It is too easy for countries simply to flip between two states of skill and creativity crisis, while attempting to model changes in the curriculum on those in distant countries. Learning from other cultures is fruitful if care is taken to go beyond surface features and slogans. But, as the chapters in this section testify, deep thought is necessary about what mathematics and what education is appropriate at any particular time or place.

To elaborate on this point, Fred Leung discusses Chinese cultural traditions in relation to mathematics and education. He contrasts the constructive and mechanistic mathematics of ancient China with the axiomatic and deductive tradition of ancient Greece, and suggests that the former may have some value, particularly for the majority, now that technology can remove the drudgery of the 'mechanics'. More generally, he draws attention to the high status of education in Pacific Rim countries which arises from the Confucian view that everyone is educable, and 'perfectible'. Thus, in the Confucian tradition, education serves the higher goal of the perfection of the self, which in turn implies a concern for the welfare of all. This tradition is clearly informing the developments in Korea and, while some purists in the west may demur from such 'extrinsic' motivation, the alternative motivation for many students in the West has been little more than the acquisition of some practical skills and a 'logical mind'. Leung suggests that there will be benefit in making explicit the values, both intrinsic and extrinsic, that underpin any new curriculum that is developed — a message for all those engaged in curricular change.

Chapter 17

New Goals and Directions for Mathematics Education in Korea

Hee-Chan Lew

Korea's 7th National Curriculum was issued as a government mandate in December 1997. It is planned that two years will be needed for developing textbooks and instructional materials, after which the new curriculum will be operated in schools from the beginning of the 21st century.

The rationale for the new curriculum has three interrelated strands. The first is the view of the mathematics education community that the mathematics curriculum should support Korea's national goals practically, and not just pay lip service to them. The urgent national goal is to construct an advanced civilized society, where there is rapid circulation of information, highly developed technology, and openness to other cultures. This society is expected to be dedicated to the welfare of mankind, a traditional dream of Korean people throughout their history. It is not clear that mathematics education has previously supported this national vision.

Secondly, compared to that of 30 years ago, the current curriculum shows few changes either in content or in methods of teaching and evaluation. It is skill-orientated, relying on the expository method to transfer fragmentary pieces of knowledge. In the opinion of the designers of the new curriculum, this orientation has led students to learn mathematics meaninglessly and as a result mathematics education in Korea is in total crisis. An example of the depth of this crisis is the level of achievement in the college entrance examination operated nationally by the government. This examination consists of multiple-choice questions each with four possible answers, yet the average score is only about 25 per cent.

Thirdly, the current curriculum leaves no room for taking account of individual differences in the abilities, needs, and interests of students. The majority of mathematics educators in Korea want a curriculum which is structured to maximize the potential for growth in each individual student — in short, a level-based, differentiated curriculum.

These three strands have led us to consider the models provided by the *Standards* of the United States (NCTM, 1989 and 1991) and the National Curriculum of England and Wales (Department for Education, 1995). We have adopted a constructivist view emphasizing students' own learning processes and their own ways of appreciating the values of knowing. This chapter describes the new goals and direction of mathematics education in Korea, together with the structure of the 7th curriculum.

The New Goals of Mathematics Education in Korea

The current (6th) curriculum has three main aims: first, that through the mathematical observation of various phenomena, students should be enabled to understand basic mathematical concepts, principles, and rules. Second, to enable students to use accurate mathematical terminology and symbols and to foster their ability to think mathematically and deal with various problems faced in their everyday lives. Third, that students should maintain a continuous interest in mathematics, should use their mathematical knowledge and skills, and should acquire a positive attitude to logical problem solving.The first of these aims has a humanistic perspective, in which knowledge about number and shape is itself a goal. The second might be termed social-utilitarian, where the purpose of teaching basic skills and concepts is for one's daily life. The third represents the standpoint of the developmentalist, who focuses on the development of the mathematical mind rather than on practical use. None of these aims expresses the contribution that mathematics education has to make to the wider goals of social reform mentioned earlier. In particular, social-utilitarian and humanistic approaches alone are not enough to construct an advanced, civilized society which can engage actively with other cultures rather than accept them passively.

In view of this national goal, it is felt that the mathematics curriculum should focus on cultivating people with the following abilities:

- creativity in solving problems
- rationality in communication with others
- openness to the ideas of others
- self-regulation or metacognition in problem solving
- resolution to cope with difficulties in solving problems
- autonomy in learning
- power to synthesize mathematical contents during the problem-solving process
- appreciation of mathematics as a tool for solving problems.

In addition, a more accurate analysis of social structures is required in order to reach a consensus on what our concrete social goals are and how mathematics education might contribute to their achievement. This analysis must include an understanding of the variability of our social structures and the social disagreement that exists between its different substructures. The mathematics curriculum needs to be broad enough to take account of this variability, so that each student can become a productive member of our future society. It is felt that the current uniform curriculum amplifies social disagreement, and should be reformed.

Problems with a Skill- and Fact-orientated Curriculum

To outward appearance mathematics education in Korea seems to be a success. Very recently Korea was ranked second in the Third International Mathematics and Science Survey (see Harris et al., 1997) and ninth in the International Mathematics Olympiad. Of course these results require close analysis, but we already have evidence of the harmful effects of our present inflexible skill- and fact-orientated curriculum. Lew and Kim (1996), for example, investigated the quality of understanding of fractions among sixth-grade students. Three kinds of test were administered: computation, estimation, and making up a word problem. The computation test consisted of questions involving the four arithmetic operations, such as the following:

$$\frac{1}{2} + \frac{1}{4} = \Box, \quad 5\frac{2}{3} - \frac{1}{2} = \Box, \quad \frac{1}{3} \times 6 = \Box, \quad 2 \div \frac{1}{2} = \Box$$

The students' average score on this test was 82.3 per cent showing that they had learned these operations well. However, in the estimation test consisting of problems such as

Estimate the sum of $\frac{1}{2}$ and $\frac{1}{3}$; estimate the sum of $\frac{12}{13}$ and $\frac{8}{9}$;

the average score was only 46.2 per cent. For the sum of $\frac{1}{2}$ and $\frac{1}{3}$ most of the wrong answers (79.7 per cent) were either $\frac{1}{5}$ or $\frac{1}{6}$. For $\frac{12}{13} + \frac{8}{9}$ one student wrote on the answer sheet $1\frac{95}{117}$ (the exact answer) but then chose 1 as the estimate. More serious were the results for making up word problems, where the average score was 38.4 per cent. Students who could carry out the computations composed nonsensical word problems as illustrated in the following examples:

Make a word problem using $\frac{1}{3} \times 6$.
The age of her father is one third the age of Minji. The age of Minji is 6. How old is her father?

Make a word problem using $4\frac{1}{6} + \frac{3}{4}$
There are $4\frac{1}{6}$ gorilla in the zoo. The owner has bought $\frac{3}{4}$ gorilla more. What is the total number of gorilla in the zoo?

These examples show that our skill- and fact-orientated curriculum does not guarantee that these students derive any meaning for the skills and facts.

Secondly, students' attainment is far less than what is intended by the curriculum. Lew et al. (1993) studied students' responses to textbook problems set in the

Table 17.1 *Average success rates (%) of 10th grade students attempting textbook problems, analysed by student gender, by problem type, and by problem difficulty*

| | Student Gender | | | Problem Type | | Problem Difficulty | | |
	Male	Female	Fact	Understanding	Application	High	Middle	Low
City	36.0	40.0	46.5	35.0	32.4	29.9	36.4	50.0
Suburb	36.0	40.4	46.1	36.1	33.4	30.5	36.4	49.1
Rural	27.1	28.4	32.1	25.5	26.0	23.5	27.1	32.9
Total	32.7	37.8	43.6	33.5	29.0	28.4	33.8	46.4

10th and 11th grades (see Table 17.1), and found the average success rate for 10th-grade students to be about 35 per cent. Since the curriculum in Korea is the textbook, this means that 10th-graders on average achieve only 35 per cent of its intended goal. Even on 'low-difficulty' problems the average success rate is about 46 per cent. On application problems the rate is below 30 per cent. Moreover, the average score for students in rural areas is far less than for students in city areas. In rural areas the average success rate on low-level problems and those involving factual recall alone is about 32 per cent on the other types of problem it is about 25 per cent.

The main culprit appears to be the nature of the curriculum, which focuses on skills and mathematical facts without attaching meaning to mathematical learning. No attention is paid to differences between students' cognitive abilities, or between the educational environments in city and rural areas.

The New Direction of Mathematics Education

Emphasis on Problem-solving Ability

It is felt that the direction of the mathematics curriculum in Korea should change from emphasis on computational skills and the 'snapshot' application of fragment-ary knowledge to emphasis on problem-solving and thinking abilities. It is true that since the 5th curriculum, one or two chapters of each semester in elementary school have been assigned to problem solving, but this is not enough. It is still supposed that problem solving can be taught only after mastery of calculation skills. But, on the contrary, calculation can be taught *during* the problem-solving process. In a society where calculators are widely available, it cannot be that calculation skills are a prerequisite of problem solving.

The problem-solving activities of elementary school do not at present extend into secondary school. Here creative problem solving is not emphasized. Indeed, in Korea the principal purpose of secondary education in mathematics appears to be to prepare students for a college entrance examination of a definite form. Students are trained to choose or find the right answer at the expense of heuristic. What is required instead is that students should develop problem-solving ability in an in-vestigative arena in which both high and low achievers can give full play to their abilities to organize a problem situation, and that teachers should provide sugges-tions to help students to overcome the many obstacles that arise.

Emphasis on Communication Skills

It is widely accepted that what is most necessary in a modern society is that its members should be able to communicate with one another. People cannot obtain information without communication. Knowing and communicating are different, and knowing by itself is not enough. Communication needs to be emphasized as much in mathematics classes as it is in social studies and language classes.

Mathematics education must cultivate students' attitudes and abilities to enable them to explain their ideas clearly, to listen carefully to others' ideas, to criticize reasonably, and to provide alternatives. Accordingly, communication skills such as representing, talking, listening, writing, reading, and compromising need to be integrated into mathematics education. These skills are also related to the development of thinking: students clarify their ideas by discussion. Additionally, higher achievers should learn to appreciate the power and elegance of mathematical symbolism and its role in mathematical processes.

The Use of Computers

The computer can be a very powerful tool in the teaching and learning of mathematics. It can provide students with rich opportunities to link the abstract with the concrete. Chapters 11 and 12 of this book, together with their references, give many examples.

In June 1989 the Korean Ministry of Education set up a plan to supply by 1996 some 300,000 standard computers to approximately 11,700 schools, at a cost of 200 million US dollars. The aim was that every school should have a computer laboratory with at least one computer for every two students using it. This plan has been achieved, with every school now equipped with a computer laboratory with between 30 and 60 computers. The current mathematics curriculum, however, does not presuppose computer use, although teachers are permitted to use them in their classes if they wish. This means that computer use depends on the interests and abilities of individual teachers, and many teachers are not rising to this challenge. Thus, we need a compulsory curriculum related to the computer.

Of course, before making such a curriculum, we need agreement in the mathematics education community on the benefits that the computer offers. Then a necessary condition for the practical use of computers in mathematics education will be a computer-integrated curriculum, which lists topics where computers can help students to understand the mathematics in ways that are better than other methods, and provides concrete standard ways to teach these topics with the computer.

Until very recently, software developed in Korea has focused on low-level computational skills and simple explanations of the contents appearing in textbooks. Now, as a result of trial and error over the last 10 years, the direction is turning towards the development of:

- game-related software to promote student motivation in the learning process
- tool-like software to support an investigative environment
- simulation software to raise students' intuitive comprehension
- a database package for use in assessment

Emphasis on Discrete Mathematics

It is true that the current curriculum does include work on matrices, mathematical induction, number sequences, sets, and logic, but these topics need to be taught in such a way as to bring out their application and meaning, not merely their operation. The creation of algorithms for problem solving, in particular of finite processes such as computer programs, can be very effective in developing mathematical thinking. Also discrete mathematics provides tools for modelling social and natural phenomena. Thus graph theory, matrices, and fractals are better sources for modelling activities to make students think mathematics is alive than traditional algebra and geometry. In discrete mathematics there are many topics on which teachers and students can work together.

Estimation and Mental Computation

In mathematics education in Korea emphasis has traditionally been placed on skill in producing exact values with written algorithms, although most numerical problems faced in daily life can be solved by estimation and mental computation. This does not mean that rote implementation of algorithms is not necessary: rather that mathematics education must enable students to operate more effectively with the meaning of a calculation in an everyday situation. Estimation strategies using front end, clustering, compatible numbers, and special numbers are practically useful, and estimation and mental calculation are tools for checking the results of rote calculations with calculators and written algorithms.

The most serious shortcoming of current education in geometry is its emphasis on a formal approach without regard to students' cognitive abilities in the sense of van Hiele levels (see, for example, van Hiele, 1986). If the purposes of teaching geometry include the cultivation of logical thinking and of geometrical intuition then the inductive approach of investigation and conjecture is as important as the deductive approach of proving theorems that other people have discovered. We should distinguish clearly between following other people's proofs and the students' own deductive activities. To encourage the latter the geometry curriculum should encompass informal activities with geoboard, tangram, and other technology such as dynamic geometry software.

The advantage of using such investigative computer software is that by enabling students to manipulate geometrical figures it provides them with a holistic perspective on geometrical meaning and relations. They can carry out investigations that are almost impossible with pencil and paper. To conjecture theorems in this way and then formalize them makes geometry more interesting and enables the mathematics classroom to become more like a science laboratory. The geometrical content of the new curriculum will need to be reordered and guidelines provided for the developers of classroom materials.

Emphasis on the Application of Mathematics

Students want to know why they learn mathematics. Although it is not easy to identify clear answers to satisfy everybody, if students are to be persuaded that mathematics can be interesting and meaningful it is surely necessary to show them the application of mathematics to a variety of situations and the connections between mathematical topics. Without such motivation effective learning cannot be expected.

The modelling process is fundamental to the application of mathematics. For descriptive purposes mathematical modelling has commonly been split into five steps, with possible iteration of part or all of the process.

- First, observe carefully the phenomenon under consideration and describe it as a concrete problem situation.
- Second, select some variables to influence the situation.
- Third, identify the mathematical model to represent the relation between the variables.
- Fourth, manipulate the mathematical model represented in symbols and deduce some results.
- Fifth, interpret the results with respect to the original situation and conclude something.

Current mathematics education in Korea highlights the fourth step only: the other steps also need to be emphasized. Although dealing skilfully with equations is important, representing a social or natural phenomenon as an equation and interpreting the solution of that equation are important also.

The new curriculum also needs room to integrate different mathematical topics (internal connection), and to integrate topics in mathematics with topics in for example, physics, chemistry and geography (external connection).

Emphasis on the Calculator in the Teaching and Learning Process

After the fourth grade, where formal calculation with whole numbers is supposed to be completed, the curriculum should permit students to use calculators freely. Generally, two dangers are considered. It is feared, first, that computational skill will decrease and, second, that this decrease will be attended by a parallel decrease in problem-solving ability and conceptual understanding. Although long-term research into this concern is needed, if effective calculation practice can be maintained the concern may not be serious. On the other hand, systematic research is needed also to check the extent to which problem-solving ability and understanding depend on computational skill.

The introduction of calculators into the mathematics curriculum offers a number of advantages.

- First, the time saved on lengthy computation can be used to focus on problem solving and understanding.
- Second, the educational circumstance can be made more natural for students by the use of realistic data.
- Third, appreciating that calculation and estimation are necessary tools to solve problems encourages students to practise these skills.
- Fourth, we may expect an improvement in students' attitude to mathematics: the burden of unnecessary calculation leads many students to think that calculation is equal to doing mathematics.
- Fifth, the calculator is not only a tool for calculation: there are many other problem-solving activities that it supports.

Introduction of New Kinds of Statistics Education

The problems of the current curriculum in Korea are more serious in probability and statistics than in the other areas of mathematics. There is a large difference in level between what is taught in junior high school and what is taught in senior high school. The junior high school curriculum deals with descriptive statistics such as mean and standard deviation. It is relatively easy and the textbook offers few interesting applications. On the other hand the work in senior high school on estimation and significance testing is very difficult for ordinary students.

To overcome such difficulties, topics such as estimation and significance testing should be eliminated. The connection between subject content and everyday experience needs to be strengthened so that students believe that probability and statistics are meaningful. Topics at progressive levels of difficulty must be developed to improve the transition from middle school through to senior high school.

Games

There are a number of advantages to using strategy games in the mathematics classroom.

- First, games have a strong appeal for students of all abilities: most people enjoy them. If it includes strategy games, students are likely to consider mathematics more familiar and interesting.
- Second, by introducing friendly competition, strategy games can strengthen motivation.

- Third, they provide enjoyable opportunities for thinking and so help improve problem-solving abilities.
- Fourth, strategy games involving number can improve mental calculation skills.

The current curriculum contains no topics that relate computation with problem solving. Skills acquired in enjoyable conditions are likely to be retained longer than skills acquired under stress.

The Structure of the New Curriculum

The epochal change in the 7th curriculum is the adoption of a level-based differentiated structure similar in principle to that of the National Curriculum of England and Wales. The aim is to maximize educational effect and the potential growth of each individual student by paying close attention to differences in individual abilities, needs, and interests. The curriculum will have two parts. One is the 'common core' from first to tenth grade, which is divided into 20 levels. Students advance by means of a level-transfer examination administered by government. The second part consists of 'electives' on different topics and with different difficulties, which students in the 11th and 12th grades opt for according to their interests.

Generally, a student who fails the level transfer test by scoring below 60 per cent must remain at that level and take the course again. Exceptionally, by request of the student or the parent, or on the teacher's decision, such a student may transfer to the next level, in which case a special course will be offered by the school at the end of the semester, operated according to minimum criteria laid down by the national curriculum. A given level in the common core may be repeated only once. To avoid unnecessary competition and a sense of incongruity among students and parents, skipping levels is not permitted. Instead, for advanced students and low achievers, special enrichment and supplementary sections will be provided during the course at the teacher's discretion. The 11th- and 12th-grade students who have not finished the common core will follow special programmes at the appropriate level provided in school or district units.

This system is accepted by the mathematics education community as a Copernican conversion from the current *laissez-faire* policy which guarantees automatic grade promotion regardless of a student's achievement scores to a policy which controls level transfer according to criteria set up in advance.

Much further discussion is required to clarify the detail of how to assign mathematical content to levels, how to determine pass or fail and who determines this, how to organize students at different levels into one class, and so on.

Conclusion

This chapter has summarized the goals, direction, and structure of the new mathematics curriculum which is being developed in Korea. The main focus is on the development of mathematical thinking abilities. This is related to the national strategy to construct a highly developed country in the near future. Mathematics provides tools for propelling the development of science and for solving quantitative and qualitative problems faced by people in their lives. To use these tools properly in appropriate situations, fragmentary knowledge and skills are not enough: we have set ourselves the specific educational objective of providing the mathematical thinking experiences which students need in order to synthesize their knowledge and skills. If this is to succeed, students need to appreciate that mathematics is a subject that is *really* necessary for them and we need firmer control over grade promotion than is afforded by the current *laissez-faire* policy.

These changes to the curriculum take place in the context of strong governmental intent for educational reform. To my knowledge it is the first time that the mathematics education community has experienced strong external pressure for change. Nobody knows that this kind of curriculum revision will succeed, but the community acknowledges that revision is necessary and will try its best for success.

What needs to be changed in mathematics education for the new millennium? The answer from Korea is to change the criteria for determining content and teaching method in order to develop mathematical thinking for all students. Why? Because mathematical thinking is a tool for all kinds of creative problem solving for all.

References

DEPARTMENT FOR EDUCATION (1995) *Mathematics in the National Curriculum*, London: HMSO.

HARRIS, S., KEYS, W. and FERNANDES, C. (1997) *Third International Mathematics and Science Study: Second National Report Part 1. Achievement in Mathematics and Science at Age 9 in England*, National Foundation for Educational Research, UK.

LEW, H.C. and KIM, O.K. (1996) 'A study of the conceptual understanding of fraction among 6th graders, and instructional methods for fraction' (In Korean), *Journal of the Korea Society of Educational Studies in Mathematics*, 6, 2.

LEW, H.C., PARK, M.H. and LEE, S.H. (1993) 'A study of achievement levels in textbook problems for high school students' (In Korean), *The Seminar of Mathematics Education*, 3, Institute of Mathematics Education, Korea National University of Education.

NCTM (1989) *Curriculum and Evaluation Standards for School Mathematics*, Reston, VA: National Council of Teachers of Mathematics.

NCTM (1991) *Professional Standards for Teaching Mathematics*, Reston, VA: National Council of Teachers of Mathematics.

VAN HIELE, P.M. (1986) *Structure and Insight*, Orlando, Florida: Academic Press.

Chapter 18

EXAM MATHS Re-examined

Fou-Lai Lin and Liang-Chi Tsao

Prologue: One-Task-One-Rule

One of the tasks set in the Taiwanese driving test is to drive around an S-shaped path. To help their students to pass this test, driving instructors have developed a set of procedures corresponding to each sub-task. These procedures can be formulated in what are called P–N rules, i.e. when you see the point P, you rotate the steering wheel to the left or to the right through N turns, where N is a multiple of one half. Since the tests are taken in artificial testing areas away from real roads, an effective strategy for success in obtaining a driver's licence is to memorize. However, a licensed person usually needs a great many more driving lessons on the roads in real traffic in order to be able to drive safely on the streets. Additionally, it is not certain that somebody who has driven with a Taiwan driver's licence for, say, more than 10 years, will be successful in driving through the S-shaped path of the driving test.

In Taiwan the phenomenon of developing one rule to perform one task is not restricted to driving instructors. Indeed, it can be characterized as a general strategy chosen by the majority of teachers trying to help people to pass tests of all kinds. Mathematics teachers certainly conform to this pattern. For example, Mr Chen, who is recognized as a star mathematics teacher by his colleagues in a junior high school, bases his teaching on a meticulous and fine-grained classification of mathematics content. He has classified simultaneous linear equations into 20 categories, some based on coefficients such as integral, decimal, fractional, with or without symmetric pattern, some on types of substitutions, some on the form of expressions, etc. He has devised a solution procedure for each type. Experience shows that good performance is achieved in any test if a student is familiar with all these types and the corresponding solutions.

The teaching strategy of one-task-one-rule both in car driving and in mathematics lessons, where passing tests is likely to be the unique aim, characterizes learning as essentially skill training. However, it is argued here that passing tests does not guarantee that one can drive a car on the road or indeed understand or use mathematics beyond the test situation.

Training by P–N rules inevitably means that if one misses any point P, then one has no alternative way to succeed in the task. Learners are not educated to develop the flexibility to be able to adapt to different problem situations. This is found all too often in Taiwanese mathematics classes, where mathematics problems in different contexts but with the same underlying structure are regarded by students as completely new topics which have not been taught.

The Mathematics Performance of Taiwanese Students

In the International Assessment of Educational Progress study (IAEP) (Lapointe et al., 1992), Taiwanese and English 13-year-old students achieved an average number of correct items of 73 and 61 respectively. Statistically, these two populations were found to have performed differently in this test. If, however, we take one more piece of information into account, namely the average days of instruction per academic year as in Table 18.1, we may feel that the performances of these two populations are somehow as one would expect: the percentage correct ratio of 73/61 is roughly equal to the instructional time ratio of 222/192.

Of the factors that could conceivably have an impact on mathematics achievement, the average number of days of instruction in each year would not necessarily be the first to come to mind: the amount of contact with mathematics in each week might be more appropriate. The IAEP study provides the average number of minutes of mathematics instruction in school each week for each population and the percentage of students who spend four hours or more on mathematics homework each week. These figures are given in Table 18.2. They suggest that 13-year-old Taiwanese students work harder on mathematics homework than English students do.

Moreover, in considering the number of hours of mathematics studied each week, we should also take into account the hours borrowed from non-mathematics lessons for mathematics quizzes in school as well as mathematics lessons provided in cram schools or by private tutoring. After interviewing a small numbers of mathematics teachers and students in Taiwanese junior high schools, we concluded

Table 18.1   IAEP mathematics data for students aged 13 years: % of items correct and number of days of instruction per year

	Average % of items correct	**Average number of days of instruction in a year**
Taiwan	73	222
England	61	192

Table 18.2   IAEP mathematics data for students aged 13 years: teaching and learning practices

	Average minutes of math instruction each week	**% of students who spend 4 hours or more on maths homework each week**
Taiwan	204	24
England	190	6

that the majority (about 70 per cent) of Taiwanese 13-year-old students spend as many as 15 hours per week on mathematics 'learning'. This seems to be much greater than the corresponding number for English 13-year-old-students.

The test papers in the entrance examination for senior high schools are mathematics, Chinese, English, natural sciences, and social studies. The study of these five school subjects is the focus of work for Taiwanese students. Indeed, the typical daily life of Taiwanese students aged 14, in the last year of junior high school, could be characterized as follows: wake up at 6:00, go to bed at 24:00 and study subjects in test papers whenever you are not in bed! Most parents regard this study schedule as absolutely essential for school success and few want to or feel able to make different arrangements for their children. The Chinese traditionally place a very high emphasis on education (see Leung, Chapter 18); they also believe that working hard is virtuous.

If they took into account the daily life of Taiwanese youth, would educators still applaud their good mathematics performance? Clearly there is room for different views. Nevertheless, it is necessary to recognize that there is a complexity underlying any interpretation of Taiwanese student mathematics performance as presented in, for example, the data in the IAEP study, which goes beyond merely noting the scores. For further interpretation, the following two questions need to be addressed:

1   How are Taiwanese students encouraged to study so hard in school subjects?
2   What *is* school mathematics education in Taiwan?

Thinking about question 1, it is fair to say that everybody, whether educator or parent, agrees that the entrance examination system is the key factor dominating students' lives. A brief description of this system is given in the next section. It is then argued that this examination system induces a rather special approach to school mathematics, which begins to answer question 2.

EXAM MATHS in Taiwan

The Examination Culture in Taiwanese Secondary Education

A teenager who studies school subjects from day to night throughout the whole year is not doing so because he or she is interested in the subjects studied, but because he or she is encouraged or even forced to do so by certain pressures. In Taiwanese secondary schools, everyone knows that the pressure comes mainly from the entrance examination for further education.

Compulsory education in Taiwan starts at age 6 years and ends at age 15 years. After that, about one quarter of the students leave school for employment, while the remaining three quarters take entrance tests to go on to further education, i.e. senior high schools, vocational schools, or junior colleges. At 18 years of age, students have to take yet another entrance test to go on in education and about half of them successfully obtain a place at a university or college. The real competition, however, is for the very few good national universities, with the best teaching staff and laboratories, and with tuition fees half those of the private universities. The competition for these prized university places filters downwards, as three quarters of the students who obtain them come from a few star provincial senior high schools, and everybody therefore wants a place in one of these. So entrance tests at both 15 and 18 years are highly competitive.

For the past 40 years, these entrance tests have come to be a central and unchangeable event in our society. They undoubtedly generate a unique and special examination culture in Taiwanese secondary education, which must be appreciated in any interpretation of Taiwanese students' performance in school. In this examination culture, the typical practice is to administer a huge number of tests simply to train the students. In general, during the last year of junior high school (9th grade) and senior high school (12th grade), students have to take two to three tests every day. Taiwanese secondary education is devoted almost entirely to preparing and taking examinations.

Students' out-of-school activities are inevitably overwhelmed by the next day's tests: they prepare the test items prescribed by their teachers and this takes the whole evening. When asked in our interview 'What do you want to do tonight if there is no test tomorrow?' a typical 9th-grade students' response is 'I do not know.' Then, they add, 'But it is impossible.' No wonder the IAEP study (Lapointe et al., 1992) showed that the Taiwanese 13-year-old students ranked the lowest among the 20 IAEP populations on the two measures reading for fun and hours watching the television.

Examination Cram Schools in Taiwan

In Taiwan, there are a great many 'cram schools' to help prepare students for public examinations. Many famous cram schools for TOEFL (Test of English as a Foreign Language) and GRE (Graduate Record Examinations) help university graduates go on for further study in the United States. There are also cram schools for secondary and university entrance tests in almost every city in Taiwan. Even for primary-school children there are cram schools which focus on their transitional learning to help them to go on to junior high schools. To prepare for entrance examinations for the Masters degree programme in universities in Taiwan, many candidates register at cram schools too; in fact cram schools for the Masters degree in business management are so popular that one has to pre-register and pay fees at least six months in advance in order to secure a place. Not only are cram schools set up for school and university students: they also exist to prepare people for examinations used to recruit government officials, lawyers, etc.

This culture of setting up cram schools is copied and hence praised by Taiwanese immigrants in foreign countries: for instance, Taiwanese cram schools have recently been established in Los Angeles in the United States to prepare students for SATS.

The teaching approach used in these cram schools usually includes the strategy of one-task-one-rule. For instance, Wang et al. (1985) carried out a study for policy makers of the present situation in science education in Taiwan. This study distinguished the 'extra classes' from the formal school classes. Although some extra classes are taken within school after the end of normal classes, most of the information gathered in Wang's study was from cram schools. Analysing the material used in extra classes, Wang et al. found that the teaching activities in the extra classes included: 'revision of key points of each topic/chapter', 'analysis of test items', 'trends in entrance test items', 'how to memorize rules', and 'how to apply rules to solve test items'. It is not expected that any activity involving concept construction will be employed by teachers in those extra classes outside school (Lin, 1988). It is highly unlikely that the culture of the Taiwan cram schools, and certainly their teaching approach, will change as we move into the new millennium.

The Mathematics in the Examination Culture

Mathematics is an important subject in entrance tests at both 15 and 18 years and accounts for about one sixth of the total score. What kind of mathematics is prescribed in this examination culture? We will discuss it in terms of content, teaching, and learning.

Content

Whilst the intended curriculum, presented in the only set of text books in Taiwan, is developed carefully by government authorities, the implemented curriculum in most of the secondary mathematics classrooms is characterized by what we may term 'pseudo-text books'. In pseudo-text books there is no trace of knowledge construction, but rather a glossary of mathematical knowledge that emphasizes problem-solving algorithms, augmented by well chosen examples and followed by exercises for drill and practice. An extreme example is the classification of simultaneous linear equations that we described at the beginning of this chapter.

Teaching

It is a common practice for a teacher to show as many examples as possible in a lesson of 50 minutes, so there is no time for students to undertake any explorations or extensions. In such examples, stating the problem, providing the most elegant solution, and ordering students to memorize forms a typical teaching cycle.

The intended teaching approach advocated by curriculum developers is again distorted in classrooms. An example in our junior high school's intended curriculum is to find the value of $\sqrt{11}$, first by trial and error, then by successive approximation using decisection. But at the implemented level, most teachers teach it as follows: first teach students the algorithm to find $\sqrt{11}$ — this is before students have learnt $(a + b)^2 = a^2 + 2ab + b^2$, therefore they do not understand the algorithm — then ask students to write out $3.316 < \sqrt{11} < 3.317$ as verification. In our interviews, the teachers justified their approach by claiming that trial and error wastes time, and the students do not have calculators. Examples such as the above are common practice in mathematics classrooms from grade schools through to colleges.

Learning

For most of the secondary students we interviewed, learning mathematics was about passing entrance tests. There are about 15 problems in the 80-minute university entrance test, and about 24 problems in the 70-minute senior high school entrance test. Mr Chu came ninth in the Asian Pacific Mathematics Olympiad when he was an 11th-grade student but did not have enough time to finish all the problems in the entrance test he took for senior high school, in contrast to the large number of students who received full marks.

Familiarity with most of the problems in the test papers is a prerequisite for good performance. You need to be able to apply the appropriate algorithms to get the right answers quickly. For this purpose, the best strategy is to learn as many different types of problems as possible, paired with elegant solutions. Since it is too much for students to generate these classifications and solutions on their own, and there is no room in mathematics lessons for students to develop their own thinking, many students simply absorb what is required of them.

Lin (1988) has shown that Taiwanese students are heavily dependent on taught algorithms to solve mathematics problems. Solving problems using informal approaches was hardly found among Taiwanese students. So it is not surprising that the IAEP study (Lapointe et al., 1992) reported that more than half of Taiwanese 13-year-old students agreed that learning mathematics is mainly memorizing.

The IAEP Maths Test Is an EXAM MATHS

From the point of view of the students interviewed, mathematics means computation, problem solving becomes choosing the right problem routine, and learning mathematics is memorizing. When put together, the outcome is a Taiwanese student's image of mathematics, which we will describe as 'EXAM MATHS'. EXAM MATHS simply comprises sets of rules. We suggest that it militates against problem solving, since memorizing rules must work against the principle of thinking mathematically. Activities such as mathematical investigation and problem solving are considered inappropriate within this examination culture simply because they cannot be included in any entrance test. So teachers believe they are a waste of time.

Even high mathematics achievers only experience solving problems of a particular nature — well formulated and very difficult, up to, for example, the level of the Mathematics Olympiad. They have relatively little chance to develop a multifaceted view of mathematics using different representations. To them, EXAM MATHS is a cluster of difficult problems. There is some evidence that this kind of image can block high mathematics achievers from doing well at the advanced mathematics they encounter in university mathematics departments.

Low achievers in mathematics suffer the same pressures to stay in the competitive educational game — from their family, school, and even from society.

Thus EXAM MATHS gradually becomes a major source of pressure in their lives. Many students therefore look forward to the day when they can give up mathematics altogether. Sadly, this attitude is shared by many high achievers as well. But from an item developer's point of view, the items in the IAEP written mathematics test can be regarded as just another kind of EXAM MATHS, so it would be expected that Taiwanese students would perform well.

Reflections on EXAM MATHS

In this examination culture, Taiwanese children have no choice but to attend out-of-school lessons in cram schools or receive private tutoring. EXAM MATHS becomes the source of pressure, not only for the child but also for the child's family. It becomes a natural responsibility for parents to look for star tutors or good cram schools for their children. It is very clear that Taiwanese society suffers from equating school mathematics with EXAM MATHS. So why do schools and the education system in Taiwan continue in this way? Where is the opposition? Given that every social phenomenon has its societal background, we need to try to clarify this point.

Japan's entrance tests are just as competitive as those in Taiwan but they do not have the same influence on classroom practice. Why is this? We suggest that the answer lies in the law-abiding character of Japanese teachers who observe their national curriculum faithfully, refuse to distort it under test pressure, and so help to keep EXAM MATHS out of school. They refuse to teach to the test since the curriculum suggests otherwise. Outside school, though, the students receive special classes very similar to our EXAM MATHS. In fact, our early pseudo-text books contain translations from Japanese practice books.

The Taiwanese, by contrast, are famous for their ability to create a grey zone or law-free zone in every aspect of their lives. For example, the underground economy is rampant. This means that rules will not in practice be followed and it is not realistic to expect them to be. On the other hand, the Taiwanese are quite clever in dealing with problems in everyday life, including what could be regarded as genuine mathematical problems. In fact, after leaving school, they often start to develop their own methods intermingled with any vestiges of EXAM MATHS left in their minds. But the affective shadows linger on and they remember themselves as mathematics losers even though they probably are not! Hence it is a serious responsibility for our mathematics educators to show that learning 'genuine' mathematics is important for achievement in life and moreover can lead to test success. The phenomenon of EXAM MATHS is a vivid reflection of the weakness of Taiwanese mathematics education.

Current Reform

Lifelong Learning

In the current examination culture in Taiwan, students spend most of both school and out-of-school time on subjects tested in entrance examinations for further education. They disregard other subjects; they do very little outside reading; they refrain from extra-curricular activities.

In September 1994, a national education reform committee called the Council on Education Reform, Executive Yuan, was organized and directed by Dr Y.T. Lee, a Nobel Prize laureate of 1986. One of the main themes of this council, proposed to the Government in December 1996, was to build up a lifelong learning society. Graduation from school was to mean the commencement of lifelong learning, rather than the end of education. Thus, one of the main purposes of school education was seen to be the development of students' interests and abilities for further learning (Lee, 1996).

Curriculum and admissions policy for further education are now subject to reform. Many developing countries take relevant publications from developed countries as their main references for curriculum reform. For instance, both the newly implemented elementary school mathematics curriculum in Taiwan in 1996 and the new mathematics curriculum of the Republic of Korea (see Lew, Chapter 17) refer to the *Standards* published by NCTM (1989) in the United States. The council on education reform insists that any curriculum reform should conform to the rationale of lifelong learning. Its recommendations are that contents and time periods should be reduced for all the major test subjects, Chinese, English, mathematics, natural sciences, and social studies, which dominate the current curriculum and examination culture. This will leave room for students to master the basic requirements of the major subjects as well as to develop their own interests. A national curriculum reform committee was organized in 1997. As announced by the Ministry of Education, this committee will propose a restructured school curriculum framework.

Some Thoughts on Mathematics Curriculum

From the point of view of lifelong learning, school mathematics, besides basic skills, should emphasize appreciation of the process of scientific activities through mathematical concepts and modelling, methods of acquiring knowledge through problem solving, and connections with culture and everyday life. Of course, mathematics provides calculating tools, a language for expressing rules, and the means to model various branches of science. These are aspects which are more or less emphasized in our current mathematics education. Mathematics also provides training in logical inference and plausible reasoning.

Mathematics becomes a playground through problem solving, where one can learn about observation, guessing, experiment, induction, analogy, hypothesis, analysis, verification, deduction, monitoring, etc., besides logical inference and plausible reasoning. All of these are scientific methods of acquiring knowledge. Experience in these scientific methods gained through problem solving in mathematics cannot simply be transferred directly to dealing with problems in other fields. However, such experiences provide a good background for solving problems in other fields scientifically. There are numerous mathematical problems suitable for this purpose, requiring little time and only elementary techniques.

Great discoveries, such as Kepler's laws and Mendel's experiments were time-consuming and expensive, and hence those processes could not be repeated by students. In contrast, in a biology text-book we read: 'Drosophila can be reproduced easily and quickly, and their phenotypes are distinctive. Furthermore, in their salivary glands, there are large chromosomes that can be clearly seen and so easily studied. Because of these characteristics, they are used both in experimental studies and in teaching genetics.' By analogy, we argue that mathematics problems designed for problem solving can play a similar role in mathematics education to that played by drosophila in genetics education. This means that in mathematics education the emphasis will shift to problem-solving and process-monitoring and away from memorizing and plugging into formulae.

Problem solving through which one can learn the methods of acquiring knowledge is one aspect of mathematics education that has been more or less neglected in Taiwan, but is now gaining attention alongside the emphasis on mathematics education for lifelong learning. Mathematics has developed as part of our culture and has been connected to everyday life ever since the beginning of civilization. Therefore one aspect of mathematics education should be to help students become familiar with the impact of mathematics on Taiwanese culture and its connections with their everyday life.

We suggest there are at least three perspectives from which to view the impact of mathematics on human culture: environmental activities, categories of argument, and aesthetics.

Under environmental activities we include number, time and space, all mentioned by Bishop (1991). Number, as the numbering, naming, computing and recording of systems of numbers, has considerable cultural content. The real number system provides a model for time. Geometry (with or without coordinates) and trigonometry can be used as tools to measure or model space. The iterative methods of fractal geometry can be used to simulate details of the geometry of natural objects.

Considering categories of argument we can distinguish three: deterministic versus probabilistic; deductive systems; and the ability to move from the simple to the difficult by making successive approximations. The first two categories are self-explanatory but the final one needs some elaboration. A theorem is good for infinitely many cases. From simple axioms one can deduce the whole system of plane geometry; using only the sine and cosine laws, one can place a yardstick not only on every corner of the world, but also in remote space beyond our solar system. The common feature of so much of mathematics is that one must grasp simple (or essential) principles in order to tackle the more difficult (or variant) problems. Most real numbers and most function values are not rational numbers and cannot be represented by finite methods. Newton's method of finding a root, the series method of finding a function value, and other iterative methods provide an approach of successive approximation to a goal, giving also an estimation of distance from the goal. These two features of mathematics, progression from the simple to the more difficult, and successive approximation to a goal, can be applied to other fields as well as to everyday life.

Thirdly, there is the aesthetic perspective, the beauty in mathematics. It is impossible to explain beauty to everybody's satisfaction. Mathematics provides a special kind of beauty: order from chaos. One needs some aesthetics education to be an educated person and mathematics can provide one such environment.

As for connections with everyday life, numeracy, including estimation, is very important and gaining attention in mathematics education in Taiwan. In addition, mathematical terms in everyday life and links with other subjects also are important and we offer some examples. In medieval times, maps were drawn with the 'Orient' at the top, from which the word and the meaning of 'orientation' were derived. Now, because maps are drawn with north at the top, in some languages, such as Chinese, 'up-bound' and 'down-bound' are used instead of 'north-bound' and 'south-bound' respectively. 'Clockwise' is another interesting example. When one looks at a clock with its face designed as the mirror image of a usual clock, one realizes that 'clockwise' is nothing more than a convention. When the stock market index surges sharply, people may say 'it is growing exponentially', perhaps without knowing that they are talking about one of the essential properties of an important function in mathematics.

In an era of the pedagogical global village, basic spherical geometry could be taught in school in conjunction with geography, with students taught the method of measuring the size of the globe, alongside study of latitude, longitude and time zones. A good investigation would be to determine for an aeroplane the shortest route, distance, and flying time between two cities. Or, where is the furthest place in the world from here and how can it be determined through a consideration of latitudes and longitudes? Relative to Taiwan, it is the province of Formosa in Argentina, and relative to England, it is the Antipodes Islands to the south-east of the South Island of New Zealand. Making these links visible can be a fascinating exploration into history, geography, language and cultural practices, and is surely educational in the widest sense.

Some Alternative Test Problems

Will the EXAM MATHS of the present day have a place in the future mathematics curriculum? Let us first look at two typical examples of problems developed in the present examination culture.

1 Let α, β, γ be the three roots of the cubic equation $x^3 - 6x^2 + 3x + 3 = 0$.
   What is the cubic equation with $1/\alpha^2$, $1/\beta^2$, $1/\gamma^2$ as roots?
   (Entrance test paper, 1987)
2 Solve the following inequality
   $2\log 2 + \log(x^2 - 5x + 3) < 2\log(12 + 5x - x^2)$
   (Entrance test paper, 1987)

These two problems are certainly mathematically meaningful but, even though they involve more than basic skills, we suggest they have nothing to do with mathematical literacy, science, or culture and they have no connection with everyday life. Although they might be appropriate for some students aiming to be scientists they are certainly irrelevant for the majority of mathematics students. Our suggestion is that much of this type of content, which consumes more than half of the students' time in mathematics, should be removed. This will create the space for some of the areas we have described, which we believe are more geared towards a mathematics curriculum catering for lifelong learning.

But under the new system what kind of problems could be posed in examinations, in particular in national tests? We will venture two suggestions, simply to test the water.

a David Livingstone, a 19th-century missionary, was a great explorer of the African continent (Hugon, 1992). Somehow he believed that the source of the Nile should be somewhere to the south-west of Lake Tanganyika, and took the Lualaba, a river in that area, to be the Nile. But he was unable to prove his claim. After he died, another explorer, Verney Cameron, came to Nyangwe, a trade town on the Lualaba. After determining the altitude of Nyangwe, he confirmed that the Lualaba could not be the upper reaches of the Nile, because this town was lower than Condokoro on the middle reaches of the Nile.

Question: In the above story, what kind of mathematics and mathematical reasoning are involved?

b Columbus (Lequenne, 1992) sailed across the Atlantic in order to find a sea route to Asia. In his first two crossings, he was disappointed to find only islands (in what is now the Caribbean Sea). On his third attempt in 1498, he sailed into a body of water (Paria Gulf) behind an island (Trinidad). This was where a river (the Orinoco) met the ocean, and 40 miles off-shore the water was fresh. He figured that the river must be a large one, and that the land the river ran through probably should be a continent. He thought he had reached Asia.

Question: It is known that in Columbus's time the circumference of the Earth was estimated to be about 30,000 km, (in reality, it is 40,000 km) and the distance across the Eurasian land mass was estimated to be 23,000 km (in reality it is about 17,500 km). On the basis of what kind of logical inferences did Columbus believe that he had discovered a continent? Why did he come to the wrong conclusion that he had reached Asia?

Exam Maths in the Future

We are left with the question whether problems like those at the end of the last section could become so standardized that they eventually are treated as EXAM

MATHS. It seems that there is much work still to be done. The main reason that EXAM MATHS prevails is that the total score received on the entrance examination is the principle determinant of whether a university place is offered and, if so, of which university and department is assigned. As long as this admission policy continues, any innovation in problem posing is almost bound to be countered by one-task-one-rule methods of solution. These problems will then soon become just another part of EXAM MATHS.

However, in recent years other admission policies have been developed, and universities and departments are beginning to recruit some of their students in a more independent way. It is therefore not always possible for high school and cram school teachers to keep a one-task-one-rule teaching strategy. We hope that the method of problem solving through explorations will be taken up by teachers. Clearly this cannot be achieved overnight, but we believe change will happen.

In the long run, under the pressures for lifelong learning and with the internet opening up the learning environment, it would seem impossible in a national test to continue to pose problems that simply emphasize memorization and specific skills. A nationwide test should be used as a screening tool: as such, it should contain problems involving only basic concepts and procedural knowledge. Universities and departments, whenever necessary, could then pose their own problems reflecting what they need in recruiting their students. About 7 per cent (more than 5,000) of freshmen in 1997 were screened in this way into colleges. We hope that this admission policy will become prevalent in the near future. Only then, might the examination culture gradually fade and the image of mathematics education in Taiwan no longer be that of EXAM MATHS.

References

BISHOP, A.J. (1991) *Mathematical Enculturation: A Cultural Perspective on Mathematics Education*, Dordrecht: Kluwer Academic Publishers.

HUGON, A. (1992) *The Exploration of Africa* (English Translation), London: Thames and Hudson Ltd.

LAPOINTE, A.E., MEAD, N.A. and ASKEW, J.M. (1992) *Learning Mathematics*, IAEP, Educational Testing Service.

LEE, Y.T. (Chair) (1996) *Final Report on Education Reform: The Council on Education Reform*, Executive Yuan, R.O.C., 1996 (in Chinese).

LEQUENNE, M. (1992) *Christopher Columbus* (English Translation), London: Thames and Hudson Ltd.

LIN, F.L. (1988) 'Societal differences and their influences on children's mathematics understanding', *Educational Studies in Mathematics*, **19**, pp. 471–97.

NCTM (1989) *Curriculum and Evaluation Standards for School Mathematics*, Reston, VA: National Council of Teachers of Mathematics.

WANG, K.P., MAO, C.L., TSAO, L.C., CHANG, Y.F., LIU, K.T., LIU, Y.C., TSAI, Y.B. and TAN, T.T. (1985) *A Study of the Present Situation of Science Education in Taiwan, R.O.C. Science and Technology Advisory Group*, Executive Yuan (in Chinese).

Chapter 19

The Traditional Chinese Views of Mathematics and Education: Implications for Mathematics Education in the New Millennium

Frederick Leung

With the advance of communication technology such as the World Wide Web, the global village is shrinking rapidly. Different cultures are brought into closer contact or confrontation with each other, exposing the deep-rooted differences in the values in these cultures. As we contemplate what the mathematics curriculum should be for the new millennium, such cultural encounters not only help us to understand each other better, but also are fertile grounds for us to learn from each other's cultural traditions.

This chapter discusses the tradition of the Chinese culture, the dominant culture in the countries of East Asia and one of the major cultures of the world. The chapter attempts to explore the implications of the traditional thoughts in this great culture for education in the modern world. In particular, it investigates what the traditional Chinese views of mathematics and education have to offer in the current discussion of mathematics education in the new millennium.

The Traditional Chinese View of Mathematics

The Place of Mathematics in the Chinese Culture

Mathematics was never held as a highly regarded academic discipline of study in ancient China. Low-rank officials had to learn it in order to deal with those aspects of the running of the government that involved calculations. Merchants learned it for accounting purposes, and fortune-tellers studied it to do their business through calculations involving astrology. It was said that in ancient China, the professional mathematician had only two prospects: either to join the government as a low-ranking official, or to become a fortune-teller (Ding, 1989, p. 36). Mathematics was viewed as a set of techniques or tricks of the trade rather than as a discipline of study.

This is in sharp contrast with the Greek tradition, where mathematics was viewed as a school of thought and was a highly respected subject. Of course the Greeks were aware of the applicability of mathematics in everyday life, but the application aspect of mathematics was not emphasized and was even despised. In his Republic, Plato wrote of mathematics:

> . . . this branch of learning [logistic] should be prescribed by our law and that should induce those who are to share the highest functions of state to enter on that study of calculation and take hold of it, not as amateurs, but to follow it up until they attain to the contemplation of the nature of numbers, by pure thought, not for the purpose of buying and selling.' (Fowler, 1979)

For the Greeks, mathematics was a philosophical system, essential for the training of intellectuals and 'philosopher kings'.

Characteristics of Ancient Chinese Mathematics

Wang and Sun (1988) traced the development of mathematics in China from prehistoric times to the Yuan Dynasty, and extracted the following five major characteristics of ancient Chinese mathematics:

1 pragmatic
2 mystical
3 algorithmic, numerical and discrete
4 primitive dialectics
5 conformity to orthodoxy (pp. 149–62)

Most scholars in the field of mathematics education in China (for example Ronan, 1978; Siu, 1995) would agree to the list, with the possible exception of 'primitive dialectics'. In the view of the present author, the fact that 'primitive dialectics' is on the list reflects more an attempt to put down what is currently politically correct (or the orthodoxy) rather than a characteristic of ancient Chinese mathematics. Interestingly, it exemplifies well the 'conformity to orthodoxy' mentioned in the list!

The Nine Chapters

Traditionally in China, the orthodoxy in mathematics was not materialist dialectics, but the *Nine Chapters* and its various accepted commentaries. The *Nine Chapters*, throughout the dynasties, was the most important text for the study of mathematics in the imperial court or national college of study as well as the prescribed text for the national examinations. It was one of the classics, and so students were supposed to memorize the text, just as they memorized other classics. As a result, subsequent development of mathematics in China was greatly influenced by the *Nine Chapters*. As Ding pointed out, 'until the importation of western learning in the late Ming and early Ching Dynasties, mathematics in Chinese was merely an augmentation of *Nine Chapters* without any substantial variation' (Ding, 1989, p. 9).

The *Nine Chapters* is regarded by some as one of the two most influential mathematics books ever published, the other being Euclid's *Elements* (Wang and Sun, 1988, p. 80). The *Nine Chapters* is actually a collection of problems, divided into nine sets or chapters according to the nature of the problems. In each set, the problems are categorized according to the rules or techniques involved in the solution. For each problem, in addition to the statement of the problem and its solution, the rules or techniques for the solution also are given. The approach is to start with everyday problems and then, through analysis and synthesis, arrive at rules or theories for solving different kinds of problems. The rules or theories are then applied to other problems. This approach is in sharp contrast to that adopted by Euclid's *Elements*. The starting points for *Elements* are definitions, axioms, and common notions, and through deductive reasoning a system of mathematical theorems is arrived at. But the starting points for *Nine Chapters* are problems instead of axioms, and the method used is that of problem solving rather than proof. The process is constructive and mechanistic rather than axiomatic and deductive.

Wang and Sun (1992) extracted the following characteristics of the mathematics in the *Nine Chapters*:

1   an open, inductive system
2   algorithmic
3   use of mathematical models (pp. 51–8)

Thus the *Nine Chapters*, through the use of mathematical models to solve problems of everyday life, marks the two most important characteristics of traditional Chinese mathematics: its algorithmic nature and its emphasis on application. This pragmatism had a profound and sustained influence on the mathematics that developed in China subsequently. Indeed so powerful was this pragmatism that pragmatism itself became the orthodoxy in traditional Chinese mathematics. Siu (1995) pointed out that mathematicians who wanted to go beyond the application problems, had to 'clothe' the mathematics in an application format in order to discuss advanced mathematics. Pure mathematics was unorthodox and was not acceptable. The example cited by Siu is a problem involving the solution of equations of 10th degree by the famous Chinese mathematician Qin Jiushao in 1247. Qin posed a question that originally could be solved by setting up a cubic equation. Yet Qin introduced the square of a variable as the unknown and set up an equation of the 10th degree to solve the problem. Siu made the following comment,

> it seems unlikely that a mathematician of the calibre of Qin Jiushao would miss noticing that the problem can be set as an equation of third degree rather than

one of tenth degree. . . . he wanted to offer an example to illustrate his method of solving equations of higher degree, but in the good old Chinese tradition, a problem should not be discussed in a purely theoretical context but should arise 'naturally' in a practical context. (Siu, 1995, p. 229)

This orthodoxy of pragmatism dominated the mathematics of China until Greek mathematics, and in particular Euclid's *Elements*, replaced the *Nine Chapters* and its pragmatism as the orthodoxy of Chinese mathematics.

Implications for Mathematics Education in the New Millennium

The two characteristics of traditional Chinese mathematics or mathematical thinking discussed above are highly relevant to our discussion of mathematics education for the new millennium. One item on our agenda for discussion has been 'mathematics education for all'. The Greek view of mathematics as a philosophical system essential for the training of the mind may fit well with an élitist system of education. But the Chinese tradition of stressing problem solving and the application of mathematics may be more suited for the general mass. Indeed the discussion above echoes the emphasis on problem solving and the use of mathematical modelling advocated in recent decades by educators all over the world.

Moreover, with the advance of computer technology, the mechanistic aspect of mathematics is attaining more importance. Wu (1993) pointed out that just as the relatively non-mechanical ways of solving difficult problems in arithmetic were made obsolete by algebra, Euclidean geometry (which is highly non-mechanical) should give way to the relatively mechanical coordinate geometry. In fact in ancient China, algebra, and in particular theories of equations, was highly developed, and geometry problems were tackled in an algebraic manner. The use of variables to denote dimensions in geometry in solving geometric problems was devised in the 10th and 11th centuries. Of course, this way of tackling geometric problems was very clumsy and complicated (and the use of Chinese characters as symbols complicated the process even further). Nevertheless, once turned into algebraic problems, these geometric problems can be solved in a mechanistic (albeit complicated) manner. With the advance of computers these mechanical processes, no matter how complicated, are easily accomplished in seconds. So this ancient Chinese notion of reducing problems into a mechanistic form may attain new importance.

The discussion above is of particular relevance to the debate on the future of the mathematics curriculum in China (and in most of the East European countries), where there is a strong emphasis on Euclidean geometry and other non-mechanistic aspects of mathematics (for example, various ingenious ways or tricks to solve difficult arithmetic problems) and a lack of emphasis on the applications of mathematics. With the advent of mass education and computer technology, it is high time for China and other countries in that tradition to re-evaluate their curriculum in the light of the ancient Chinese tradition in mathematics.

The Traditional Chinese View of Education

The Chinese Emphasis on Education

The Chinese are known to place high emphasis on education, and sometimes researchers use this to explain the superior achievement of students of Chinese origin in international comparative studies (see for example, Stevenson, 1987). Actually, this emphasis on education can be traced to the Confucian view of education, and such emphasis can be found in all Confucian-influenced places such as Japan, Korea, Singapore, Taiwan, and Hong Kong.

Lee (1996) pointed out that the Chinese emphasis on education 'rests upon the Confucian presumption that everyone is educable' (p. 28). Confucius acknowledged that there are individual differences in intelligence, but he believed that 'differences in intelligence . . . do not inhibit one's educability' (p. 29). Confucians not only believe that everyone is educable, they also believe that everyone is perfectible. The Chinese believe that 'sagehood is a state that any man can achieve by cumulative effort' (Chai, 1965). It is this positive view of the learner that motivates the Chinese to exercise their effort and will-power in their study.

The Confucian Ideal of the Scholar

The Chinese can be said to hold a rather utilitarian view of education, in the sense of education being for the actualization or perfection of the self (sagehood). The aim of education is not the pursuit of knowledge for knowledge's sake, but the development of the character of the learner.

The Chinese ideal of the scholar is that 'a man should discipline himself first, after that he could regulate his family, then govern the State, and finally lead the world into peace'. (*Analect*, trans. Legg, 1930). 'Discipline himself' may not be the best translation here. It may be better translated as 'attain personal virtue'. The saying stresses that one should have the grand goal of 'leading the world into peace', but that goal can only be achieved through stages. One needs to prove one's worth in personal virtue and family matters before one can attain the grand goals of 'governing the State' and 'leading the world into peace'.

So the Chinese have this tradition of studying for the sake of developing virtue or self-actualization, and for serving the community and the country. The Chinese are familiar with stories in their history: in times of national crisis, there was a tradition of intellectuals studying hard for the sake of 'saving the country'.

It is interesting to note that even during the Cultural Revolution in China in the 1960s and 1970s when there was a national movement to 'criticize Confucius', there was at the same time an advocacy of 'red and expert', meaning it was not enough to be an expert, one had to have the right virtue which at that time meant having the 'correct' political attitude (red). So although the content of the virtue was different from the traditional Chinese values, the insistence that virtue had to go hand-in-hand with (or even supersede) knowledge had not been changed. It is this deep-rooted Chinese value that Sun (1983) termed the 'deep structure' of the Chinese culture.

Aims of Mathematics Education

As pointed out above, mathematics has never been a highly regarded subject of study in China, but the Chinese view of education discussed above seems nevertheless to apply to mathematics. For example, in analysing the current mathematics syllabus in China, Leung (1992) found that intrinsic aims of mathematics education were totally lacking. In their place, he found extrinsic aims of inculcating 'virtues' such as 'to foster in students good qualities of character and elementary dialectical materialistic viewpoints' (State Education Commission, 1988).

Incidentally, it is interesting to find that in the Republic of Korea, a country substantially under the influence of the Chinese culture, such value-laden aims appear in the latest effort of their reform of the mathematics curriculum as well. Lew (in Chapter 17), discussing the 'rationale' for the new Korean curriculum, points out that it is the view of the mathematics education community in Korea that 'the curriculum should support the national goals', and that the Korean society is expected to realize 'a devotion to the welfare of mankind, which is a traditional dream of Korean people throughout history'.

Implications for Mathematics Education in the New Millennium

Such value-laden, extrinsic aims of mathematics education are alien to many mathematics educators outside the Confucian culture, and the Chinese have sometimes been criticized by these educators as promoting extrinsic rather than intrinsic motivation for studying mathematics. Under the western paradigm of education, this criticism is understandable. It is widely accepted that providing stimulation to students so that they enjoy the learning of mathematics itself is very important. But experience tells us that it is not always easy for students to appreciate the mathematics they are doing. And the study of mathematics often involves ample practice of skills before students are able to learn further mathematics based on those skills. At the time of practising the skills, it is difficult for students to derive intrinsic motivation for the study. In this case, extrinsic motivation, if properly provided, would be an encouragement to students in their studies. Besides, the distinction between internal and external motivations is not always clear-cut and may even be complementary (Lynn, 1988).

It is not the intention of this chapter to argue that in the new millennium people from other cultures should adopt the Chinese views and values in respect of education. We may not subscribe to the Chinese ideal of sagehood or service to the community. But this Chinese attitude towards education may well be an antidote to the 'technique-oriented' curriculum (Bishop, 1991) that is so prevalent in many western countries. The problem with many mathematics curricula in the west seems to be that they give the impression that mathematics is a purely technical subject which may help students acquire practical skills and a logical mind, but which has nothing to do with the values we want to inculcate in students. This impression tends to divorce the study of mathematics from value education, and deprives students of one kind of motivation to learn.

The lesson to learn from the discussion above is perhaps that we should consider and make explicit the values, both intrinsic and extrinsic, that we would like to promote in mathematics education in designing the curriculum for the new millennium. In fact, whether we are conscious of it or not, our curriculum carries with it implicit values (Bishop, 1991). With a deliberate effort to make explicit to students the goals for their study and with due encouragement for them to achieve those goals, we may help alleviate the problem of lack of motivation to study which is so prevalent in many countries.

Educators from countries outside the Confucian culture may not feel comfortable with the value-laden attitudes towards education in China, but in our discussion of mathematics education for the new millennium the Chinese experience should be taken seriously. For, in the final analysis, China seems to be able to produce students who are motivated to study and attain high achievement.

References

BISHOP, A.J. (1991) *Mathematical Enculturation*, Dordrecht: Kluwer Academic Publishers.

CHAI, C. (1965) *The Humanist Way in Ancient China: Essential Works of Confucianism*, New York: Bantam Books.

DING, S.S. and ZHANG, Z.G. (1989) *Mathematics and Education*, Changsha: Hunan Education Press. (in Chinese)

FOWLER, D.H. (1979) 'Ratio in early Greek mathematics', *Bulletin of the American Mathematics Society* (New Series), **1**, pp. 807–46.

LEE, W.O. (1996) 'The cultural context for Chinese learners: Conceptions of learning in the Confucian tradition', in WATKINS, D.A. and BIGGS, J.B. *The Chinese Learner*, Hong Kong: CERC and ACER.

LEGG, J. (1930) *The Four Books*, Shanghai: The China Book Company.

LEUNG, F.K.S. (1992) 'A comparison of the intended mathematics curriculum in China, Hong Kong and England and the implementation in Beijing, Hong Kong and London', PhD thesis, The University of London Institute of Education.

LYNN, R. (1988) *Educational Achievement in Japan*, Basingstoke: Macmillan.

RONAN, C.A. (1978) *The Shorter Science and Civilisation in China: An Abridgement of Joseph Needham's Original Text*, Cambridge: Cambridge University Press.

SIU, M.K. (1995) 'Mathematics education in Ancient China: What do we learn from it?', *Historia Scientiarum*, **4**, 3, pp. 223–32.

STATE EDUCATION COMMISSION (1988) *Mathematics Syllabus*, Beijing: People's Education Press. (in Chinese)

STEVENSON, H.W. (1987) 'America's math problem', *Educational Leadership*, **45**, pp. 4–10.

SUN, L.K. (1983) *The 'Deep Structure' of Chinese Culture*, Hong Kong: Chap Yin Co. (in Chinese)

WANG, H.J. and SUN, H.A. (1988) *Ways of Thought in Chinese Ancient Mathematics*, Nanjiang: Jiangsu Education Press. (in Chinese)

WANG, H.J. and SUN, H.A. (1992) *Introduction to Ways of Thought in Mathematics*, Beijing: People's Education Press. (in Chinese)

WU, W.J. (1993) 'The modernisation of mathematics education', in *Mathematics Education in the 21th Century*, Beijing: Beijing Normal University Press. (in Chinese)

Notes on Contributors

Johnston Anderson

Johnston Anderson, who was born in Edinburgh, gained a Bachelor's degree (1959) and a Ph.D (1963) in Mathematics from The Queen's University of Belfast. He joined the staff of the Mathematics Department at the University of Nottingham in 1962, where he is now Senior Lecturer in Mathematics. His research interests are now in Mathematics Education.

Margaret Brown

Margaret Brown is a Professor of Mathematics Education at King's College London. After teaching in primary and secondary schools, and being involved in teacher training, she has directed more than 15 research projects on teaching, learning and assessment in mathematics. She has been a member of two government committees on mathematics, has chaired the Joint Mathematical Council of the UK, and been President of the Mathematical Association and the British Educational Research Association.

Mike Clayton

Mike Clayton graduated in Mathematics from the University of Cambridge in 1964, and joined the Telecommunications Research Laboratory of GEC Hirst Research Centre in 1965 to work on modelling and performance prediction for microwave trunk radio communication systems. From 1973 to 1997 he was leader of the Systems Studies Group, responsible for carrying out theoretical modelling for a wide range of telecommunications systems, including analogue and digital trunk radio systems, stored-program-controlled exchanges, fibre-optic communications, and networks. As well as supervision of students on industrial placements, Mike's involvement with mathematics education has included membership of mathematical sub-committees of the University Grants Committee and the Science and Engineering Research Council, work with SCAA (now QCA) on A-level and National Curriculum mathematics, and technical advice for the Nuffield Advanced Mathematics project.

Bernard Cornu

Bernard Cornu is the Director of the IUFM (Institute Universitaire de Formation des Maitres — University Institute for Teacher Education) of Grenoble, France, in which all primary and secondary teachers, in all disciplines, are trained for two years. He is a mathematician at Grenoble University; he studied the influence of computers and informatics on mathematics and its teaching, and also worked in didactics of mathematics. He is the Chairman of IFIP Working Group 3.1 ('Informatics Education at the Secondary Education Level').

H. Brian Griffiths

Brian Griffiths became Professor of Pure Mathematics in Southampton University in 1964, Professor Emeritus in 1992 and later Visiting Research Fellow at the Mathematics Centre, Bognor. In 1966 at Southampton he introduced options in Mathematics Education into the Honours Mathematics course, with the aid of various colleagues — notably A.G. Howson with whom he wrote the book *Mathematics: Society and Curricula* (1974). A guiding principle of the group was to root the discipline of Mathematics Education in reflection on their daily teaching of Mathematics itself. His other activities included starting (with H. Halberstam), and nurturing, the Nottingham Conferences on the Undergraduate Mathematics Teaching; and chairing the Steering Committees of the projects LAMP and RAMP. Apart from continuing work in Geometry, he has most recently been involved in helping V. Villani to edit the recent ICMI publication 'Perspectives on the Teaching of Geometry for 21st Century' (1998).

Rogers Hall

Rogers Hall is an assistant professor of Education at the University of California, Berkeley, where he teaches and does research on representation and quantitative reasoning. His work compares representational practices in classrooms and workplaces where people use quantitative reasoning to design things, with a particular focus on learning and teaching.

Gillian Hatch

Gillian Hatch has been involved in the training of teachers for more than twenty years. She now works at Didsbury School of Education, Manchester Metropolitan University. She has done research in both primary and secondary classrooms. Her research interests include the needs of mathematically able children, games in the mathematics classroom, the development of notions of proof in the classroom, teachers attitudes to the teaching of mathematics.

William Higginson

William Higginson is Coordinator of the Mathematics, Science and Technology Education Group in the Faculty of Education at Queen's University in Kingston, Ontario. A graduate of Queens', Cambridge, Exeter and Alberta he has taught in schools in Canada (secondary mathematics teacher, Kingston and Toronto), the United Kingdom (infant class assistant, Duxford C of E Primary), Kenya (acting headmaster, Kabarnet Boys Secondary School), and the United States (visiting professor, MIT Arts and Media Laboratory). A committed peripatetic (cf David Lodge's academic novels) in the earlier years of his career he has more recently become a reluctant expert on the diseases of roses in a cold climate.

James J. Kaput

Professor Kaput was initially trained in mathematics, but turned to mathematics learning and thinking in the 1970's and to the use of interactive technologies to further teaching and learning in the 1980's. His particular interests are in the use of new technologies to create new notation systems and forms of interaction to render much more mathematics learnable by many more people than has been historically possible.

David Klug et al.

Phil Ramsdem, Phillip Kent and Margaret James (now retired) are members of the METRIC project team who implemented the computer aided mathematics courses in the Chemistry and Biochemistry Department. Their collaborators Richard Templer, David Klug and Ian Gould, run the mathematics provision in these Departments.

Frederick Leung

Dr. Frederick Leung is the Dean of the Faculty of Education at the University of Hong Kong. He is also the Chairman of the Hong Kong Centre for IEA Studies and the National Research Co-ordinator for the TIMSS project in Hong Kong.

Hee-chan Lew

Hee-chan Lew is an associate professor in the Department of Mathematics Education at the Korean National University of Education. He was a senior researcher in the Korea Educational Development Institute after studying in Seoul National University, Korea and Temple University, USA. He has carried out research on practical change in mathematics education related to computers and assessment. He was a director of the Elementary Textbook Development Project based on the 6th national curriculum and currently directs the government sponsored IMC Project which produces a range of materials to support school use of computers and performance assessment to improve mathematics creativity.

Fou-Lai Lin

Fou-Lai Lin, Professor and Chairman of the Mathematics Department, National Taiwan Normal University, has been involved in many aspects of mathematics education research projects and developmental works, such as students' formation, diagnostic teaching, conceptualizing of mathematics teaching, values in mathematics education, curriculum development. He was the Chief editor of the *Chinese Journal of Science Education*, and managing director of Yuan-T Lee Foundation (Science Education for All).

Jeremy Roschelle

Dr. Roschelle works in educational software design, math and science education, collaborative learning, and video analysis methodology. At MIT, he designed and implemented the graphics subsystem for Boxer, a successor to the Logo programming language. In his Berkeley Ph.D, he analyzed cognitive learning processes by which students develop mental models of velocity and acceleration vectors, and authored a simulation called 'The Envisioning Machine' that utilized dynamic graphics and multiple representation. In his work at the Institute for Research on Learning, he investigated the conversational processes which enabled collaborating learners to build shared understandings of scientific concepts. He developed VideoNoter, a pioneering video analysis tool and later produced CVideo which now is a leading commercial video analysis product. He is now employed at SRI International, where he manages software development for the SimCalc Project, leading the team in its applications of advanced technologies including 2D and 3D simulations, linked multiple representations, dynamic edittable graphs, scripting, drag and drop, and interoperable components. Dr. Roschelle is a founding member of the Educational Object Economy, and co-leader in the Center for Innovative Learning Technologies, and an associate editor of the *Journal for the Learning Sciences*.

Kenneth Ruthven
Kenneth Ruthven works at the University of Cambridge School of Education where he trains mathematics teachers and educational researchers, and researches issues of curriculum, pedagogy and assessment.

Daniel Sandford Smith
At the time of the conference Daniel Sandford Smith taught Science in a London (Haringey) Comprehensive and was in charge of Physics and KS3 co-ordinator. Since then he has been Head of Science at an Upper School in Borehamwood, Hertfordshire. He has recently been appointed Director of Curriculum Support for the Association of Science Education.

Geoff Wake
Geoff Wake is a Research Fellow of the Centre for Mathematics Education at the University of Manchester. His main areas of activity include Post-16 Mathematics, both at Advance Level and for students for whom mathematics is not the main focus of their study programme. His work in this area has recently included the production of curriculum support materials, analysis of curriculum content and delivery, and the design of new curricula for government agencies.

Julian Williams
Julian Williams is Director of the Centre for Mathematics education at the University of Manchester. His research activities have included applied mathematics, modelling, vocational mathematics and teaching, learning and assessment in mathematics in general. His current research projects include the development of new teaching methods, the study of dialogue in classrooms, assessment and testing, and the relationship of College mathematics and workplace practices.

Index